D1489029

Women and Interreligious Dialogue

REGIS COLLEGE LIBRARY
100 Wellesley Street West
Toronto, Ontario
Canada M5S 2Z5

Interreligious Dialogue Series

Catherine Cornille, Series Editor

VOLUMES IN THE SERIES:

1 Criteria of Discernment in Interreligious Dialogue (2009)

2 Interreligious Hermeneutics (2010)

3 The World Market and Interreligious Dialogue (2011)

4 Interreligious Dialogue and Cultural Change (2012)

5 Women and Interreligious Dialogue (2013)

REGIS COLLEGE LIBRARY
100 Wellesley Street West
Toronto, Ontario
Canada M5S 2Z5

WITHDRAWN

Women and Interreligious Dialogue

edited by
CATHERINE CORNILLE &
JILLIAN MAXEY

BL
458
W57
2013

CASCADE *Books* · Eugene, Oregon

WOMEN AND INTERRELIGIOUS DIALOGUE
Interreligious Dialogue Series 5

Copyright © 2013 Wipf and Stock Publishers. All rights reserved. Except for brief quotations in critical publications or reviews, no part of this book may be reproduced in any manner without prior written permission from the publisher. Write: Permissions, Wipf and Stock Publishers, 199 W. 8th Ave., Suite 3, Eugene, OR 97401.

Cascade Books
An Imprint of Wipf and Stock Publishers
199 W. 8th Ave., Suite 3
Eugene, OR 97401

www.wipfandstock.com

ISBN 13: 978-1-60608-294-2

Cataloging-in-Publication data:

Women and interreligious dialogue / edited by Catherine Cornille and Jillian Maxey.

Interreligious Dialogue Series 5

vi + 254 p. ; 23 cm.

ISBN 13: 978-1-60608-294-2

1. Women and religion. 2. Multiculturalism—Religious aspects. 3. Religion—Relations. 4. Religious pluralism. 5. Dialogue—Religious aspects. I. Cornille, C. (Catherine). II. Maxey, Jillian. III. Title. IV. Series.

BL458 W5635 2013

Manufactured in the U.S.A.

Contents

Introduction: On Women and Interreligious Dialogue
CATHERINE CORNILLE   1

1   Women and Interfaith Relations: Toward a Transnational
    Feminism
    ROSEMARY RADFORD RUETHER   11

2   Gift to The Prophet from a King: The Politics of Women
    in Interreligious Dialogue
    JEANNINE HILL FLETCHER   27

3   Epistemology and Embodiment in Women's Interreligious
    Dialogue
    MARA BRECHT   49

4   Dialogue in Times of War: Christian Women's Rescue of Jews
    in Hitler's Germany
    KATHARINA VON KELLENBACH   70

5   Abraham and His Family at the Interfaith Border Edge:
    Asking the Overlooked Question of Gender
    NANCY FUCHS KREIMER   88

6   Meeting at the Well of Spiritual Direction: A Jewish
    Feminist Perspective
    SUE LEVI ELWELL   108

Contents

7 Constructive Interreligious Dialogue Concerning Muslim
Women
ZAYN KASSAM 127

8 The Qur'anic Rib-ectomy: Scriptural Purity, Imperial Dangers,
and Other Obstacles to the Interfaith Engagement of Feminist
Qur'anic Interpretation
AYSHA HIDAYATULLAH 150

9 Women Negotiating between Religions and Cultures:
The Case of Chinese Muslims in Hong Kong
WAI CHING ANGELA WONG 168

10 Beyond Beauty: Aesthetics and Emotion in Interreligious
Dialogue
MICHELLE VOSS ROBERTS 188

11 The Knowing Body: Currents of Connection and Women
in Religious Dialogue
ANNE CAROLYN KLEIN (RIGZIN DROLMA) 209

12 What Do Women Bring to the Dialogue Table?
RITA M. GROSS 231

List of Contributors 251

Introduction

On Women and Interreligious Dialogue

Catherine Cornille

By all appearances, dialogue between religions is conducted mainly by and between men.[1] The images of high-level meetings between religious leaders tend to depict males, dressed in colorful religious robes, displaying solidarity and mutual respect in spite of their differences in beliefs and practices. Theologians and intellectuals involved in theoretical reflection on interreligious dialogue also appear to be predominantly men, as evident also in the previous volumes in this series.[2] And many of the public grassroots interfaith initiatives are attributed to men. This is largely unsurprising. In so far as the leadership of most religions continues to be predominantly male, and official dialogues tend to involve religious leaders, it is to be expected that women appear absent or underrepresented in official dialogues between religions. And the majority

---

1. This has been observed by many scholars and further thematically developed in books such as: Maura O'Neill, *Women Speaking, Women Listening: Women in Interreligious Dialogue* (Maryknoll, NY: Orbis, 1992); Maura O'Neill, *Mending a Torn World: Women in Interreligious Dialogue* (Maryknoll, NY: Orbis, 2007); Doris Strahm and Manuela Kalsky, eds., *Damit es anders wird zwischen uns: Interreligiöser Dialog aus der Sicht von Frauen* (Ostfildern: Matthias-Grunewald, 2006).

2. The volume on *Criteria of Discernment in Interreligious Dialogue* (2009) had two women contributors; *Interreligious Hermeneutics* (2010) two; *The World Market and Interreligious Dialogue* (2011) one; and *Interreligious Dialogue and Cultural Change* (2012) one.

of scholars working on topics in the area of interreligious dialogue are men.[3]

However, the reality of interreligious dialogue is much broader than the formal engagement between religious leaders and scholars, and women have been involved in various ways in the dialogue between religions, just as this dialogue has had a significant impact on the lives and the self-understanding of women in particular religions. This volume focuses on various dimensions of women's involvement in interreligious dialogue. It discusses examples of women who have been engaged, wittingly or unwittingly, in dialogue with members of other religions. It explores the complex relationship between interreligious dialogue and feminist developments within different religions, and it considers the difficult question of whether women have something distinctive to contribute to interreligious dialogue in general. The volume brings together the voices of women from different religious traditions, and from different generations. The authors are deeply involved within their respective traditions while also engaged in prolonged and in-depth dialogue with at least one other religion, or in reflection on dialogue itself. As such, they bring both personal experience and historical insight to bear on various questions involving women's participation in interreligious dialogue.

Women and Interreligious Dialogue "from below"[4]

Even though women may not feature prominently in public displays of interreligious dialogue, many women have been active in various forms of dialogue and collaboration that emerge from the grassroots and in the margins of religious traditions. Women from different religious traditions have often spontaneously formed dialogue groups, sharing their faith and their joys and struggles with one another. And in the course of history, women have often played heroic (but unacknowledged) roles in reaching out across religious boundaries. Katharina Von Kellenbach

3. In my recently edited *The Wiley-Blackwell Companion to Inter-Religious Dialogue* (Oxford: Wiley-Blackwell, 2013), 9 out of the 29 contributors are women. This indicates some improvement in the participation of women in scholarly interreligious dialogue, but women still number less than one-third of the contributors.

4. Annette Wilke also uses the expression "Dialog von unten" in her article "Interreligiöses Verstehen: Rahmenbedingungen für einen gelingenden christlich-muslimischen Dialog," in *Damit es anders wird zwischen uns*, 14–26.

offers gripping examples of Christian women, some ordained, who during the second world war spearheaded the resistance against anti-semitism by helping Jews escape captivity and by speaking up against the horrors of Nazi treatment of Jews. The contribution of these women to the Christian-Jewish dialogue has often been forgotten. It was only in the last decade that the famous 1935 memorandum, warning the church of the impending genocide and calling for prophetic action, was properly attributed to the protestant pastor Elisabeth Schmitz. And few Roman Catholics are aware of the fact that Gertrud Luckner, a Roman Catholic woman who helped many Jews, played an important role in the genesis of the Vatican II document *Nostra Aetate*. Being theologically uneducated and outside of the mainstream leadership, these women operated in the margins of their respective traditions, a place which is often seen as a fertile ground for interreligious dialogue.

In addition to these individual instances of interfaith heroism, women have been actively engaged in dialogue groups of all kinds and in different places. They are active in more deliberate dialogue groups such as the "Daughters of Abraham" which have spread throughout the United States, drawing Jewish, Christian and Muslim women together to read texts and thus come to a deeper understanding of one another, and in events such as Women's Interfaith Conference which yearly gathers hundreds of women from different religions in cities such as Saint Louis and Irvine. But they are also involved in more spontaneous initiatives which emerge in different localities and which focus on creating community and mutual understanding. Mara Brecht describes one such community in Philadelphia which she studied for an extended period of time. She discusses the ways in which, rather than focusing solely on doctrinal differences, these women attempted to understand one another through probing into the meaning of particular beliefs in daily life and through participation in one another's festivities. This form of participatory learning was seen to create not only a deeper mutual understanding but also a personal bond. Also in Philadelphia, Nancy Kreimer mentions the emergence of interfaith walks or pilgrimages, which allow members from different religions to get to know one another and develop a sense of a shared ritual practice and experience.

One area in which dialogue between different religions, and between women in different religions has born most direct fruit is that of spirituality. Sue Levi Elwell focuses specifically on the development or the recovery of the practice of spiritual direction in Judaism as one of the immediate results of the dialogue with Christianity. While spiritual direction is of course not exclusive to women, those who initiated or reintroduced spiritual direction into Judaism happen to be women. Elwell suggests that it is the traditional marginalization of women within their respective religions that may lead to a greater desire for and cultivation of interiority.

In the process of engaging in such grassroots dialogue with other religions, women often come to develop their own personal synthesis and religious identity, born from different religious sources. This comes clearly to the fore in Angela Wong's contribution, which discusses the ways in which women in Hong Kong have come to negotiate their Chinese and Muslim identities. While deeply identifying with recent developments in global Islam (such as veiling), Chinese Muslim women also apply a typically Chinese attitude of pragmatism toward certain Islamic injunctions such as the primacy of domestic roles for women. Many of the women Wong interviewed paid lip service to this principle while occupying important professional roles in the community. Several women had initiated a divorce, finding justification for this in the Qur'an and in the desire to lead a more observant life. One of the areas in which their Muslim and their Chinese identities coalesced was that of commitment to family, involving respect and responsibility for parents and siblings. In all of this, it is the women themselves who engage in an internal and implicit dialogue, juggling the demands and the values of the broader culture, their personal faith and the practical demands of everyday life.

Though women have thus played an active role in interreligious dialogue, Jeannine Hill Fletcher reminds us of the various ways in which women have been and continue to be the objects, rather than the subjects of interreligious dialogue. Women have been used as pawns in the exchange between male religious leaders, and male leaders continue to often display agreement and solidarity in matters that deeply affect women but over which they have no say. Hill Fletcher points to the essentially political nature of dialogue as always harboring the interests and investments of some. She also argues that a focus on doctrine tends to depoliticize interreligious dialogue since it merely reinforces the patriarchal systems that produced these doctrines. Hill Fletcher nevertheless or therefore insists on the importance of active participation of women in interreligious dialogue, so as to draw attention to the "material impact of dialogue on bodies sexed and gendered female and on the multiplicity of women whose different social locations mean that impact is felt differently."

Even though women play an important role in the dialogue of daily life, or in grassroots interreligious activism and solidarity, there seems to be a disconnect between what is happening on the ground and what transpires in the dialogues between official representatives of different religions. Women's interreligious dialogue remains mainly personal and interpersonal and rarely affects or changes the religions to which they belong. However, dialogue from below often yields important insights and experiences which could be highly instructive and inspiring for the broader tradition, and genuine dialogue can only profit from the participation of all voices.

Interreligious Dialogue and Religious Feminism

Several articles in this volume point to the marginalization of women within their own respective traditions as an incentive and an opportunity for interreligious dialogue. Not only do women, or some women, feel less constrained by institutional and doctrinal strictures, but the shared confrontation with the structures of religious patriarchy also creates an immediate topic for exchange. Dialogue between religions indeed often emerges from a sense of interconnection, from a particular challenge or concern common to individuals from different religions. For feminists from different religions, this sense of commonality expresses itself in the experience of exclusion from religious authority and knowledge, and of control over their sexuality. While these expressions of religious patriarchy tend to be legitimated through internal religious teachings and traditions, the dialogue between women from different religions reveals more universal patterns of subordination which suggest deeper anthropological reasons. It is thus not surprising that some of the earliest examples of constructive interreligious dialogue or comparative theology may be found within the area of feminist thought. Works such as *Womanspirit Rising: A Feminist Reader in Religion* (1979) or *Speaking of Faith: Cross-cultural Perspectives on Women, Religion and Social Change* (1986) attempt to deal with topics regarding women in particular traditions from the perspective of broader, interreligious questions of religious patriarchy. And in the course of the past decades, a large number of volumes have appeared comparing and reflecting on the position of women in various religions.[5]

Rosemary Radford Ruether, herself one of the pioneers of Christian feminist thought and interreligious dialogue, sketches in her article "Toward A Transnational Feminism" some of the significant developments which have taken place in feminist thought in various religions, from Judith Plaskow's appeal for Jewish women to be recognized as standing alongside men at Sinai to Rita Gross's call to return to the liberating center of essential Buddhism. Though dealing with their own expressions of patriarchy, these feminists were often inspired by the same tools of feminist critique and by the bold steps taken by women in other traditions to critically engage their traditions. They tended to distinguish an originally or essentially egalitarian tradition from later patriarchal overlays and to tap into religious resources which could be used to establish the dignity of women and their religious equality. While affirming the importance of these expressions of religious and interreligious feminism, Ruether also acknowledges the postcolonial critique of liberal feminism and the ways in which it has been abused in the interest of vested powers.

This critique is developed in greater detail by Zayn Kassam, who in her article "Constructive Interreligious Dialogue Concerning Muslim Women" discusses the ways in which Muslim women have become the target of both Islamophobia and reactionary ideologies within Islam. Kassam exposes three myths about Muslim women which are prevalent in the West: that the war in Afghanistan will lead to a liberation of Muslim women, that capitalism will improve life for Muslim women and that Islam is essentially misogynist and the liberation of Muslim women will require secularism. Each of these myths points to the ways in which

5. Arvind Sharma, ed., *Women in World Religions*, McGill Studies in the History of Religions (New York: SUNY Press, 1987); Jean Holm with John Bowker, eds., *Women in Religion*, Themes in Religious Studies Series (London: Printer Publishers, 1994); Ursula King, ed., *Women in the World's Religions, Past and Present*, God, the Contemporary Discussion Series (New York: Paragon, 1987); Judith Plaskow and Carol Christ, *Weaving the Visions: New Patterns in Feminist Spirituality* (New York: HarperOne, 1989); Lucinda Joy Pach, *Women and World Religions* (Boston: Pearson, 2001); John Stratton Hawley, ed., *Fundamentalism and Gender* (New York: Oxford University Press, 1994); Arvind Sharma and Katherine K. Young, eds., *Fundamentalism and Women in World Religions* (London: T. & T. Clark, 2007); Arvind Sharma, ed., *Feminism and World Religions*, McGill Studies in the History of Religions (Albany: SUNY Press, 1998); Paula Cooey et al., eds., *After Patriarchy: Feminist Transformations of World Religions*, Faith Meets Faith Series (Maryknoll, NY: Orbis, 1991).

feminist ideals have been co-opted by a broad anti-Islamic rhetoric of fear in the West. On the other hand, Islamist ideologies have come to hold women in particular responsible for upholding Islamic identity, morality and family. Kassam argues that the path to change for Muslim women will have to emerge from within, from Muslim women engaging their own religious resources and participating in the public and political sphere. This may not lead to a mimicking of Western feminist ideals. As seen in examples of women in Malaysia and in Egypt, women may develop their own ways of negotiating with traditional authority, and of engaging in activism based at times less on distinctly feminist than on particular spiritual goals. Ruether similarly points to the situation of women in Botswana whose priorities at times appear to be different from those of Western feminism. This emphasis on particularity and difference, not only between but also within religions has come to characterize postmodern feminism, thus rendering the dialogue between women of different religions even more complex, but also more authentic.

A clear example of development and difference in feminist reflection within particular religions may be found in Aysha Hidayatullah's article "The Qur'anic Rib-ectomy," which critically examines the ways in which earlier Islamic feminists have at times idealized Islamic sources and set them over against Jewish and Christian traditions. Since the story of the secondary creation of Eve from the rib of Adam does not appear in the Qur'an, feminists such as Riffat Hassan have argued that the Qur'an presents an essentially egalitarian understanding of genders, and that the later appearance of the (crooked) rib in the Hadith must be attributed to Biblical influences. While Hidayatullah recognizes the anomaly of the sudden appearance of this story in the later tradition, she also warns against the danger of exonerating the tradition, and argues for the importance of acknowledging misogynistic tendencies in the texts and the traditions that have allowed such texts to become normative. Though feminists engaged in interreligious dialogue are certainly justified in pointing to resources within their own traditions which may become an example or a source of inspiration for others, it is also true that few traditions are free from traces of patriarchy and that dialogue may become an additional tool for discerning this in one another's traditions. This critical and self-critical function of dialogue is also evident in Jeannine Hill Fletcher's contribution which takes issue with the ways in which topics of particular concern to women have been, and continue to be discussed among all-male religious leaders. While such gender imbalance and injustice may be noted by women from any one religion, the combined critical effort by women from different religions may carry greater weight and efficacy.

Focusing on the history of dialogue, feminists may also shed critical light on the ways in which particular texts or figures have been used. Nancy Kreimer, for example, problematizes the habitual reference to the story of Abraham in the dialogue between Judaism, Christianity and Islam. While all three religions evoke him as a central example of faith, she points to the elements of sexism, violence and exclusion which are also an integral part of the Genesis story. Some scholars have attempted to ignore or to expand some details of the narrative in order to soften its exclusivist and sexist elements. Kreimer herself, however, insists on the importance of acknowledging the difficulties associated with this story while moving forward and tapping into other, more aggregative symbols from the different religions. The article also points to the creative imagination of women in developing new rituals, both within and between religions. Kreimer discusses the ritual of feet-washing as the analogue to the *berit milah* for female infants. She also points out how the development of new rituals at times opens up new meaning, which may eventually come to enrich the tradition at large.

Women's Contribution to Interreligious Dialogue

While women have thus played an important role in dialogues from below, and while dialogue has played an important role in the development of feminist reflection within different religions, one may still ask whether women actually bring something distinctive to interreligious dialogue. The question may seem overly general and disturbingly essentialist. What contemporary gender theory and the papers in this volume make clear is that one cannot speak of "women" as a fixed and universal category. Women's experiences and orientations differ according to race, class, sexual orientation, cultural norms, socialization, etc. However, the critique of women's absence from official dialogues contains some suggestion that women might offer a distinct perspective or approach, or at least that the presence of women would make a difference.

In her paper "What do Women Bring to the Dialogue Table?," Rita Gross categorically rejects the idea that women might have something unique to offer to interreligious dialogue. Reflecting on decades of involvement in both interreligious dialogue and in feminist thought, she suggests that the exclusion of women from dialogue may not only be blamed on the traditions themselves or on the predominantly male participants in dialogue. Gross argues that feminist thinkers have often themselves been less than eager to engage in dialogue with other religions, often due to a general distrust of all religions as essentially patriarchal. However, she still believes that it is absolutely necessary for women to participate in interreligious dialogue. Not only does their presence signal the reality of women's importance and role in every religion, but their experiences may also warn against the exclusivistic tendencies of religions, which she regards as the greatest impediment to interreligious dialogue. Beyond this, however, Gross denies (whether or not on Buddhist grounds) that women would bring anything distinctive, either in form or in content, to the dialogue table.

While neither Michelle Voss Roberts nor Anne Klein suggest that attention to the affective or non-verbal dimensions of dialogue would be distinctive of women, their contributions to this volume focus at length on the role of emotion and currents of energy in the process of interpersonal, intercultural and interreligious understanding. Inspired by the Hindu term *rasa* or emotion, which has a long tradition in Indian aesthetics, Voss Roberts suggests that this category may be invoked to shed some light on affective responses to religious difference. In the process of engaging the religious other, the term *rasa* invites a non-utilitarian and other-centered understanding. Rather than judging the religious other, it allows participants in dialogue to savor the emotion of wonder itself, and to enrich their own experiential life with particular religious emotions. This attention to emotion points to a more holistic understanding of interreligious dialogue as not only an exchange of ideas, but as an attempt to also tap into the experiential dimension of the religious life of the other.

Anne Klein uses Tibetan Buddhist notions of currents in an attempt to break through the traditional dichotomies of male–female, mind–body, intellect–affect as well as the teachings and practices that divide religions. Within Tibetan Buddhism, the various levels of currents that form the most subtle material dimension of being have been

9

thematized and integrated in personal practices and interpersonal communication. She suggests that they may also be used to engage in a deeper level of understanding and communication across religious traditions. Far from arguing that women have special access to these currents, she proposes that a greater attention to them may move beyond or beneath the traditional focus on gender differences which tend to have disadvantaged women.

Though it may be impossible to determine whether and exactly how women's participation in interreligious dialogue would make a difference, it is clear from the contributions to this volume that women from different religions do bring something distinctive to the dialogue, based on their particular location within or between religions and on their particular experiences of dialogue. Some reflect critically on their own tradition and on the intersection of feminism and dialogue, while others bring the resources of respective traditions to bear on the broader dialogue. The questions asked and the examples and sources selected certainly shed new light on the dialogue and offer new avenues for reflection. And if the Boston College Symposium on Women and Interreligious Dialogue in September of 2012 was any indication, women also bring a distinct style to actual dialogue: rather than engaging in polemical discussions, the authors of the papers in this volume attempted to find connections with other papers, building upon one another's thoughts and insights in an ongoing process of constructive reflection. It is only by bringing these voices, perspectives, and style into the mainstream of interreligious dialogue that women will actually make a difference, and render dialogue more complete.

1

Women and Interfaith Relations

Toward a Transnational Feminism

Rosemary Radford Ruether

Second wave feminist theology has been developing since the 1960s, initially focusing on Christianity. Mary Daly, with her 1968 book, *The Church and the Second Sex*, was a pioneer in the feminist critique of Catholicism. This was followed in 1973 with her more radical tome *Beyond God the Father*.[1] By this time Daly had decided that Christianity could not be reformed and was calling for women to leave not only the Church but all patriarchal religions. But many other Christians were also writing on feminist rethinking of Christianity. In the 80's and 90's women in other religious traditions, Judaism, Islam and Buddhism, among others, began to do feminist critique and reconstruction of their faiths. Feminist theology today is a global and interfaith discourse.

In this essay on women and interfaith relations, I will first summarize and compare four major groups of feminist theologians writing in the Christian, Jewish, Muslim and Buddhist traditions. I will then discuss global intercultural relations between Western and third world feminisms, lifting up African and Middle Eastern women's perspectives on their historical cultures and their challenge to Western feminism as colonialist. I will explore the question of transnational feminist relations.

---

1. Mary Daly, *The Church and the Second Sex* (New York: Harper, 1968); Daly, *Beyond God the Father* (Boston: Beacon, 1973).

To what extent is interfaith and global dialogue between feminisms possible that can overcome such misunderstanding and move toward mutual collaboration?

I begin my discussion of feminist theology with my 1983 book, *Sexism and Godtalk: Toward a Feminist Theology*, as an example of feminist critique and reconstruction of Christianity. In this book I propose as the critical principle of feminist theology "the promotion of the full humanity of women." I elaborate this principle in the following way:

> Whatever denies, diminishes or distorts the full humanity of women is, therefore, appraised as not redemptive. Theologically speaking, whatever diminishes or denies the full humanity of women must be presumed not to reflect the divine or an authentic relation to the divine, or to reflect the authentic nature of things, or to be the message or work of an authentic redeemer or community of redemption. This negative principle implies the positive principle: what does promote the full humanity of women is of the Holy, it does reflect true relation to the divine, it is the true nature of things, the authentic message of redemption and the mission of the redemptive community.[2]

Having enunciated this critical principle of feminist theology, I go on to say that the meaning of the term "full humanity of women" is not fully known. It has been negated within the histories we have known by the denigration and marginalization of women. Still women's humanity has not been totally destroyed. It has constantly reaffirmed itself, even if in limited and subversive ways. These partial appearances are touchstones by which we can test and criticize all that diminishes us and begin to imagine a world without sexism.

Although patriarchy and the subjugation of women have shaped both the sources and history of Christianity, the Christian tradition has not lacked critical principles that are usable for feminist theological development. Foundational to such critical principles is what I call "the prophetic principle." The prophetic principle is not a marginal idea in the Bible. Rather it can be said to be the central tradition of Biblical faith, the critical pattern of thought by which Biblical faith constantly criticizes and renews itself and its own vision.

---

2. Ruether, *Sexism and Godtalk: Toward a Feminist Theology* (Boston: Beacon, 1983), 19.

There are four components of prophetic faith: 1) God defends and vindicates groups of people who are oppressed and unfairly exploited. 2) This implies a critique of systems of power and their power-holders who are responsible for this oppression. 3) It also involves a critique of the ideology by which oppression is justified and a repudiation of the assumption that this domination comes from God and is based on divine will. 4) Finally, there is a vision of a new age to come in which the present system of injustice is overcome and God's intended reign of peace and justice installed in history.[3]

Significantly, prophetic language in Hebrew Scripture and the New Testament is not directed against other religions, but it is self-critique. It is directed against teaching and practices of its own people and its leaders. God is depicted as repudiating these writings and practices and their assumptions about who God is and what God wants. Thus the God of the prophet Amos thunders: "I hate, I despise your feasts and I take no delight in your solemn assemblies . . . Take away from me the noise of your songs, to the melody of your harps I will not listen. But let justice roll down like waters and righteousness like an ever flowing stream" (Amos 5:21, 23–24).

But prophetic critique is not a static set of ideas. Rather it is a principle of discernment of truth and falsehood, justice and injustice that has to be constantly applied to new circumstances and contexts. Prophetic critique insightfully applied in one context can become language justifying triumphalism and oppression of others in another context, when those who are the heirs of that language become the power-holders that assume that their self-interests speak for God. Thus, for example, Jesus' critique of the Scribes and Pharisees has one meaning as the view of a Jewish prophet within and critiquing his own religion. It takes on a totally different meaning when Christianity becomes a separate gentile religion and uses this language to reject Judaism and establish a triumphalism of Church over the Synagogue within a Christian Roman empire.

The Hebraic prophetic tradition formulated its vision of oppression and hope for liberation in the context of the socioeconomic oppression of the poor by the wealthy and of a small colonized nation by the great empires of antiquity. It was not used to question the subjugation of women and slaves within the Jewish patriarchal system. Although Jews

3. Ibid., 22–24.

saw themselves as liberated slaves, and called to liberate Jews who are enslaved, they need not liberate gentiles who they enslave. In the Jesus movement these begin to be included. In early Christianity there is a vision of a new humanity in Christ that overcomes the privileged status of male over female, Jew over Greek or Hellene over barbarians, free over slave. But Christianity eventually developed a new system of hierarchy within a Christian empire that ignored these innovations. Christianity has to rediscover and reapply this prophetic liberating principle in new contexts in its ongoing history.

Feminist theology in the late twentieth century is the first time that patriarchy as a whole was seen as contrary to God's will. The domination of male over female is distinguished from God's power and will; hence identification of God as a patriarchal male must be questioned. Yet, feminism also must recognize the inadequacy of thinking of all women as equally 'oppressed' by patriarchy and discern the complexity of gender hierarchy within class, race, ethnic and sexual hierarchies among others. The rapid diversification of feminist theologies within ethnic and racial contexts, class hierarchies and gay and lesbian groups, often using distinct names, such as 'womanist' or 'mujerista,' represent this coming to voice of distinct groups in different contexts of oppression within patriarchy.

In the 80s and 90s, American Jewish women also began to develop a feminist critique of Judaism. American Jewish women had long been leaders of American feminism, but for Jewish women trained in their religious tradition to reconstruct Judaism from a feminist perspective is more recent. Some issues, such as patriarchal God language, are shared by Christians and Jews, but other issues are distinct. Jewish women do not have to deal with the Christian linking of original sin to Eve as woman's representative since original sin is not a part of Jewish anthropology. But ceremonies, such as circumcision and Bar mitzvah, have privileged the Jewish male as the normative Jew. Rabbinical laws have excused women from the time bound commandments of prayer on the grounds that women are busy with housework and child care. Jewish religious feminists thus saw themselves as needing to create inclusive language, ceremonies, and religious observances to include women more fully in Judaism.

Judith Plaskow in her 1990 work, *Standing Again at Sinai: Judaism from a Feminist Perspective,* has written one of the foundational works in

Jewish feminist theology.[4] The title of this book comes from the founding event in Jewish history in which the Jewish people stand at Sinai to receive the covenant from God as a people. To prepare for this reception, Moses gives the men the commandment "Be ready by the third day. Do not go near a woman" (Exodus 19:15).

To be fit to approach God, men must abstain from sex for three days. But this command raises the question of whether women were present at Sinai at all. Did both men and women abstain from sex and were present side by side? Or were women banished to some other place, so men could be free to approach God? Clearly it is men who are seen as the representatives of the people Israel, and hence those who should make themselves pure to approach God and receive his commandments. Thus, for Plaskow, a feminist Judaism must call for Jewish women to be acknowledged as standing at Sinai, to receive the covenant as equal members of the Jewish people before God.

For Plaskow, it is not enough to reform particular *halakhah* or Jewish laws. One must challenge the fundamental presuppositions of the legal system, namely that women are not normative Jews. That women are not called to the Torah, are silent in the marriage ceremony and shackled when it comes to divorce are not just disabilities that can be reformed, as they have been in Reform Judaism. More fundamental is the basic presupposition of 'otherness,' of women's lack of normative status as Jews and as human beings.

This is given dramatic expression in Jewish language about God. Although said to transcend sexuality and to be One, God is nevertheless spoken of in language that is patriarchal, with male pronouns and images. Although Jewish mysticism integrated female imagery about God, this is still seen as unacceptable in religious liturgy. To do so is to raise the specter of paganism, of the suppressed and negated 'Goddess' of negated religions of the ancient world. But unless we can speak of the divine in female terms, God remains seen as a male, and only males are normatively 'images' of God.

For Plaskow, these two issues, women's 'otherness' and the male imagery for God are connected with a third issue, that the Jewish tradition is not the product of the Jewish people as a whole, but of men alone. Of course women have lived Jewish history and carried its burdens. But

4. Judith Plaskow, *Standing Again at Sinai: Judaism from a Feminist Perspective* (San Francisco: Harper & Row, 1990).

15

women's experiences are not the history passed down and recorded in the texts. The maleness of God and of normative Jews who shaped the tradition silences women as shapers of the Holy.

A feminist Judaism demands a new understanding of Torah, God and Israel. The male bias of Torah and view of God must be overcome. Women must be fully integrated into the people of Israel and its memory and life. Feminism demands a new understanding of God that is foundational to a new understanding of women as equally participating members of Jewish humanity, shaping its thought and practice. Only then will reforming Jewish law be rooted in the larger reality of Jewish life. Only when Jewish women can speak and name their own experiences, and this becomes a part of Jewish memory passed down in texts of Jewish life, will women truly become integral members of the people Israel. Such a holistic feminist Judaism will also be a part of a larger struggle for a more just world.

Christian and Jewish feminists in Christian countries or in the state of Israel, face right-wing critics that would disallow propositions for reconstructing their faith. But they are relatively secure in the liberal wings of their communities and schools. Islamic feminists by contrast face a more embattled situation, particularly in some Islamic states. Since the l970s movements of Islamic fundamentalism have challenged patterns of secular modernization and sought to reestablish the reign of a particular view of Muslim Law (*Sharia*) that would mandate women's subordination and confinement in the patriarchal family as normative.[5]

Some Islamic fundamentalists, such as the Taliban in Afghanistan, have even engaged in violence, such as throwing acid in women's faces, when they appear in public with uncovered head and secular dress. They have destroyed girls' schools and killed female teachers. Yet despite these threats, the Islamic feminist movement has grown apace over the last thirty years, and its outspoken advocates unequivocally claim that gender equity should be normative for Islam.

Riffat Hassan is one example of such Muslim feminists. Born and raised in Pakistan, Dr. Hassan has taught religious studies at the University of Louisville, Kentucky for many years. Her research has focused on the Qur'anic understanding of the original creation of humanity as male

---

5. See Judith Plaskow, "Jewish Feminist Theology," in Rosemary S. Keller and Rosemary R. Ruether, *In Our Own Voices: Four Centuries of American Women's Religious Writings* (Louisville: Westminister John Knox, 1995), 451–55.

and female by God and how this firmly establishes gender equity of men and women as normative for Islam, despite later Islamic exegesis to the contrary. Until recently the Quran, the *Hadith* (oral tradition attributed to the Prophet) and *Fiqh* (jurisprudence) have been interpreted solely by men. Women are said to have been created from the left rib of Adam and to have been created subordinate to serve men.

Yet a study of the Qur'an itself shows that these views are not present in it. The Qur'an does not contain the 'rib' story of Eve's creation. It only speaks of the creation of Adam and Eve at the same time as equals. The rib story and the idea of women's secondary creation as subordinate came into Islamic tradition later, probably from Christianity. For Hassan this is of prime importance. The creation of man and woman at the same time as equals needs to be understood as the foundational Islamic viewpoint. In Hassan's words, "The only way that Muslim daughters of Hawwa' (Eve) can end the history of their subjugation at the hands of the sons of Adam is by returning to the point of origin and challenging the authenticity of the *ahadith* that make women derivative and secondary in creation, but primary in guilt, sinfulness and mental and moral deficiency. They must challenge the later sources that regard them, not as ends in themselves but as instruments created for the convenience and comfort of men."[6]

Two other leading Muslim feminist theologians, Amina Wadud, author of the *Qur'an and Women* (1999) and *Inside the Gender Jihad: Women's Reform in Islam* (2005) and Asma Barlas, *"Believing Women" in Islam: Unreading Patriarchal Interpretations of the Qur'an* (2002) have focused particularly on God-language in the Qur'an in their vindication of women's equality with men in the sacred text. Central to the Qur'an and to Islam as a whole is the absolute unity or oneness of God (*Tawhid*). Islam rejects the Christian Trinity and the divinity of Christ as violations of this oneness of God. God is understood to be incomparable and unrepresentable, particularly in anthropomorphic terms. This understanding of God establishes oneness in relation to creation, and to male and female as equal in relation to one another. Imaging God as male and the male as particular representative of God is forbidden. God is said to do no injustice (*Zulm*) by setting up one group as superior to another. This forbids understanding God as setting men as superior and

6. Riffat Hassan, "Muslim Women's Hermeneutics," in ibid., 459.

women as secondary in relation to men.[7] Reform of law and practice in Islam must be rooted in the primacy of the Qur'an as the foundational source for understanding who God is and how God created humanity, male and female.

Turning to Buddhism, we see that it too is a complex tradition with conflicting views of gender. It is said that the Buddha was reluctant to allow women to become nuns, and was finally persuaded to do so only on the condition that the nuns would be strictly subordinate to monks. Even the oldest and most mature nun must defer to the youngest monk. Yet, according to the original Buddhist texts, the existence of nuns is regrettable. Buddhism would have lasted 1000 years, rather than falling into crisis after 500 years, if women had not been admitted to monastic life. Because female monastic life is seen as less worthy, nuns' orders receive much less financial support from Buddhist laity than male monks. The Buddhist understanding of karma, derived from Hinduism, makes the very existence of women the product of bad karma. Rather than being liberated from rebirth, people are reborn in inferior social status, such as female, because they have failed to live purely in the previous life. Some Buddhist traditions throw into question whether women can become Buddhas or become fully enlightened because of their inferiority as female.

Yet many Buddhist women feel these negative traditions are more than fully offset by other traditions that insist that men and women are equally capable of enlightenment, and that the view of women as inferior to men is an illusion of false consciousness and egoism. For Buddhist feminist theologian, Rita Gross, author of *Buddhism After Patriarchy* (1993), what is particularly attractive is the lack of a God to whom the believer must submit. One does not have to struggle with the maleness of God and how to include the female as image of God, since there is no anthropomorphic deity. Rather the divine is a life process of coming to be and passing away. Buddhist meditational practice, leading to enlightenment and "compassion for all sentient beings," entails giving up ego clinging that seeks to hold on to one's selfhood as if it were eternal life. Freed of such possessiveness, one can affirm the life process as it actually

7. Asma Barlas, *Believing Women in Islam: Unreading Patriarchal Interpretations of the Quran* (Austin: University of Texas Press, 2002), 13–16.

exists. This meditational practice is the same for men and women or in Gross' words, "The Dharma is both male and female."[8]

For Gross, Buddhism in its essence is not only egalitarian, but can even be said to be identical with feminism.[9] Like feminism, Buddhism begins with experience and directs one toward a process of dissolving and discarding ego clinging that blocks liberation. Yet Gross admits that Buddhism has been shaped by patriarchy in Asia; Buddhism in its Asian patriarchal setting would not have been her 'religion of choice.' But in late twentieth-century United States, where converts to Buddhism have been drawn from progressive feminists, it becomes possible to discard these patriarchal overlays and discover the liberating center of essential Buddhism.

For Gross, Buddhism and feminism in her life and practice have become a process of mutual transformation. Buddhism can be deepened by bringing in prophetic concern for injustice and hope for social transformation. At the same time Buddhist meditational practice has enabled her to relax and to discard the anger and distress she once felt about gender injustice. In her words, "perhaps we can envision a marriage of compassion and righteousness in social ethics, a gentle and active approach to such issues as gender inequity, privilege and hierarchy."[10]

These feminist theological thinkers teach in the United States, in religious studies departments of universities or ecumenical settings. They differ from each other. Many Christians might disagree with the Islamic rejection of the Trinity and the divinity of Christ, although Judaism would agree with this. Islam disagrees with Judaism on its view of the election of the Jews, believing that God's relation to humanity includes all people equally, a view that would be compatible with the Christian teaching that people of all nations are one in Christ. Christians, and perhaps Jews and Muslims, might have problems with the Buddhist denial of any ontological status to the divine or to the self. But these differences are differences between these religions, not differences between the writer's views as feminists.

---

8. Rita M. Gross, *Buddhism after Patriarchy: A Feminist History, Analysis, and Reconstruction of Buddhism* (Albany: SUNY Press, 1993), 207.

9. Rita M. Gross, "Buddhism and Feminism," in Keller and Ruether, eds., *In Our Own Voices*, 259.

10. Ibid., 463.

As feminists, they draw on similar principles. All the writers across the four religions would agree with the quest for an inclusive God who is not male and does not choose males as superior and representative of the divine, but establishes the equality of men and women in relation to one other and to God. Yet differences and conflicts between feminisms have appeared across global regions, particularly as they have been divided by the colonialism of Europe and North America toward Asia, Africa, the Middle East and Latin America. It is to these challenges of feminism as colonialist that I turn to discuss the question of a transnational feminism.

Several African scholars, male and female, have vehemently disputed the way in which western scholars, including western feminists, have interpreted African social history as "primitive" and oppressively patriarchal toward women. Nigerian sociologist Oyeronke Oyewumi, in her 1997 book, *The Invention of Women: Making African Sense of Western Gender Discourse*,[11] argued that the western categories of gender have no relevance in Africa. On the basis of her study of the Oyo-Yoruba in Western Nigeria she concluded that gender was totally absent from pre-colonial Yoruba society. The central organizing principle of social relation was not gender, but seniority.

Ifi Amadiume, also a Nigerian sociologist, argued against what she saw as western distortions of African social development. In her 1997 book, *Reinventing Africa: African Matriarchy, Religion and Culture*,[12] she sees pre-colonial African society as having complementary systems of matriarchy and patriarchy in ways that coexisted and supplemented one another. Women had their own systems of power that included land ownership, women's councils and rule. The Goddess was central to women's religion. The interaction of female and male systems of power created gender fluidity, allowing men and women to cross gender boundaries and exchange roles and status. Amadiume explores this gender fluidity in her 1987 book, *Male Daughters, Female Husbands: Gender and Sex in an African Society*.[13] Here she explores pre-colonial African practices of allowing females to play roles usually monopolized

11. Oyeronke Oyewumi, *Invention of Women: Making African Sense of Western Gender Discourse* (Minneapolis: University of Minnesota Press, 1997).

12. Ifi Amadiume, *Reinventing Africa: African Matriarchy, Religion and Culture* (Minneapolis: University of Minnesota Press, 1997).

13. Amadiume, *Male Daughters, Female Husbands: Gender and Sex in an African Society* (London: Zed, 1987).

by men, including taking on a woman as wife and being classified as males for purposes of power.

Exclusive patriarchy was introduced by Arab slave trading societies from the eleventh century, but more thoroughly by European colonialism—British, French and Belgian—in the nineteenth century. African women's organizations, such as market women's associations, vehemently resisted European colonization and were violently repressed. Western scholars of Africa, including feminists, have often ignored or misunderstood this rich and complex history of African societies, and imagined themselves to be bringing modernity and the liberation of women to Africa.

But the relations of western feminism and colonialism are more complex than westerners dominating third world societies and western feminists reading them through the lens of ignorant paternalism. There are also cases where the leaders of a third world country entered into colonial relations with the west and became advocates of western feminism in order to dominate their own society. A fascinating example of this is Iran whose shifting history in relation to both colonialism and feminism is traced by Iranian historian Nima Naghibi in her 2007 book, *Rethinking Global Sisterhood: Western Feminism and Iran.*[14]

Naghibi begins her story with British women adventurers to Persia in the late nineteenth and early twentieth centuries, such as Gertrude Bell and Ella Sykes, who traveled to Persia when Britain was competing with Russia for Persian resources. They saw the West as bringing redemption to Muslim women by freeing them from the subordination and passivity supposedly imposed on them by Islam. Women from the West were seen as having a special role in this conversion and liberation of the Muslim woman of Persia since they, unlike the male missionaries, could enter into the harem and bring the Christian and Western message of education, health care and fuller humanness to the secluded Muslim women. Islam and Persian society were seen as embodying "primitive" and "backward" human systems of an earlier era, while Christianity and the West brought modernity ad enlightenment.

This relation of western colonialism and feminism took on a different meaning in the 1930s to 1960s in Iran. In 1936, Reza Shah Pahlavi, after a trip to Turkey where he was impressed by Ataturk's

---

14. Nima Naghibi, *Rethinking Global Sisterhood: Western Feminism and Iran* (Minneapolis: University of Minnesota Press, 2007).

modernization policies, legislated the "Unveiling Act," where he forbade women to wear the veil in public and commanded his soldiers to arrest veiled women or tear the veil off their head if they appeared in public with any form of *hijab*. This meant that more conservative women who wished to wear the veil could not function in public with it on. Rural or lower class women were banned from public activity, even though they needed to do so as shoppers and sellers of goods.

Under the new Shah, installed in 1941, wearing the veil became a choice. Women could choose to wear it or not. But the class aspect of this choice remained. Unveiled women in western dress were the educated upper class. The veiled woman was assumed to be uneducated, belonging to lower class or rural families. Royal women and their upper class allies championed feminism and saw themselves as bringing modernity to Iran. The result was an identification of feminism with colonialism and Western imperialism in Iranian history. In 1983 when the Shah was overthrown and an Islamic anti-colonial regime introduced, the revolutionary leader Ayatollah Khomeini implemented the Veiling Act, which prohibited women from appearing in public unveiled. Now they could be arrested and sanctioned if they appeared without the veil and without Islamic dress in public.

The veil becomes identified not only with Islam but also with anti-colonial nationalism. This identification means that today it becomes difficult not only in Iran and other Muslim states, but globally, to distinguish the decision of a Muslim woman not to wear the veil from a modernity identified with western colonialism, or to affirm an indigenous feminism that might include wearing the veil as a choice for one's own identity and not submission to Islamic male coercion. How does transnational feminism cut through these confusions and affirm the choice for Muslim women to wear or not wear the veil that is not loaded with these feminist or anti-feminist colonial or anti-colonial messages?

Today a plurality of feminisms has become present in cultures and societies around the world. The 2012 book, *South Asian Feminisms*, edited by Ania Loomba and Ritty Lukose, documents the variety of local feminisms in India, Pakistan, Sri Lanka, Kashmir and Bangladesh.[15] Feminisms not only have distinct perspectives across these nations but are in internal conflicts within nations. In India, for example, right wing

15. Ania Loomba and Ritty A. Lukose, eds., *South Asian Feminisms: Contemporary Interventions* (Durham: Duke University Press, 2012).

Hindu women may appropriate militant feminist language in ways that vilify Indian Muslims, including Indian Muslim women.

But even in mainline liberal feminism in countries such as India, feminism is in tension between two goals that are not always in harmony. On the one hand, Indian feminists hope to bring about gender equality for all Indian women, but on the other hand feel it incumbent for Indian feminism to establish its nationalist credentials; that is, to show that the goals of feminism are compatible with the Indian ideals of femininity in the family and culture. These two goals are not easily compatible; more specifically, the second goal may limit what can be achieved toward the first.

This conflict of feminist goals in India is a version of the problem we encountered in Iran. India seeks to be a modern and progressive nation, but also a nation born from the struggle against colonialism; hence feminist liberation must be reconciled with nationalist anti-colonialism. How do western feminists enter into understanding and collaboration with feminism across this divide between modernization and anti-colonial nationalism? To explore this dilemma, I will discuss my recent experience in Botswana in southern Africa. From June 5–25, 2012, I participated in a course in Botswana with a focus on the theme of "Gender, Leadership and Culture." As western women studying or teaching at the Claremont Graduate School, we went to Botswana, not to teach them about gender, but to immerse ourselves in its history and culture to try to understand how issues of gender and leadership were developing in this country today.

Botswana is a country in southern Africa that is a third larger than Zimbabwe to its east, but lightly populated, with less than 2 million people. Botswana is notable because throughout its forty-five years of existence as an independent country, it has been a multi-party democracy, the only country in Africa that has not gone through a period of one-party dictatorship. Also, unlike its neighbors, South Africa, Namibia and Zimbabwe, it never had apartheid and white colonization of its land imposed on it.

From 1885–1966 it was ruled as a British Protectorate, called Bechuanaland. But it evaded white colonization and apartheid thanks to the determined resistance of its indigenous chiefs. In the 1890s the British intended to hand Bechuanaland over to Cecil Rhodes' British South African Company, who would have treated it as it was treating Rhodesia, confiscating the best land for white settlers and marginalizing Blacks on poor land or making them serfs on white estates. This was blocked by three Batswana chiefs who traveled to England with missionary W. C. Willoughby as their interpreter. The chiefs demanded that Bechuanaland not be transferred to Rhodes, that their lands not be confiscated, their status as chiefs be preserved and alcohol be prohibited in their areas. Chamberlain, the Colonial Secretary, tried to ignore them, but they traveled all over England speaking to audiences. This evoked an avalanche of letters of support, and Chamberlain had to back down and not hand the area to Rhodes, although some land was ceded to build a railroad between the two countries.

In 1910 after the Boer War, Britain intended to hand over Bechuanaland to South Africa, but again the Chiefs protested and threatened to take their case to England and fight in the British law courts. Again Britain delayed. Then in the 1950s with the creation of more severe apartheid laws in South Africa unpopular with most Britons, transfer to South Africa become unacceptable to the British government. By the 1960s the British determined to give self-government to its colonies. Botswana came into existence as an independent state in 1966 without having to fight for their independence or having passed through colonization or racial segregations. Its historical leadership groups and their control of their lands was largely intact. Thus, Botswana became an independent state less scarred by white colonization than many other African states.

Although the British had exercised a protectorate over Botswana for eighty-two years, it had invested almost nothing in its development. British policy was to get its colonies to pay for any development, and to invest as little of its own funds as possible. Botswana was seen as largely worthless, so little was done in the way of economic or social development. Britain neglected services such as education or health. Missionaries did build some schools and hospitals, and local chiefs also built schools and hospitals not controlled by missionaries. But at independence Botswana was seen as one of the world's poorest countries with few educated people.

Once independent, the democratically elected Botswana government dedicated itself to rapid development of their country. A constitution was written that remains largely unchanged to the present. The President as head of state also presides over the national assembly.

A national Judiciary is represented by law courts throughout the country. The traditional chiefs or *Dikgosi* remain as an advisory council to the national government, and continue to play an important role in administering welfare services and presiding over law courts in local communities.

In 1967, after two years of independence, diamonds were discovered, and this new wealth was put under a national company whose large revenues are used to fund national development. Social and economic development has been extensive. A national land policy gives every household the possibility of acquiring a plot of land for farming. A road system links all major villages. A national water system makes potable water available in every village. An education system makes schools free for all Batswana from primary school to University. And a health system produces health services for everyone with a very nominal consultation fee of 5 Pula (62 cents).

In 1985 HIV/AIDs appeared in Botswana, mostly from men working in South Africa, and soon spread to a fourth of the population. The Botswana government invested millions to cover AIDS medication for all who needed it. AIDS deaths were sharply reduced, although today about a fourth of Batswana are living with AIDs. The economic development of the country has been so rapid and successful that the United Nations has recently reclassified Botswana as a "middle income nation" which means that some international NGO grants for poverty alleviation are no longer available for Botswana.

In 1980 Botswana began to build its own university. To do so it appealed to every citizen to give one cow to fund this national institution, which today is a progressive and well developed school located in Gaberone, the national capital. A life-sized statue of a Batswana peasant walking with his cow, located in front of the Administration building, commemorates this contribution of the ordinary people of Botswana to building their university.

Our three-week course based at the University of Botswana focused on lectures by eight university faculty from different departments on issues of gender and social development in Botswana. From these lectures we became aware that the Botswana government is strongly committed to gender equality as integral to its self-understanding as a democratic state. Botswana signed the UN declaration against all discrimination against women. The Citizenship Act reformed Botswana law that had made the children of Batswana women married to foreigners, citizens of their father's country, and make Botswana citizenship inheritable by the children of these Batswana women. The Marital Power act of 2004 reformed the laws that gave dominant power to husbands in families, according equal ownership and power to both husband and wife. Legislation in 2008 made domestic violence a crime.

And yet Botswana legislators have stopped short of reform of family relations in two areas. The effort to make rape of a wife by her husband a crime was not passed by a narrow margin, and homosexual relations remains illegal. Thus traditional views, based on ideas of what is seen as appropriate for the "African" or Botswana "family" as heterosexual, giving husbands the right to sexual access of their wives, remain intact. Moreover the increasing independence and empowerment of women has evoked anxiety in young Batswana men, resulting in a spate of cases of young men in their late teens and early 20s killing girlfriends who broke up with them and then committing suicide. Violence to women and girls is high in Botswana families and society, although not higher than many other countries throughout the world.

As US students immersed in gender studies in Botswana, what should be our response to this mixed history? These are realities that we seek to understand in their Botswana context. It is not our job to be reformers there. Only Batswana can further the process of gender reform in their country. In areas such as marital rape and homosexual relations they have to do so in a way that can be seen as compatible to Botswana society, not as practices imported or imposed by the West. Needless to say, changes in these two areas are not universally endorsed by all people in western societies either.

In this context what does "transnational feminism" mean? In my view, it means that western feminists, and women and men concerned about gender equality in countries such as Botswana, meet as equals. Westerners do not come assuming they have the superior modern culture to impart to "less developed" people. This doesn't mean that western liberal feminists deny principles to which they are committed, but these are points of discussion, not domination. Our first agenda is to understand how our friends in Botswana are working in their own historical and cultural context. Only in that way can we really work together as colleagues. This is the rich promise of an emerging transnational feminism.

2

Gift to The Prophet from a King

The Politics of Women in Interreligious Dialogue

Jeannine Hill Fletcher

In January 2012, the Interfaith Center of New York hosted a day of reflection for Muslims and Catholics who had been engaged in joint service projects in which interreligious dialogue and interfaith action came together.[1] The event covered a range of topics and included perspectives that were scholarly, historical, pastoral and practical; it gave evidence of a vibrant past and future of collaboration. Women had been engaged in the different projects around the city, and so their reflections were included in this public dialogue.[2] They powerfully discussed their

1. One immediate question raised by the topic of "women in interreligious dialogue" is precisely what constitutes "interreligious dialogue" and how one might have access to a sufficient body of data in order to make judgments/assessments. Interreligious dialogue takes numerous forms, including but not limited to: formal public venues for exchange of ideas, texts with various religious viewpoints, online posting sites, informal/local venues for exchange/conversation (classroom, home, church/synagogue/mosque), everyday practices where persons of different religious traditions are in conversation (even if not expressly on religion). This essay looks at some highly visible political statements as representative but not exhaustive evidence of "women" in interreligious dialogue.

2. As evidenced in writings on women in interreligious dialogue and data from high-profile forums, women are frequently underrepresented or absent in interreligious dialogue. See Ursula King, "Feminism: The Missing Dimension in the Dialogue of Religions," in John D'Arcy May, ed., *Pluralism and the Religions: The Theological and Political Dimensions* (London: Cassel, 1998), 40–55; Jeannine Hill Fletcher, "Women

experiences and raised crucial concerns surrounding women's lives and bodies—access to food, immigration status, and the integrity of bodies sexed female and under assault—among them. But the presence of "women" was more than what met the eye. Women and women's concerns were also invoked and imagined, demonstrating that "women" in interreligious dialogue can sometimes be fictive and functioning in a variety of ways.

In the course of this day-long event, as participants tried to envision future collaborations as a positive extension of the history of Christian-Muslim relations, the complicated nature of "women" in interreligious dialogue was captured with the imaginative presence of one particular woman. One of the speakers very sincerely shared the story of what must have been among the first Muslim-Christian encounters: the Prophet Muhammad is remembered to have sent an envoy to Egypt and its Christian ruler, and although the King refused the invitation to convert to Islam, he sent to Muhammad a young girl as a token of friendship and good will. The speaker didn't elaborate on the fate of this young girl in history or her figuring in the tradition, but she hovered in this dialogue at the precarious place of connecting Christians and Muslims past and present. If her name was uttered, it wasn't sufficiently compelling to warrant holding her person in memory. She was simply there: an object passed from one tradition to another; a broken sign of past possibilities and future failings.

If the name of the young girl who passed as gift between two powerful figures was unremembered in the dialogue setting, the episode has not been forgotten in Islamic tradition. The political setting is paramount in this story, where the Prophet as statesman desired peaceable relations with surrounding rulers, sending envoys not only to Egypt but to all neighboring kingdoms.[3] One account of the Egyptian King's po-

---

in Interreligious Dialogue," in Catherine Cornille, ed., *Wiley–Blackwell Companion to Interreligious Dialogue*, Wiley–Blackwell Companions to Religion (New York: Wiley–Blackwell, 2013). It is also easy to see this in the published programs of many high-profile interreligious dialogue events, for example, World Day of Peace in Assisi (2002), http://www.vatican.va/special/assisi-participants_20020118_en.html; and Munich (2011) http://www.santegidio.org/index.php?let=A&pageID=2426&idLng=1064&langID=1064&pv=0.

3. Christopher James Wright indicates that the term used to identify the Egyptian leader (*muqawqis*) has had a variety of uses at various times (including "prince" and "patriarch") and refers in this case to letters sent to "kings of the non-Arabs." Wright cites *Futuh Misr* by Ibn 'Abd al-Hakam. Christopher James Wright, unpublished

lite refusal to convert to Islam indicates his response with the following words: "I send you now as a gift from me two (slave) girls who occupy a special place among the Copts, along with a robe of honor and a saddle beast for a mount."[4] Tradition holds that these two young women were of a family highly regarded in Egypt[5] and names them regularly as Mariyya and Sirin. Because Mariyya finds special favor with the Prophet and eventually bears a son, she is remembered more centrally than her sister, and likely is the young girl referenced in the January 2012 meeting. Yet, as Aysha Hidayatullah has demonstrated, we know more about how Mariyya is remembered and recounted down through the centuries than we do of her actual, historical reality.[6] Rooted in accounts from the hadith (c. 845), considered authoritative transmission of the sayings and stories of the Prophet, we can see how the retelling of Mariyya's story reflects values and interests of the community holding her in memory.

Hidayatullah identifies one of the values Mariyya regularly conveys as an advocate for interfaith relations.[7] With this role and her story as point of departure, we might follow this strand to investigate those places where interfaith dialogues continue to exhibit male political agendas taking place over women's bodies. But Mariyya's story offers more points for examination, as she also figures as an exhibit of the Prophet's virility as, "The Holy Prophet took one of these sisters for his own wife."[8] So, we might ask what function sexuality and sexual difference plays in interreligious political exchange and dialogues. Further, Mariyya's story

dissertation "Ibn 'Abd al-Hakam's "Futuh Misr": An Analysis of the Text and New Insights into the Islamic Conquest of Egypt" (University of California, Santa Barbara, 2006). Aysha Hidayatullah names him as "governor of Alexandria" in "Mariyya the Copt: Gender, Sex and Heritage in the Legacy of Muhammad's *umm walad,*" *Islam and Christian–Muslim Relations* 23 (2010) 223 (221–43).

4. Hajjah Amina Adil, *Muhammad, The Messenger of Islam: His Life and Prophecy* (Washington, DC: Islamic Supreme Council of America, 2002), 432.

5. See, for example, http://www.cyberistan.org/islamic/muqawqis.html: "The Prophet's letter to Muqawqis, the ruler of Egypt was similar to that sent to Emperor Heraclius, as he was a Coptic Christian. Muqawqis answered to the Prophet (pbuh) evasively. However, he sent a rich present of a thousand measures of gold, twenty robes of fine cloth, a mule, and two Coptic Christian ladies who were held in great respect in Egypt. The young ladies were sisters, Mariyah and Sirin. The prophet gave Sirin to Hassan ibn Thabit, the poet, and he took Mariyah as his wife. The mule was named Duldul and the Prophet rode it in the Battle of Hunain."

6. Hidayatullah, "Mariyya the Copt."

7. Ibid., 223.

8. Amina Adil, *Muhammad, The Messenger of Islam*, 432.

sends her also into a network of the Prophet's wives, first as a slave/ servant/concubine and later as the mother of a son to Muhammad, in some renderings elevating her to a wife among wives.[9] The complexity of female relationships in this context invites us to consider women in interfaith encounter from another angle. By opening up avenues for investigation, Mariyya unexpectedly brings gifts of insight for a feminist consideration of interreligious dialogue.

The Gift: Political Exchange over Women's Bodies

In forging an amicable link between Egypt and Medina, Mariyya serves as an advocate for peaceful relations across religious and political lines, the brokering of her body a vehicle for "international affairs" among male leaders. Even today, women's bodies continue to function as pawns in male-dominated interreligious political games. Frequently cited as example of this is the invocation of the plight of women in Afghanistan by First Lady Laura Bush on the eve of a U.S. invasion.[10] In this case, the helplessness of "women and children" (a phrase Bush employs six times in her short speech) builds the bridge of concern between the United States and Afghanistan, playing on the expectations of American Christians regarding their Muslim Afghani sisters. As Mandy McKerl suggests, "For most Western listeners, who have been exposed to representations of Islam as a religion that subordinates women, such speeches only uphold these views and perpetuate notions of 'religion and culture' being responsible for abuse rather than the actions and behaviours of other human beings."[11] As a form of "interreligious exchange," international relations and public discourse about them might constitute a "dialogue" of sorts. Here, "religion's" supposed impact on

9. Barbara Stowasser names her "Mariya the Copt," mother of Ibrahim, in "Mothers of the Believers in the *Hadith*," *Muslim World* (January–April 1992) 9 (1–36).

10. See Janet R. Jakobsen, "Ethics after Pluralism," in Courtney Bender and Pamela E. Klassen, eds., *After Pluralism: Reimagining Religious Engagement* (New York: Columbia University Press, 2010), 47. Jakobsen cites Laura Bush's November 2001 address from http://www.presidency.ucsb.edu/ws/index.php?pid=24992. Mandy McKerl, "Multiculturalism, Gender and Violence: Multiculturalism—Is It Bad for Women?" *Culture and Religion* 8/2 (2007) 201 (187–217). McKerl cites also S. Hussain, "The War on Terror and the 'Rescue' of Muslim Women," in N. Lahoud and A. H. Anthony, eds., *Islam and World Politics* (London: Routledge, 2005), 93–104.

11. McKerl, "Multiculturalism, Gender and Violence," 201.

women's bodies masks the male political interests driving the antagonistic international relationship.

Although Mariyya and the women of Afghanistan are seen in explicitly political contexts, they can serve to illuminate the fact that each interreligious encounter is always embedded in a wider material and political landscape. Since there are no persons who stand apart from their embodied positions in a global network of privilege and dispossession, the persons who meet for dialogue are always politically constituted and invested.[12] Interreligious dialogue, even in its neutral settings of academia or public fora, always harbors the investments and interests of its participants. And yet, interreligious dialogues too often mask the investments and interests which shape actions, when members of the dialogue attribute actions to "the religions" or "religious belief." Because "the religions" have been formulated in history predominantly by men, hypostatizing "religions" and personifying "traditions" masks the human actors whose interests continue to be served. Static notions of "the religions" invites dialogue to focus on doctrine, which can serve to (seemingly) depoliticize interreligious dialogue: discussion about differences among authoritative stances on key issues too often forgets to ask whom these authoritative stances serve, and too often the interests of women are eclipsed in the process.

A focus on doctrine and exchange at the level of belief too easily elides the difficult questions of practice, masking unjust practices in the process. For example, in the exchange of dialogue rooted in doctrine, Christians and Muslims may come to the agreement that, "Spelled out clearly in the teachings of both traditions is the right of every individual for true development in all dimensions, social, cultural and spiritual, with justice and equality for all so that every person will have the opportunity to experience the divine gifts of dignity and peace."[13] While seemingly a positive place from which to build the well-being of all persons, how this "doctrine" plays out in practice must be placed under

---

12. Mark Lewis Taylor helpfully constructs humanity ontologically as "political," given that our very being as humans is within networks of shifting power and the struggle for well-being. See Taylor, *The Theological and the Political: On the Weight of the World* (Minneapolis: Fortress, 2012).

13. Dr. Mohammad Aslam Cheema, President of the American Muslim Council and Archbishop William H. Keeler, President of the National Conference of Catholic Bishops, "Muslim and Catholic Leadership Issue Joint Statement on Cairo Conference on Population and Development" (1994), 2–3. Http://old.usccb.org/seia/is2.pdf.

considerable suspicion when issued from male representatives of two traditions which reserve leadership roles to men. That this doctrine of "the right of every individual for true development in all dimensions" is invoked in a paragraph preceding the discussion of abortion raises further questions about whose full flourishing is in view, and whose interests are served in particular interpretations of "the divine gifts of dignity and peace." When Muslim and Christian issue a public statement on abortion, interfaith harmony takes place over women's bodies.[14] Here is a place where we must insist that interreligious dialogue is an immanently practical discourse—and a political one—and must be interrogated for how affirmations are uttered in a religio-political landscape which regularly and explicitly denies justice and equality to women. It is insufficient to attend to interreligious dialogue on the level of doctrine, belief or religious experience without situating these articulations in the embodied, practical and political.

In the story of Mariyya the Copt, it is her body which functions to promote the public reconciliation of male leaders; thus her story can function to interrogate contemporary interreligious reconciliations when they take place over others' bodies. For example, the U.S. Supreme Court hearing of Hosanna-Tabor Evangelical Lutheran Church v. Equal Employment Opportunity Commission (January 2012), ruled that under the principle of 'religious freedom' religious institutions need not abide by national laws that protect the dignity of persons from unjust discrimination in employment.[15] Instead, largely male-led religious institutions will have the benefit of a "ministerial clause" in which the religious body will determine who counts as a "minister" in their congregation and for whom legal rights of employment which govern citizens in this country will simply not apply.[16] As argued in an amicus

14. "Muslim and Catholic Leadership Issue Joint Statement on Cairo Conference on Population and Development" (1994), 3.

15. Http://www.pewforum.org/Church-State-Law/The-Supreme-Court-Takes-Up-Church-Employment-Disputes-and-the-"Ministerial-Exception".aspx.

16. Adam Liptak, "Religious Groups Given 'Exception' to Work Bias Laws," New York Times, January 11, 2012. http://www.nytimes.com/2012/01/12/us/supreme-court-recognizes-religious-exception-to-job-discrimination-laws.html?pagewanted=1&_r=1. See also the ACLU website which describes how, "ministerial exception grants religious organizations immunity from employment discrimination suits brought by 'ministerial' employees, i.e., those employees principally engaged in leading the faith and advancing its religious mission and functions." Online: https://www.aclu.org/religion-belief/hosanna-tabor-evangelical-lutheran-church-and-school-v-equal-employment-opportunity.

brief by religion and law professors, "The ministerial exception deprives religious employees of basic employment protections."[17] This is especially a concern for female religious employees, as a separate amicus brief presented by the American Civil Liberties Union describes,

> Female employees in ministerial positions have encountered similar obstacles under the blanket exception, which has prevented redress for sexual harassment even where the defendants have asserted no religion-based justification for the harassing conduct. *See, e.g., Elvig v. Calvin Presbyterian Church*, 375 F.3d 953, 966–69 (9th Cir. 2004) (ministerial exception prevented associate pastor from redressing adverse-employment actions following sexual harassment, and even from inquiring into defendant's motivation for the harassment). When applied to scenarios like these, the exception transcends the protection of religious liberty and instead resembles "a limitless excuse for avoiding all unwanted legal obligations." *Africa v. Com. of Pa.*, 662 F.2d 1025, 1030 (3d Cir. 1981) (citation omitted).[18]

Despite strong concerns that a ruling in the Hosanna-Tabor case would disadvantage female employees in male-centered religious institutions, and arguments that the ministerial clause would place religious institutions above the law, the amicus briefs of those who petitioned in support of Hosanna-Tabor Evangelical Lutheran Church and School represented a range of religious institutions including the United States Conference of Catholic Bishops, the American Jewish Committee, and the Muslim-American Public Affairs Council.[19] Legal, political agreement on the disadvantaging of women forges a convenient link for di-

---

17. "Brief of *Amici Curiae* Law and Religion Professors in Support of Respondents," August 9, 2011, p. 2. Online: http://www.americanbar.org/content/dam/aba/publishing/previewbriefs/Other_Brief_Updates/10-553_respondentamculawandrelprofs.authcheckdam.pdf.

18. Document No. 10-553 in the Supreme Court of the United States, HOSANNA-TABOR EVANGELICAL LUTHERAN CHURCH AND SCHOOL, *Petitioner, v.* EQUAL EMPLOYMENT OPPORTUNITY COMMISSION, ET AL., *Respondents*. On Writ of Certiorari to the United States Court of Appeals for the Sixth Circuit, "Brief of Americans United for Separation of Church and State, American Civil Liberties Union, ACLU of Michigan, National Council of Jewish Women, Sikh Council on Religion and Education, and Unitarian Universalist Association as *Amici Curiae* In Support of Respondents." August 9, 2011. Online: https://www.aclu.org/files/assets/brief_amici_curiae_of_americans_united_et_al_no__10-553.pdf.

19. For a full list, see: http://www.scotusblog.com/case-files/cases/hosanna-tabor-evangelical-lutheran-church-and-school-v-eeoc/.

verse religious leaders, 'religion' and 'interreligious agreement' serving as cloak for unjust and unlawful practices.

Another public, political event in early 2012 hosted a range of interreligious leaders to consider policies directly related to women's bodies. This time, a Congressional hearing on healthcare reform that would include rights to reproductive technology saw leaders from Christian denominations and a Jewish representative argue again for a "religious freedom" that would enable employers to decide whether or not to provide access to these reproductive rights. The first and most high profile of the panels to address Congress was made up exclusively of male religious leaders.[20] In this most public, political, interreligious setting, women's bodies were the object of discussion, yet women were not among the subjects influencing policies on "religious freedom" which would impact women's lives physically, materially, socially and economically. When religion is mobilized by men across religious traditions for policies directly impacting women, there is serious concern as to whose "religious freedom" is in view and whose "deeply held beliefs" are at stake.[21] As Mariyya is passed from one powerful male to another powerful male, we are reminded of the ways that women's bodies continue to serve as sites over which male political agendas can be enacted.

20. It was to this panel that representative Carolyn Maloney asked, "Where are the women?" The panel was described thus: "From left, Reverend William E. Lori, Roman Catholic Bishop of Bridgeport, Conn., Reverend Dr. Matthew C. Harrison, President, The Lutheran Church Missouri Synod, C. Ben Mitchell, Graves Professor of Moral Philosophy Union University, Rabbi Meir Soloveichik, Director Straus Center of Torah and Western Thought, Yeshiva University and Craig Mitchell, Associate Professor of Ethics of the Southwestern Baptist Theological Seminary, testify on Capitol Hill in Washington, Thursday, Feb. 16, 2012, before the House Oversight and Government Reform Committee hearing." In "Lines Crossed: Separation of Church and State. Has the Obama Administration Trampled on Freedom of Religion & Freedom of Conscience." (Carolyn Kaster—AP); http://www.washingtonpost.com/blogs/guest-voices/post/womens-religious-freedom-violated-photo-of-all-male-birth-control-witnesses-tells-the-viral-truth/2012/02/16/gIQAeyykIR_blog.html. A subsequent panel did include two women.

21. For example, Catholic Bishops publicly oppose the revised health-care mandate with the argument that Catholics object to the use of contraception on religious and moral grounds, while a gallop poll indicates that 82% of U.S. Catholics do not find the use of contraception morally objectionable: "Eighty-two percent of U.S. Catholics say birth control is morally acceptable, nearing the 89% of all Americans and 90% of non-Catholics who agree." Http://www.gallup.com/poll/154799/Americans-Including-Catholics-Say-Birth-Control-Morally.aspx.

While these very public examples of interreligious functioning over the bodies of women clearly serve patriarchal interests at the cost of women, it is not a stretch to envision that these patriarchal public agreements have been forged in less politicized interreligious dialogues, especially when the leaders making public political statements are also those called upon to represent their traditions in local interreligious dialogues. Like the focus on the Prophet and the King, high profile interreligious dialogues have been largely concerned with the authoritative perspectives emerging from leaders of religious traditions. When nearly every religious tradition of the globe has reserved leadership and authority to men, women too often have been barred from the training necessary to be considered "authoritative." Furthermore, the "doctrines" that serve as point of departure for many interreligious dialogues (even those with women's participation), serve to confirm male privilege as male interests are embedded deeply within the traditions. For who has shaped the doctrine, belief and practice of traditions but male leaders who knowingly or inadvertently shore up privilege to the exclusion of women, and at the expense of women? As Chung Hyun Kyung concludes, "So-called, all higher world religions are patriarchal and are institutionalized under the patriarchal light. So we have patriarchal Buddhists and patriarchal Christians having interreligious dialogue, and we have nice patriarchal conclusions there."[22] The focus on doctrine and male representative leaders to explain them creates exclusions for women who are barred from the education necessary to appear "representative." With the expansion of feminist theology and women's activism across the traditions, the absence of women in interreligious dialogue is increasingly evident. Yet, even the recognition of women's absence from dialogue can be blind to the male-interests interreligious dialogues have served. Thomas Michel, SJ, reflects, "[Women's dialogue] is a dialogue that was not very apparent in the first decades of the interreligious movement, probably because most encounters were organized by men, in ways that men feel comfortable doing, but with which women might feel out of place, and on topics of interest to men but perhaps of less interest to women."[23] It is disingenuous to suggest

22. Chung Hyun Kyung, "Seeking the Religious Roots of Pluralism," *Journal of Ecumenical Studies* (1997) 401.

23. Thomas Michel, SJ, "Where to Now? Ways forward for Interreligious Dialogue: Images of Abraham as Models of Interreligious Encounter," *Muslim World* (October 2010) 536.

that women have had no interests in these dialogues, except perhaps insofar as "doctrine" can continue to be abstracted from the question of whom the authoritative stance of doctrine serves. Women may have had no interest in the patriarchal conclusions being reached in expert-led dialogues, but they certainly have had investments in the application of those dialogues in life and practice, especially as they impact women's lives and women's bodies.

Sex and Salvation

Mariyya's female embodiment is key in the exchange between the King and the Prophet, undeniably bringing sexuality into the discussion as she becomes concubine to Muhammad and demonstrates his own physicality, sexuality, and virility.[24] Simultaneously, she invites a consideration of gender roles, assumptions, and constraints as she assumes a specific gender role both in relation to the Prophet and bearing a son with him. Although her precise legal status remains ambiguous, her social status is enhanced as beloved of the Prophet and further improved when she becomes a mother. As Hidayatullah notes, "The birth of Ibrahim confers on Mariyya the status of the Prophet's *umm walad* [mother of a child]. According to a Hadith of the Prophet cited by Ibn Sa'd, the birth of this child entitles her to her freedom."[25] For some interpreters, she becomes included as among the "mothers of the believers,"[26] finding a place within the sacred family of the Prophet.

The "mothers of the believers" are exemplary figures in the Islamic tradition. Yet, in critical feminist perspective, Ghassan Ascha has suggested that "the mothers of the believers" are less historical personalities and more fictive personae, functioning to project female subjectivities.

24. Hidayatullah writes, "it appears that it is not just acceptable, but also favorable, to describe the Prophet's sexual practices for the sake of demonstrating his hearty sexual appetite and manly vigor" ("Mariyya the Copt," 228).

25. Ibid., 223. Hidayatullah further parses Mariyya's liminal status: as umm walad, "her status falls somewhere below that of a married woman but above that of an ordinary slave" (225).

26. Stowasser, "The Mothers of the Believers in the *Hadith*," 9. Stowasser includes Mariyya among the "mothers of the believers" while Ghassan Ascha maintains that her "slave-concubine" status excludes her from this grouping. See Ghassan Ascha, "Mothers of the Believers: Stereotypes of the Prophet Muhammad's Wives," in Ria Kloppenborg and Wouter J. Hanegraaf, eds., *Female Stereotypes in Religious Traditions*, Studies in the History of Religions 66 (Leiden: Brill, 1995), 90 (89–108).

She writes, "Each period has its own 'Mothers of the Believers', according to the prevailing cultural and moral values and social norms. Thus, the Prophet's wives do not derive their importance from their historical personalities, but from the continuous modifications, retouchings and modernizations that these personalities have undergone. They have been used throughout the centuries, as we have seen, in order to justify a great variety of attitudes about the Muslim woman. They are ideal, obedient, gentle, affectionate, content, pious, dwelling inside the marital house and veiled."[27] When Mariyya gains status in very distinctive gender roles as one among these mothers, her story reinforces those roles for women.

We can look for ways that "women" in interreligious dialogue function the same way—as fictive figures rhetorically constructing roles for women. For example, Muslim and Catholic religious leaders met for dialogue and produced a document on "marriage" in which male and female stereotypes are writ large. Consider the following. From a Catholic perspective:

> Husbands and wives have complementary roles to play in the family. Wives should be loved for their dignity as women. As mothers, they should have every opportunity to exercise a vital role in the upbringing of their offspring. As partners with their husbands, they share in the management of the household. At the same time, wives and husbands are called to live a special form of personal friendship. Husbands likewise should be loved for their dignity as men and as fathers. Along with his spouse, a father should also serve an important role in the nurture and education of his children. He must be attentive to his wife and family, and should not be absent for long periods except in circumstances realistically beyond his control. When he is with his family, a husband and father should avoid any sense of superiority that might threaten the equality of his marriage partnership.[28]

---

27. Ghassan Ascha, "Mothers of the Believers: Stereotypes of the Prophet Muhammad's Wives," in Ria Kloppenborg and Wouter J. Hanegraaf, eds., *Female Stereotypes in Religious Traditions* (Leiden: Brill, 1995), 107 (89–108).

28. "Marriage: Roman Catholic and Muslim Perspectives," document of the Mid-Atlantic Catholic–Muslim Dialogue Group, 2011, pp. 10–11. http://old.usccb.org/seia/Mid-Atlantic-Dialogue-Marriage-Roman-Catholic-and-Sunni-Muslim-Perspectives-2011.pdf, pages 10–11.

And, in an Islamic view:

> The husband is responsible for the financial support of his wife. This is in fact established as a wife's right by the authority of the Qur'ān itself and the Sunnah (i.e. the words, deeds, and approval of Prophet Muhammad, pbuh). It is inconsequential whether the wife is Muslim, non-Muslim, rich, poor, healthy, or sick. This responsibility is inherent to a man's role as "*qawam*" (leader); he is to bear the financial responsibility for the family in such a way that his wife is assured economic security.[29]

> The wife may not refuse her husband sexually, as this can lead to marital problems, including a grave risk of adultery. The husband, of course, should take into account his wife's health, showing her kindness and consideration. Without her husband's knowledge and consent a wife may not receive or entertain unrelated males in the domicile. She should never be alone with an unrelated male.[30]

> The husband has been given the right to be obeyed because he is the leader and not because he is superior. Obedience does not mean blind obedience. It is subject to two conditions: (a) A wife is required to obey only within the morally permissible categories of action. (b) She must obey only with regard to matters that fall within the scope of the husband's legal and moral rights.[31]

The document is authored by two male religious leaders, and it comes unaccompanied by any list of participants in the dialogue, thus masking the gendered positionality, social locations and life experiences of the persons for whom the document supposedly speaks. What is unclear is whether women as wives within the religious traditions represented would agree to the portrait presented of themselves and their married lives. What is clear is that patriarchal interests of complementarity and gender dualisms are served by this interreligious dialogue.

This binary of complementarity that emerges from "doctrine" through "dialogue" assigns woman a particular gendered place in relation to a man that is not too far from Monique Wittig's feminist assessment: "For what makes a woman is a specific social relation to a man, a relation that we have previously called servitude, a relation which

29. Ibid., 36.
30. Ibid., 38.
31. Ibid., 39.

implies personal and physical obligations as well as economic ones."[32] The Catholic–Muslim document on marriage constructs 'woman' fictively in this complementary relationship, assigning very specific gendered relationships and resisting any variety to the way families might be constituted. It comments disapprovingly: "The long-held belief that marriage is the union of a man and a woman open to the transmission of life has been challenged by many in today's world. The prevalence of divorce and the normalization of single-parent households have eroded this traditional model of family life. Some believe that same sex unions can also be defined as 'marriage.'"[33] Instead the authors insist: "Catholics and Muslims affirm together that marriage is a blessing from God, established as a part of the created order and hence, as natural between man and woman."[34] Although the two communities may not agree doctrinally on the path to "salvation," they appear from this document emerging from dialogue to agree on rightly-ordered sex, and familial roles that are 'natural' for women.[35] Assigning very specific roles for women in a necessary complementarity to men not only constructs those who will be placed in the category "woman," but also defines some persons out of the "natural order."

If we return to Mariyya's story, we see that the "natural" role of woman as wife and mother secures her well-being in a foreign land. Her physical beauty, sexual relation with the Prophet and bearing a son, all save her from the fate of becoming an otherwise unknown victim of male political exchange. Yet, as captivating as Mariyya is to Muhammad, her beauty is simultaneously the source of suspicion. When one of her fellow Copts, a male, comes to visit her, charges of conspiracy and infidelity are raised. As Barbara Stowasser frames the story, "Reportedly the Copt did household chores for Mariya, and the people gossiped that there was 'an infidel man who has access to an infidel woman.' The Prophet sent 'Ali ibn Abi Talib to investigate the matter. When Ali, sword

32. Monique Wittig, "One is Not Born a Woman," in *The Straight Mind and Other Essays* (Boston: Beacon, 1992), 20.

33. "Marriage," 5.

34. Ibid., 2.

35. On the doctrinal disagreements, especially the role of Jesus in salvation see Mahmoud Ayoub and Daniel Madigan, "Jesus and Muhammad," Michael Ipgrave, ed., *Bearing the Word: Prophecy in Biblical and Quranic Perspective* (London: Church House Publishing, 2005), 87–99; and Alexander Malik, "Confessing Christ in the Islamic Context," in *Asian Faces of Jesus* (Maryknoll, NY: Orbis, 1993), 75–84.

in hand, approached the Copt, the man was either sitting on a date palm and threw his clothes away, or he climbed up on a date palm and his garment slipped off. In either case, 'Ali saw him to be without genitals, 'without a penis or testicles.'"[36] Just as Mariyya's place in a heteronormative, patriarchal sexuality is her salvation, so too the non-normative sexuality of her kinsman saves her from suspicion.[37]

The subject position of the eunuch held a variegated set of meanings in the ancient and medieval world, serving as boundary crosser on many levels. According to Cengiz Orhonlu, the eunuch was a figure who transgressed religious lines, as they were valued for particular roles in the Islamic world, while the practice of castration was denounced. To acquire a eunuch as a slave, transaction occurred across religious lines.[38] Not fitting neatly into either side of the dualistic divide that separated "male" and "female," eunuchs served a particularly fluid gender-role in societies divided by gender, serving "as intermediaries between their master and his wives and concubines."[39] Many served in courts of powerful leaders and others were consecrated as holy from a young age.[40] Constructed and exchanged across religious lines, the 'khasi' opens a new line of questioning from Mariyya's story.

That the non-normative sexuality and gender ambiguity of the eunuch is not a threat in Mariyya's interreligious setting invites questions

36. Stowasser, "The Mothers of the Believers in the Hadith," 15. Hidayatullah cites the account of this story by Ibn S'ad, an early biographer of Muhammad: "A Coptic [man] would go to her and bring her water and wood. The people said of this: 'A foreigner visits a foreigner.' [Word of] this reached the Messenger of God and he sent 'Ali ibn Abi Talib [to deal with the man]. Ali found him at a palm tree. When [the man] saw ['Ali's] sword, he [became alarmed], cast off the garment that he had on, and become exposed. [It was clear that] he was a eunuch" ("Mariyya the Copt," 233).

37. Piotr O. Schultz describes, "Eunuchs were not simply 'bedchamber attendants,' as the Greek term suggests. Nor were they always slaves, as some authors stress. They could just as well be ascetics, priests, magicians, scholars, physicians, military commanders, admirals, or senior officials at the courts of both eastern and western rulers." Piotr O. Scholz, *Eunuch's and Castrati: A Cultural History*, trans. John A. Broadwin and Shelley L. Frisch (Princeton: Wiener, 2000), ix. Scholz provides further historical sources which suggest that this eunuch's castration may have been connected with his "dedication to the church" (198). Scholz is citing Arab historian Mukaddasi.

38. "Khāṣī," in *Encyclopaedia of Islam*, 2nd ed., Brill Online, 2012. Reference. Fordham University Library. http://referenceworks.brillonline.com/entries/encyclopaedia-of-islam-2/khasi-COM_0499.

39. Ibid.

40. Ibid.

on queerness and interreligious dialogue today.[41] The challenge of persons who cannot be captured by the strict gender divisions of 'male' and 'female' similarly is not a threat to interreligious meetings because, too often they are simply excluded from them and the normative sexuality enforced through interreligious exchange. As Virginia Ramey Mollenkott describes, "the attitude of many religious leaders has been that gender is fully and adequately defined by the male-female binary. Any one who does not fit that binary doesn't even exist in any reality worthy of religious recognition."[42] The interreligious meeting along the corridor of normative sexuality is yet another potent symbolism that Mariyya's story invites us to pursue, for it is not only the dualistic categories of gender that are enforced in interreligious dialogues, but a compulsory heterosexuality as well.[43]

In January 2012, thirty-eight leaders from a variety of American congregations sent an open letter "to all Americans" entitled, "Marriage and Religious Freedom: Fundamental Goods that Stand or Fall Together."[44] Here, normative assumptions about heterosexuality and the defense of marriage as "the union of one man and one woman" brought together Jewish and Christian leaders to publically denounce legislations that might alter the civil definition of marriage. This followed previous documents that included "leaders from Anglican, Baptist, Catholic, Evangelical, Jewish, Lutheran, Mormon, Orthodox, Pentecostal and Sikh communities"[45] (2010) and a 2011 letter to John Boehner as

41. I am following Thomas Bohache in his use of "queer" to indicate the range of persons who do not fit the normative gender-complementarity of male–female binary. Bohache writes, "The queer consciousness that has recently developed goes beyond notions of 'gay' and 'lesbian' and seeks to critique heteronormativity and heteropatriarchal patterns of domination . . . To be 'queer' means to stir things up and even perhaps spoil them, in order not to settle for the easy answers of the status quo." Bohache, "Embodiment as Incarnation: An Incipient Queer Christology," *Theology and Sexuality* 10/1 (2003) 19 (9–29). See also Bohache, *Christology from the Margins* (London: SCM, 2008).

42. Virginia Ramey Mollenkott, *Omnigender: A Trans-religious Approach*, rev. ed. (Cleveland: Pilgrim, 2007), 89.

43. For a discussion of compulsory heterosexuality, see Judith Plaskow, "Sexual Orientation and Human Rights: A Progressive Jewish Perspective," in *The Coming of Lilith: Essays on Feminism, Judaism, and Sexual Ethics, 1972–2003* (Boston: Beacon, 2005), 186–87.

44. Http://www.usccb.org/issues-and-action/marriage-and-family/marriage/promotion-and-defense-of-marriage/ecumenical-and-interreligious-activities.cfm.

45. "The Protection of Marriage: A Shared Commitment," December 6, 2010.

Speaker of the House of Representatives signed by "leaders of Catholic, Protestant and Sikh communities of faith—together representing tens of millions of adherents."[46] The explicit relationship between the religious and the political is noted by the authors themselves who are employing interreligious agreement as rhetoric to resist legal changes in which, "by a single stroke, every law where rights depend on marital status—such as employment discrimination, employment benefits, adoption, education, healthcare, elder care, housing, property, and taxation—will change so that same-sex sexual relationships must be treated as if they were marriage."[47] Here, the "religious" stance is clearly "political" in its attempt to keep gay and lesbian citizens from their rights. Like the structure of local dialogues which fictively enable a single individual to speak for the whole of a tradition, such authoritative documents employ the smokescreen of representation as a rhetorical claim to power designed to sway public opinion and influence legal policies (as if these few men could know the hearts and minds of "tens of millions of adherents"). In the three distinct letters cited above, a total of forty-eight different individuals signed on to "represent" their "religion" against rights for same-sex unions. Only one of them was a woman.[48]

The legal maneuvers of politically-invested interreligious statements are part of a broader process by which the parameters of personhood are constructed and reinforced. Judith Butler describes this process of normalization:

> As an operation of power, regulation can take a legal form, but its legal dimension does not exhaust the sphere of its efficaciousness. As that which relies on categories that render individuals socially interchangeable with one another, regulation is thus bound up with the process of *normalization* . . . [Statutes] that regulate gay speech in the military are actively engaged in producing and maintaining the norm of what a man or what a woman will be, what speech will be, where sexuality will and

46. USCCB News Release, March 4, 2011, "Interfaith Group Urges Speaker of the House to Defend DOMA [Defense of Marriage Act] Legislation in Court." Http://old.usccb.org/comm/archives/2011/11-044.shtml.

47. "Marriage and Religious Freedom," par. 5.

48. This reflects perhaps much of what has already been said about the exclusion of women from leadership positions in many religious traditions. But, perhaps also those same congregations and communities which are ordaining women are also taking the lead to secure LGBTQ rights and well-being. The question of whether these communities are represented in the dialogue is a pressing one.

will not be. State regulations on lesbian and gay adoption as well as single-parent adoptions not only restrict that activity, but also refer to and reenforce [*sic*] an ideal of what parents should be, for example, that they should be partnered and what counts as a legitimate partner. Hence, regulations that seek merely to curb certain specified activities (sexual harassment, welfare fraud, sexual speech) perform another activity that, for the most part, remains unmarked: the production of the parameters of person-hood, that is, making persons according to abstract norms that at once condition and exceed the lives they make—and break.[49]

While the very public statements with political ends clearly have in view particular understandings of "male" and "female" and the relationship between them, even non-public interreligious dialogues can become a vehicle through which heterosexuality and gendered expectations are normalized and reinforced. When our interreligious dialogues promote heteronormativity and denounce homosexuality, or silently ignore the absence of LGBTQ persons within the dialogue, our interreligious dialogues are securing human rights for some and denying them to others by creating systems for what is "normal." Interreligious dialogues can function as spheres of normalization in a politically infused national and global gender-landscape.

One strategy for normalization, given the diverse worldviews of our faith perspectives, is to invoke "natural law" as common ground.[50] Subsequently, "natural law" then serves the way salvific truth has in the past, as a point of departure for religiously-based discriminations (albeit now with interreligious agreement). In the case of same-sex marriage, a conceptual replacement of sex for salvation has taken place. If inter-religious dialogues tend to highlight inclusivist and pluralist mindsets which open salvation to all people of good will (regardless of faith tradi-tion), sexuality has become the new boundary marker for who is in and who is out. Those who enter into interreligious dialogue as "women" and "men" who fit the "natural order" must be cautious of who is ex-cluded in the process.

49. Judith Butler, "Gender Regulations," in *Undoing Gender* (New York: Routledge, 2004), 56.

50. Donald W. Wuerl (Archbishop of Washington), "Unifying Threads among World Religions: The Common Ground in Search for World Peace," The Pope John Paul II Annual Lecture on Interreligious Understanding, The pontifical University of Saint Thomas Aquinas. Rome, April 4, 2008.

Into a World of Women, Reimagining the Gift

Mariyya fit into a religiously foreign land by assuming the "natural" roles of wife and mother. But, the gains she enjoys through her sexed and gendered female body are not entirely without losses. As socially subordinate slave becomes "wife" and privileged through bearing a son, tradition holds that Mariyya's status among the wives of the Prophet was the source of jealousy among them. As Hidayatullah notes, "A common concern within several accounts of Mariyya's life is the disturbance in the Prophet's household reportedly caused by the wives' jealousy of her."[51] The tension which arises among the women might be employed mimetically to remind us of the multiple social and material locations from which "women" emerge into the dialogue setting. "Women" are not singularly interested and all of one mind, but are diversely interested and may have competing and contradictory aims. This has been precisely Maura O'Neill's point in her thorough examination of women's positionality in interreligious dialogue. As she explains, "One of the intentions of this work [*Mending a Torn World: Women in Interreligious Dialogue*] is to demonstrate that the content and nature of women's dialogue is the ideal place to start the long journey of understanding the diverse factions of religious followers both within each tradition and across traditions."[52] Or, as one woman has offered in thinking about a moment in her ten-year long participation in interreligious dialogue:

> It was the first time I realized there isn't *a* Muslim faith, there isn't *a* Lutheran faith, it's what your personal spin of it is. The women who are Muslim, you know they don't wear the headscarf. And that *is* something that is in the Qur'an. They are very quick to say, "It's between me and God." They do their prayers, they do everything else. But that's where they draw the line. There was a Jewish woman . . . she says that her Orthodox religion says that women cover their hair. She says, "That's where I draw the line. I'm not covering my hair." And I realize that that's where the Catholic women, they had practiced birth control or whatever. The religion becomes personal with each person that you know.[53]

51. Hidayatullah, "Mariyya the Copt," 231.

52. Maura O'Neill, *Mending a Torn World: Women in Interreligious Dialogue*, Faith Meets Faith (Maryknoll, NY: Orbis, 2007), 7.

53. Joanne [pseud.], interview by Mara Brecht, December 15, 2007, Philadelphia, Pennsylvania; transcription of digital recording.

The multiplicity of women with whom Mariyya engages reminds us of the competing interests and diverse social locations of women in interreligious dialogue, insisting also on the multiplicity of women's lives and positionalities in any dialogue setting. "Women" in interreligious dialogue are not singular, but attached to particular life situations, stories, privileges and dispossessions. Women come not as "woman" only, but as politically invested and interested, as "men" come also with a multiplicity of interests that shape them. We are all hybrid and we are all politically entangled. Our discourses, however they attempt to appear to be extracted from the social, material, and political, are embedded within them; it is not just the Prophet and the King whose interreligious agreements are politically invested, but all of us.

Mariyya's real gift, then, is that she helps us see interreligious dialogue as always situated in a political landscape. The political is starkly in relief in the context of her story and in high profile, public, political dialogues. But thinking with her we can see that all interreligious dialogue is situated in a particular time and place and that actors in the dialogue are actors in the world, each of whom is socially and materially situated, and thus politically interested. She invites us to see how women—as living bodies and as fictions in the dialogue—figure as objects of interreligious, political maneuvering. Mariyya's gift to a politically interested interreligious dialogue is that she helps us see the employment of fictive women, which should compel actual women and men to interrupt the privileges which can characterize dialogue in its normative form, focused on doctrines which serve male/patriarchal interests and wielding the power of anonymous representation to mobilize toward specific heteronormative aims.

As mother of Ibrahim, Mariyya helps us see how participation in patriarchal social arrangements brings personal benefits. Given the constraints which otherwise characterized her situation—all but alone in a foreign land, captive to a foreign ruler—accommodating to this prescribed role seems like a wise and creative choice. This could serve to make our participation in interreligious dialogue both self-reflective on our own self-interests and cautious in too easily enjoying its gains, when the dialogue serves to exclude the personhood of others who do not fit patriarchal, heteronormative expectations.

The gift Mariyya brings to interreligious dialogue is to remind us of the bodies impacted by interreligious exchange. The story of the Prophet and the King brings into relief the way interreligious agreements materially impact real bodies. With Mariyya's witness in view, we ask ourselves whose bodies are impacted by the interreligious agreements we come to, and whose interests are served by the dialogue. We can put ourselves in Mariyya's place to interrogate those dialogues which negatively impact some for the benefit of others; but we also must place ourselves in the politically invested position of the Prophet and the King. Whose lives matter in the discourse at hand? What social, material and political benefit does any particular dialogue produce? For whom? Recognizing the politically-charged and socially-invested outcomes of dialogue frees us to participate in dialogues toward social and political ends. How might accepting the invitation to dialogue provide a platform for a counter-normalization or the disruption of heteronormative hegemonies? What willingness does each of us have to disrupt the authoritative stances of our traditions, even at the cost of further distancing from the power brokers/leaders of the traditions? Mariyya's gift of bringing the political clearly into relief asks us to participate in interreligious dialogue *with* the political in view. Mariyya's entry into the world of women and the complex relationality among them enables us to insist on the complexity of women in their concrete reality and the maintenance of this complexity in interreligious dialogue. This enables us to insist on the expanding presence of women in interreligious dialogues both to indicate the material impact of doctrine and dialogue on bodies sexed or gendered female *and* to demonstrate the internal multiplicity of women whose differing social locations mean that the material impact is felt diversely.

Mariyya's gift finally is in standing as a figure who brings together women across religious traditions in her hybridity. For even as she emerges from Christian Egypt and embodies that heritage, tradition holds that she converted to Islam en route to Medina. [54] She embodies "interreligious dialogue" in her very person, and stands as a figure to be claimed across religious lines. She might serve as reminder of the way women across traditions have already in many and diverse ways been engaging in interreligious dialogue. They've been doing this

---

54. Hajjah Amina Adil writies, "Before they even reached Madinah, [Mariyya and Sirin] had, through the instruction of the Prophet's envoy Hatib ibn Balta'a, been enflamed with ardor for Islam, and both became Muslims." *Muhammad, The Messenger of Islam: His Life and Prophecy* (Washington, DC: Islamic Supreme Council of America, 2002), 432.

"on-the-ground" in the multireligious contexts of the globe for generations.[55] They've been doing this in the virtual spaces of technology and living spaces of private gatherings.[56] They've been doing this in published works for decades.[57] They've been doing this through activism as well.[58] They've been doing this in ways outside the spotlight and far from the public eye.[59]

But, if we can see that "women" figure in patriarchal interreligious dialogue in pressing practical, and political ways, it is no longer sufficient for women in interreligious dialogue to be a hidden reality. Given the way "women" function for patriarchal aims in the public, political interreligious discourse (as bodies to be agreed over and as fictive persona for heteronormative ends), we can see that like Mariyya we are being betrayed by our co-religionists whose interests in interreligious dialogue come at a cost to the well-being of many. Mariyya's brave journey, under conditions beyond her control, through complicated and contested relationships, and into a shared heritage across religious lines, invites women in their multiplicity, their hybridity, and their complexity to enter the dialogue en masse. As we have seen, interreligious dialogue

55. Mercy Amba Oduyoye gives evidence of this in her reflections on Muslim and Christian women in Africa in *Beads and Strands*; Chung Hyun Kyung similarly reflects on this the multi-religious contexts of Asia. For an overview of women's interfaith projects see Kwok Pui-lan, *Globalization, Gender, and Peacemaking: The Future of Interfaith Dialogue* (New York: Paulist, 2012).

56. Countless grass roots groups around the globe feature women's interfaith encounter including: Millionth Circle, Women of Sprit and Faith, Circle Connections, Gather the Women, Spiritual and Women's Alliance for Hope, Women's Earth Alliance. These organizations were featured in an article in *The Interfaith Observer*, April 2012; http://theinterfaithobserver.org/journal-articles/2012/4/15/interfaith-women-exploring-new-ways-to-lead.html.

57. See, for example, Carol P. Christ and Judith Plaskow, eds., *Womanspirit Rising: A Feminist Reader in Religion* (San Francisco: HarperSanFrancisco, 1992); Paula Cooey et al., eds., *After Patriarchy: Feminist Transformations of the World's Religions*, Faith Meets Faith (Maryknoll, NY: Orbis, 1991); and the collaborations of Rita M. Gross and Rosemary Radford Ruether, *Religious Feminism and the Future of the Planet: A Christian–Buddhist Conversation* (New York: Continuum, 2001); as well as Elisabeth Schüssler Fiorenza and Judith Plaskow.

58. Women's activist organizations that cross religious lines include: WATER, Women in Black, National Organization of Women.

59. On women's interfaith dialogue practices see Helene Egnell, *Other Voices: A Study of Christian Feminist Approaches to Religious Plurality East and West* (Uppsala: Studia Missionalia Svecana C, 2007); and Jeannine Hill Fletcher, *Motherhood as Metaphor: Engendering Interreligious Dialogue* (New York: Fordham University Press, 2013); Kwok Pui-lan, *Globalization, Gender, and Peacemaking*.

is a way of shaping public sentiment, and public sentiment shapes the conferring of rights which have a direct impact on material well-being. For ourselves and for our "others" we must network and mobilize across religious lines to resist the propagation of gender-violence and gendered-exclusions in the name of religion.

3

Epistemology and Embodiment in Women's Interreligious Dialogue

Mara Brecht

The pioneering work of Maura O'Neill philosophically analyzes women's interreligious dialogue in order to demonstrate women's distinctive contributions for achieving ethically-oriented conversation goals. O'Neill argues women are uniquely equipped for promoting interreligious empathy across religious boundaries and encouraging justice within and among different traditions. This conviction rests on her belief that women are capable of accessing emotions, communicating interpersonally, and emphasizing practical solutions to problems. She writes, "I am convinced that women are better able than men to bridge the wide abyss of understanding that plagues our world."[1] Like O'Neill's project, my work draws on philosophical tools and feminist principles to analyze the distinctive contributions of women in interreligious dialogue. We differ though, in that the particular set of contributions I interrogate are not ethical, but rather epistemological.

Scholarly discussion on interreligious dialogue often centers on its social, economic, and ethical consequences. However, it is also possible and important to focus on its epistemological outcomes. That is to say: when we encounter people who are religiously different from us

1. Maura O'Neill, *Mending a Torn World: Women in Interreligious Dialogue*, Faith Meets Faith (Maryknoll, NY: Orbis, 2007), 7.

in dialogue, we inevitably are confronted with their beliefs, pushed to reflect on how those beliefs are different from our own, and to examine more deeply our own beliefs.[2]

I propose to investigate interreligious dialogue as a site of religious epistemic disagreement. My premise is that dialogue allows people to see how their beliefs are distinctive from the beliefs of others, and often in tension and conflict. In short, true dialogue is rooted in disagreement. For epistemologists, disagreements are important because they raise fundamental questions about notions of epistemic reliability, standards for belief justification, and the concepts of rationality and truth. Seeing dialogue as a site of disagreement means, first of all, that two interlocutors respect each other's views enough to engage in discussion. Blind dismissal of a conversation partner's point of view results in neither disagreement nor dialogue. Seeing dialogue as disagreement means also that one takes the epistemic nature of religious beliefs seriously— inquiring into their reliability, justification, and rationality—and that one takes the creative challenge of interreligious dialogue seriously.[3]

Unfortunately, many scholars who apply epistemological principles to interreligious dialogue tend to see dialogue as a 'fork in the road'-type

2. My understanding of "religion" is aligned with the definition articulated by Paul Griffiths in *Problems of Religious Diversity*. Religion, Griffiths argues, is "a form of life that seems to those who belong to it to be comprehensive, incapable of abandonment, and of central importance." Religious claims are statements that grow out of this form of life. When religious claims are made explicit and *required* of members of the religion, they are "doctrines"; when they are made explicit and only *suggested* for members of the religion, they are called "teachings." On this theory, the category of "religious claims" is more wide-ranging than "doctrine" and wider still of "teaching." Griffiths argues that religious claims are focused on "the setting of human life . . . the nature of persons . . . and the proper conduct of life" (Paul J. Griffiths, *Problems of Religious Diversity* [Malden, MA: Blackwell, 2001], 21–24). Because religious claims involve acceptance and/or assent by religious persons, they are epistemological in nature (17). My use of "religious beliefs" throughout this essay applies to all three of Griffiths' categories: claims, doctrines, and teachings. While the women's interreligious dialogue group (to which I refer in this essay) rarely, if ever, discuss doctrines and teachings, the religious beliefs they discuss fall into Griffiths' "claims" category and have epistemological significance as such.

3. Justification is the special epistemological property that distinguishes belief from knowledge. Sometimes, epistemologists talk about this property as the "truthmaker" for belief, or the feature of a propositional claim that makes it more than "mere belief." On another note, I am indebted to James Kraft for his language of "creative challenge," which he uses in a discussion on religious epistemic peers. Kraft, *The Epistemology of Religious Disagreement: A Better Understanding* (New York: Palgrave Macmillan, 2012), 145.

of epistemic situation. Richard Feldman presents just this kind of argument. In Feldman's view, if a believer critically reflects upon his belief in light of an epistemic disagreement, which is realized through dialogue, it becomes nearly impossible for the believer to point to justification for his belief. In disagreement we realize that no one can be certain that any particular belief is *the* true belief, and so, Feldman claims, we cannot continue retaining our beliefs; therefore, we must give them up.[4]

James Kraft develops a response that is sensitive to the problems of epistemological recommendations like Feldman's that advocate wholesale religious renunciation. Kraft states that when we meet a religious other and dialogue with them, it is possible—even likely—that we will doubt the surety of our beliefs. He explains the epistemological impact of this: "Loss of confidence is an indicator of loss of justification." Kraft states that we can only hold our religious beliefs with significantly reduced confidence.[5]

In this thinking, participants are compelled either to grip their religious beliefs more tightly or to loosen their grasp or even let go completely.[6] By contrast, I argue that although it is valuable to see interreligious dialogue as an occasion for exploring disagreements over beliefs, it is a mistake to construe dialogue as being aimed at determining which religious beliefs are more or less epistemically meritorious. Dialogue is not a zero-sum game.

Paul Griffiths argues similarly that religious diversity presents believers with an opportunity to be more thoughtful about diversity's deep implications for their own beliefs. Griffiths writes, "Epistemic uneasiness often (and properly) produced by increasing Christian awareness of deep diversity should be acknowledged as a neuralgic point of creative conceptual growth for Christian thought."[7] While I contend that disagreements are a central part of dialogue and worthy of epistemological inquiry, I reject the notion that disagreements are *all* there is to dialogue. One of the primary aims in this essay is to demonstrate

4. Richard Feldman, "Reasonable Religious Disagreements," University of Rochester;   http://www.ling.rochester.edu/~feldman/papers/reasonable%20religious%20 disagreements.pdf.

5. Kraft, *The Epistemology of Religious Disagreement*, 147–49.

6. The phrase I play on here—"hold what we know with a relaxed grasp"—comes from Maura O'Neill, *Women Speaking, Women Listening: Women in Interreligious Dialogue* (Maryknoll, NY: Orbis, 1990), 19.

7. Griffiths, *Problems of Religious Diversity*, 97.

that while dialogue necessarily involves disagreement, it is the response to those disagreements, rather than the disagreements themselves, that bear out epistemological significance.

To make this argument, I turn to women's interreligious dialogue and, more specifically, to a case study of a group I observed in the Philadelphia metropolitan area. Having watched their interactions, my thesis is that women in dialogue emphasize *processes* over *products*. In other words, they focused on ways by which they form their religious beliefs rather than on the beliefs themselves. Stated in epistemological terms, the women in dialogue highlight belief *formation* rather than *justification*. Their dialogue yielded genuine disagreement which, in turn, led to new depths of epistemological understanding of their own faith and the beliefs of others in the group. This pattern, which emerges from women's dialogue, has implications for both scholarship on interreligious dialogue broadly as well as for traditional epistemological discourse.

Drawing on qualitative interviews, I first offer a history and overview of the Philadelphia women's interreligious dialogue group, emphasizing the group's collective commitment to highlighting the distinctive nature of their plural beliefs. For the Philadelphia women, epistemic disagreements function as doors into deeper appreciation of why dialogue partners believe what they believe and how they came to do so. By naming their differences and disagreements, the women are able to negotiate disagreements in creative ways, which specifically involve developing appreciation toward their conversation partners' perspectives and epistemic processes. I contend these strategies for handling disagreements function as paradigms for both retrieving and re-envisioning the epistemological significance of dialogue.

The Philadelphia women enact two central, paradigmatic strategies. These consist in narratively leading one another through their religious beliefs and commitments and, following this, practically guiding each other through the embodied practices of their home traditions, particularly in the areas of feasting, prayer, and pilgrimage. The following section describes the women's narrative and embodied practices and, in so doing, unpacks the significance of these practices for re-imagining epistemology in an interreligious context. The final component of this essay draws on feminist epistemological principles to argue for the necessity of developing embodied epistemological models.

The Philadelphia Area Women's Interreligious Dialogue Group

For a period of two years, Jeannine Hill Fletcher and I undertook a re-search-conversation with the members of a long-standing women's in-terreligious dialogue group.[8] Our research was qualitative in nature. We used a participant-observer model of inquiry: interviewing the women about their dialogue and actively entering into their interreligious con-versations. The purpose of our research was open-ended and primarily directed toward hearing the women's insights, reflections, and wisdom on dialogue. We began the project as a sort of academic dialogue with the structure and substance of the women's group itself.

The Philadelphia area women's interreligious dialogue group has been in existence for close to a decade. The group began because a hand-ful of women from Philadelphia, having known one another through the city's longstanding Thanksgiving interfaith service, decided they wanted more interaction with a diverse range of religious people. The three women who are responsible for organizing the group did so by asking their friends, people from their church, synagogue, and assem-bly, and others that they knew from the Thanksgiving interfaith event if they would be interested in meeting regularly throughout the year. As they recruited friends for the newly forming group and held a few small meetings in each other's living rooms, they also decided that it would be beneficial to hold an event for the larger community on the topic of religious diversity. Because of the timing of the planned event, which was set to be in the late summer and early fall of 2001, their community program specifically responded to the World Trade Center terrorist at-tacks from a variety of religious perspectives.

To open a conversation about the role of religion in the September 11th attacks, they followed a traditional form for "doing" interreligious dialogue. One of the group's founding members explains: They had four speakers, "a priest, a rabbi, a Muslim, and a Baha'i" and "invited the public to come and listen."[9] The religious leaders came to the commu-nity program to speak as authoritative representatives of and for their

8. I am especially grateful to Jeannine Hill Fletcher for extending me the op-portunity to work on this research project as well as for her extensive guidance both in writing the narrative of the group and in thinking through the philosophical and theological implications of the women's voices.

9. Interview by Mara Brecht, June 25, 2007, Philadelphia, PA, transcription.

tradition. This community program took place in a Philadelphia suburb and is remembered by group members as a success. It was successful both because it brought together members of the community to talk about a sensitive subject at a critical moment and also because it was ultimately the catalyst for drawing in more women to sustain the interreligious conversation. One of the group's founding members tells why she thinks the community event planted the seed for the group today: "We all sought to express our feelings in an interreligious setting."[10]

The dialogue group is not a formal group in the sense that it has a declared title or a mission statement. It is not registered with any broader interfaith organizations (such as North American Interfaith Network or the Interfaith Alliance) and does not advertise itself or host community events. Without any formal processes, structures, or purpose in place, it is intriguing that the group should be able to maintain itself for over a decade. Group members report sticking with the group in the first years for a variety of reasons: they wanted to express their feelings about the state of the world in general, to reflect on their hopes for religious people in American culture following this crisis, and to learn about other religious traditions, in particular, Islam.

In its nascent form, the group met the basic learning needs of its members. That is to say, the women came to learn *about* religious traditions, and the group provided that possibility. As the women continued meeting, however, the group meetings shifted from being a forum to talk about September 11th or a space for a pedagogically-oriented discussion about religions *per se* to a group where members came to truly converse with each other about their own religious lives in a rather profound way.

In the group's present form, they no longer place emphasis on which tradition is being represented by whom and neither do they expect that any person can speak for an entire religious tradition. This leads to a richness of dialogue that sustains the group today. In the words of one group member, the purpose of the dialogue group is "spiritual conversation and community."[11]

The questions I attempt to answer in this essay are: How did the women accomplish the shift from pedagogical discussion among

10. Interview by Mara Brecht, June 20, 2007, Philadelphia, PA, transcription.

11. Interview by Mara Brecht and Jeannine Hill Fletcher, February 12, 2009, Philadelphia, PA, digital recording.

neighbors to the deep spiritual conversation of a community? And, following from that, what is the epistemological significance of this shift?

Attending to Difference and Disagreement

Acknowledging difference and disagreement are key aspects of how the women achieved "spiritual conversation and community" through dialogue. In other words, the women presuppose that their dialogue will be a catalyst for disagreements. Another presupposition of their dialogue is willingness to explore those disagreements. When asked whether the dialogue group emphasizes commonalities more than divisions among religious beliefs, one woman responds, "First and foremost, we are distinctive and unique human beings, each one of us, each faith tradition—and we know each faith tradition has multitudes of expressions of that. So we know even within faith traditions, within even one congregation, we are not [the same]—our experiences, our practices, our expressions of one's faith are not [the same], they are different. To me, it's about the distinctiveness, it's *all* about the distinctiveness."[12] Another member contrasts her experience of discussing religious beliefs in the interreligious dialogue group with her experience of discussing beliefs in her all-Jewish friend group. She refers to one friend in particular, "Every time I asked her about the conflicts, she says, 'I won't talk about it.' So we've been friends for fifty years. I mean a *longtime* friendship. We simply don't talk about the things upon which we disagree. Sometimes we don't even know if we disagree, because we don't talk about it!" Another dialogue member, in exasperated sympathy, replies: "You're not discovering anything!"[13] These comments demonstrate that women of Philadelphia place a premium on acknowledging difference and disagreement as a first step toward untangling those disagreements.

The disagreements do not merely exist in principle, but in actuality. For example, one participant remarks, "at times members manage to say things that I feel are objectionable."[14] For the group, the issue of

12. Interview by Mara Brecht, July 27, 2007, Philadelphia, PA, digital recording.

13. Interview by Mara Brecht and Jeannine Hill Fletcher, February 12, 2009, Philadelphia, PA, digital recording. Note the tone that "disagreement," "distinctiveness," and "challenge" take for these women: they welcome them as opportunities for discovery and further discussion.

14. Interview by Mara Brecht, December 15, 2007, Philadelphia, PA, digital recording.

women's roles and statuses in religious communities tends to be the most significant source of challenge. On many occasions, group members have questioned the "second class status" of women within other group members' faith traditions.[15] The group members explain that the women whose home tradition had been critiqued often respond by asserting that there is no such devaluation of women. The original questioners remained unconvinced and describe their conversation partners' answer as "unsatisfying."[16] But then they are willing to push further into the conversation rather than merely accept that they disagree with each other.

For one woman, this raises questions not only about others' perspectives, but also about her own. She says, "Even if you thought you were open-minded there are all sorts of things that challenge that assumption."[17] These women have found that although they often desire to reconcile their disagreements or harmonize their diverse beliefs, disagreements are, at times, insurmountable. At these times, the group emphasizes the necessity of listening even more carefully and humbly. The Philadelphia women allow for genuinely emerging disagreement because, in their experience, disagreements ultimately provide the group with fresh opportunities for learning to listen to each other with deeper appreciation.

Negotiating Disagreement through Narrative

Time and again, members of the Philadelphia group attest to the importance of allowing each group member to narrate her life of faith. To put this value into practice early on, the Philadelphia women decided to engage in an exercise that would allow them to do so systematically. They refer to this exercise as the sharing of their spiritual autobiographies or faith journeys. For several consecutive months (some members recall the process taking an entire year), they devoted each dialogue session to the spiritual autobiographies of one or two women. In a document describing the process, the Philadelphia group explains the purpose of this exercise as follows: "We are interested in stories of how our life's experiences, values and beliefs have shaped our religious identification

15. Interview by Mara Brecht, October 2, 2009, Philadelphia, PA, transcription.
16. Interview by Mara Brecht, August 18, 2008, Philadelphia, PA, digital recording.
17. Interview by Mara Brecht, August 18, 2008, Philadelphia, PA, digital recording.

and practice. Sharing our spiritual journeys promises to give life to the distinctiveness and richness of our diverse faith traditions, while deepening relationships and understanding." These narratives were emotive and emphasized embodiment as a theme of their individual journeys.

Throughout the spiritual autobiography exercise, each woman occupied the roles of storyteller and story hearer at various times. Taking the time to listen to each woman recount her journey of faith and answer questions about her story resulted in what one member calls a "qualitative difference" in the group.[18] As another member says, "The group was more superficial before [we shared our spiritual autobiographies] and our conversations were more superficial."[19] Engaging with each other through their own narratives afforded the women stronger bonds of relationships as well as conversations with greater depth.

This activity—and the kinds of practices involved in doing such an exercise—functions as a lodestone for the group. It is not only the most important experience in the group's collective memory, it is also the experience to which they continually refer and the experience that guides their follow-on conversations. The group is characterized and constituted by the spiritual autobiographies. As one women puts it, "I would say that experience in the women's dialogue . . . has been sharing stories of life's journeys and stories and faith and opinions formed out of that—there's no doubt about it."[20] In their narrative sharing, they became a community and defined for themselves a common "language" and pattern of functioning.

A group member reflects on the significance of the spiritual autobiography exercise. She states, "I think [storytelling] helps us understand each other's religions and thought processes and seeing where each other comes from . . . At the time of contention and rift in the bigger world, when we come together, we sort of put a salve on each other's wounds. And we try to find out or try to sort through the issues and how they affect us as individuals and us as members of the larger society."[21] By listening to each other's stories, the women of Philadelphia cultivate empathetic understanding for each other that, in turn, allows them to

18. Interview by Mara Brecht, July 20, 2007, Philadelphia, PA, digital recording.

19. Interview by Mara Brecht, July 21, 2007, Philadelphia, PA, digital recording.

20. Interview by Mara Brecht, July 20, 2007, Philadelphia, PA, digital recording.

21. Interview by Mara Brecht, December 16, 2007, Philadelphia, PA, digital recording.

take care of one another—to "put a salve on each other's wounds." In the foregoing comments, the Philadelphia women identify characteristics of relationality, accessibility in conversation, and openness to vulnerability as imperative elements of women's interreligious dialogue. It is clear that, at least in the case of the Philadelphia women, the interreligious dialogue group creates a setting that honors and cultivates these characteristics.

While I am not arguing that mixed-gender groups or men's interreligious dialogue groups do not or cannot engage in narrative sharing practices and, through it, achieve deep spiritual community, the women of Philadelphia—in concert with O'Neill's view of women's interreligious dialogue—insist on the special and distinctive qualities of women's dialogue for accomplishing this end. [22] One dialogue member explains why it is important to her that the dialogue group is composed of only women: "You are less afraid to humble yourself." [23] Another member echoes this sentiment saying, "The level of disclosure and permission to talk about sensitive subjects continues to grow. My sense is that women are more relational." [24] Yet another dialogue member says she feels a sense of "camaraderie" and "sisterhood" in the group because the women all bring what she calls "a softer perspective" to the difficult issues raised in dialogue. [25]

I posit that the women's culture of care and appreciation emerges through acts of shared narration and has epistemological significance as such. Although O'Neill ultimately draws out dialogue's ethical ramifications, she makes a corollary point saying, "When we tell our

22. According to O'Neill, the "female way of being" is different than the "male way of being." The situation of interreligious dialogue underscores this reality in such a way as to reveal that women are better equipped to be in dialogue and produce positive outcomes through dialogue. It is outside the scope of this paper to problematize O'Neill's assertions about the fundamental (ontological) qualities of men and women viz. interreligious dialogue. My argument does not stand or fall by the *normative* gender claims that O'Neill makes. Rather, my purpose is to use the women of Philadelphia's reflections as a platform for opening the range of possibilities for interreligious dialogue. It happens to be the case that the Philadelphia women's self-understanding dovetails with O'Neill's view of women's interreligious dialogue, and I intend this point to be a *descriptive* one.

23. Interview by Mara Brecht, December 15, 2007, Philadelphia, PA, digital recording.

24. Interview by Mara Brecht, August 19, 2007, Philadelphia, PA, digital recording.

25. Interview by Mara Brecht, December 16, 2007, Philadelphia, PA, digital recording.

stories—where we came from, our family background, our formative experiences—we are really explaining how we acquired our particular way of believing and why we perceive things the way we do."[26] O'Neill's analysis can be pushed even further to show that the interchange between listening and caring to which the Philadelphia women refer is itself an epistemological practice.

In an essay on the epistemological dimensions of narrative, Liz Stanley writes, "All [narrative] derives from, is the product of, and helps to construct lives." She continues, "all knowledge of the world is rooted in the knowledge-production processes engaged in by enquiring and experiencing and therefore knowing subjects."[27] The act of telling others about oneself—the act of telling others about one's journey of faith—is an act of construction and production of knowledge. In this case, the act focuses on one's religious beliefs. Women's interreligious dialogue uniquely draws upon this narrative style of discourse and, concomitantly, leads to the production of religious beliefs.

Feminist epistemologist Uma Narayan argues that narrative is a distinctive feature of women's interreligious dialogue, which productively conveys our "truths" that would otherwise be inexpressible. She says, "'Non-analytic' and 'non-rational' forms of discourse, like fiction or poetry, may be better able than other forms to convey the complex life experiences of one group to members of another."[28] The Philadelphia women discovered the validity of this approach by using "interreligious narration" to formulate their own, individual beliefs, and also to allow them to understand their conversation partners' religious beliefs. Helene Egnell points to this very idea in her analysis of women's dialogue; she notes, "The experience of being listened to in its turn creates a willingness to listen."[29] Narrative thus works on both of "ends" of dialogical interaction—telling and hearing.

26. O'Neill, *Mending a Torn World*, 110.

27. Liz Stanley, "The Knowing Because Experiencing Subject: Narratives, Lives and Autobiography," in *Knowing the Difference: Feminist Perspective in Epistemology*, eds. Kathleen Lennon and Margaret Whitford (New York: Routledge, 1994), 146.

28. Uma Narayan, "The Project of Feminist Epistemology: Perspectives from a Nonwestern Feminist" in *Gender/Body/Knowledge*, eds. Alison Jagger and Susan R. Bordo (Piscatawey, NJ: Rutgers Univeristy Press, 1989), 264.

29. Helene Egnell, "Dialogue for Life: Feminist Approaches to Interreligious Dialogue," in *Theology and the Religions: A Dialogue*, ed. Viggo Mortensen (Grand Rapids, MI: Eerdmans, 2003), 254.

Because of the interreligious setting, religious beliefs are articulated and clarified in the encounter with others. That is, interreligious dialogue enables persons of diverse faith to meet one another and to shed light on the theological and philosophical positions to which they adhere. This is useful both for their own self-understanding and the understanding of others. In other words, through storytelling, a close connection is drawn between narrative representation and religious beliefs both for one's own as well as others' beliefs. This narrative connection facilitates the women's commitment to cultivating appreciation.

Epistemologically, I construe appreciation as the recognition of the full worth of the way in which believers form their beliefs. This includes careful and sympathetic attention to the processes, testimonies, intuitions, and perceptions believers rely on in forming beliefs. Insofar as women's interreligious dialogue encourages this "alternative" type of discourse—a type that has been overlooked and undervalued by epistemological analyses because it does not fit the paradigm of disagreement (as it does not result in renounced or uncertain religious belief)—women's interreligious dialogue groups like the Philadelphia group offer a unique opportunity for reconsidering the epistemological significance of dialogue; namely, that it is a setting wherein religious beliefs may be challenged through disagreement, but more importantly, where they are forged and reworked through practices such as interreligious narration.[30]

Negotiating Disagreement through Embodied Practices

One Philadelphia woman compares interreligious dialogue to "exercising one's spiritual muscles." As she explains it, when a person trains her muscles—physical or spiritual—it makes it easier for her to use those

---

30. Challenges to religious belief need not come in the form of direct or "exact" contradiction to raise epistemic disagreement. Griffiths helpfully describes several possible, latent forms of disagreement among religious beliefs. "Approximate contradiction" is most relevant for this essay. Religious claims are in approximate contradiction, Griffiths writes, when they "do not have the formal appearance of contradictoriness, but can readily be made to yield a contradiction" (Griffiths, *Problems of Religious Diversity*, 33). Indeed, the women of Philadelphia do not disagree about one another's narrations; however, the religious claims implied by one person's narrative of faith might be in approximate contradiction with the claims implied by another person's narrative, particularly when the persons belong to different home traditions.

muscles and to use them more effectively and frequently.[31] The language of "exercise" is critical because it points toward the training, practices, and activities that lie at the heart of religious beliefs. In telling each other what they believe, the women of Philadelphia refer to various, active religious exercises from their home traditions.

Collectively, the women's spiritual narratives point to three discrete loci of religious practice that are central to the formation and support of their religious beliefs: religious feast, prayer and pilgrimage. Not only do the women tell each other about their formative religious practices, over time, they also invite each other *into* these practices. Building from the Philadelphia woman's insight about dialogue as exercise, I propose to frame the group's religious and interreligious practices as epistemological exercises. In describing the collective interreligious practices of the group, I stress the embodied dimensions and, in the next section, systematically address the epistemological significance of embodied exercise.

Religious Feasting

The first loci of practice—religious feasting—could also be characterized more generally as "celebration." However, because food takes center stage in the Philadelphia women's shared celebrations, the language of feast seems appropriate. In our research-conversation, recollections of celebrations around food stand as prominent and fond memories for the group. Over the years the women of Philadelphia have celebrated several different kinds of religious holidays involving feast from the Jewish, Muslim, and Baha'i calendars. (After all, the group itself grew out of a Philadelphia citywide interfaith Thanksgiving event.) One year, just before Passover, the Jewish women decided to give a Seder dinner for the entire dialogue group. In our interviews, they recall planning the meal, getting together to cook and prepare it, and inviting all to participate in the ceremony of the dinner. During the Seder meal, non-Jewish members of the group asked each of the Jewish women to describe what was special to them about the meal and the holiday and how each of their families celebrated Passover.

---

31. Interview by Mara Brecht and Jeannine Hill Fletcher, July 27, 2007, Philadelphia, PA, digital recording.

The event was such a success that the Muslim women in the group decided to plan a meal for the breaking of the fast during Ramadan. They served Pakistani and Indian food—dishes from their countries of origin.[32] While the Philadelphia women joined together over a meal to celebrate Ramadan with the fasting group members, they also enjoyed other traditional activities staged by the Muslim women. The Muslim women wore traditional dress, shared bracelets with the other group members to wear, and applied henna to the hands of "the ladies who were brave enough" to try it.[33] Through their activities and conversations at this celebration, the Philadelphia women were able to go beyond a theologically simplistic understanding of Ramadan as an austere time and instead appreciate the deeper, celebratory meaning of the holiday for the Muslim community.

Just as the success of the Seder celebration gave rise to the Eid one, the success of the Eid celebration gave rise to the Baha'i spring festival. The women remember these holidays as "special," "amazing," and "wonderful." Of them, a Christian woman said: "We felt so close to each other [during those times]. It was an evolving thing with our group."[34] The women of Philadelphia note both the importance of the celebrations around feast and, most importantly the fact that they, as a group, *worked up* to the events. In other words, they trained over time, through conversation and intentional exploration of one another's lives, to prepare themselves for meeting together at these religious celebrations. They came to understand the significance of the Passover meal, Ramadan fast-breaking, and the Baha'i new year, because they prepared themselves to participate in it together. They arrived with their physical and spiritual appetites, ready to put on different clothes, imbibe different drink, and hear different prayers.

Feasting and its spiritual partner, fasting, are of central importance to many religious traditions, and particularly those represented by the Philadelphia women. Rhythms of fasting and feasting remind religious practitioners how to both discipline and enjoy, to restrain and revel, and to remember and rejoice *through* denying and nourishing their bodies

32. Interview by Mara Brecht, December 16, 2007, Philadelphia, PA, digital recording.

33. Ibid.

34. Interview by Mara Brecht, December 15, 2007, Philadelphia, PA, digital recording.

with food. Feast involves the body in a particularly distinctive way—as it is food that gives the body life, and it stands as a way of unlocking a door to the importance of embodied practice for the women's dialogue group.

Prayer

The exercise of prayer, the second loci, is best explored through an anecdote offered by one of the women. A Jewish member of the group recalls that early in dialogue, she felt perplexed by a Christian member's description of her prayer life. She paraphrases the words of the Christian woman: "I pray all the time. I prayed on this. I had a struggle in my life, I prayed on it. Prayer is just a part of my daily life. I pray when I go to get a parking spot." The Jewish woman says this account of prayer was utterly foreign to her; something she called "out of her orbit." She elaborates, "When I heard someone who is so sophisticated, so capable, so functioning in the world, a very respected professional say that they pray for a parking space, I didn't even know how to integrate that." Eventually, the Jewish woman began to think about how to "integrate" the Christian dialogue partner's prayer practice into her life.

There are two aspects to how she achieved this integration. First, the Jewish woman listened *with appreciation* to her Christian conversation partner describe her prayer practice, despite how alien it seemed to her at first. Second, the group developed a prayer practice of its own, in which the Jewish woman engaged and by which she was transformed. The Jewish dialogue member explained how the group institutionalized lighting a candle at the beginning of each meeting and taking time to silently pray and reflect together. The Jewish woman describes the effect this had on her: "It woke me up. I am not praying for parking spaces. I am not there yet! But I know what that means. I know that it [prayer] is not something that I wait to do when I go to Synagogue."[35]

Another Philadelphia group member, a Christian, offers a reflection on prayer that unfolds its sensory, embodied elements. She recalls a time when she was very sick, undergoing both surgery and radiation treatments. She says, "I remember at one of my low points writing to this group and asking for their prayers. And it was really profound to me, because I realized that those prayers were coming from so many

---

35. Interview by Mara Brecht, July 20, 2007, Philadelphia, PA, digital recording.

different traditions. And yet . . . I very much sensed them." She concludes the account with the image of the prayers of her dialogue partners to be "really holding me."[36] Her reflection on this experience is inflected with themes of embodiment, using the language of "sense" and "holding." That she begins this remembrance with the conjunctions "and yet" implies that this woman was surprised to find herself appreciating prayers made by non-Christian dialogue members.

The self-noted transformation effected here is not unlike the Jewish woman in the previous example. While neither of the women use epistemological language such as "believe," "describe," or "maintain," their views of prayer were importantly impacted; both of the Philadelphia women found their appreciation and practice of prayer changed through dialogue. This suggests that it was *because of* the engaged, embodied exercises of the dialogue group that transformation about what prayer is—an epistemological transformation, or transformation of belief—was accomplished.

Pilgrimage

Finally, religious pilgrimage is another area of focus for the Philadelphia women's dialogue group. One Christian woman shares her initial skepticism about being in conversation with Muslims, because of the political and social climate at the time of the dialogue group's beginning (recall that the group formed just after September 11, 2001). However, she came to "appreciate the richness" of Islam upon hearing a Muslim describe her pilgrimage to Mecca. From the pilgrimage description, the Christian woman began to envision the Hajj as a "moving scene," something profound. She goes on to describe how, when she would walk around in her day-to-day life, she would imagine "all those people also walking around [the Kabaa]" and be awestruck. "It's just awesome!" she exclaims. Although as a non-Muslim, she cannot participate in the Hajj, this woman *imagines herself into* the Muslim pilgrimage experience. And this "imagining into" takes bodily form; it is by walking about herself that she realizes the profundity of millions of Muslims expressing their faith in walking.

36. Interview by Mara Brecht and Jeannine Hill Fletcher, July 27, 2007, Philadelphia, PA, digital recording.

The embodied aspects of the Hajj surface for another member of the dialogue group. Her description includes a blind pilgrim's heightened sensory experience and how his recollection influenced the way she talked about religious practices with the group. Here are her words:

> I felt so privileged to be in the presence of somebody within a month of Hajj who lived all their life waiting for this and I could appreciate it. Now, am I meant to do this? No! I want to understand the power of this pilgrimage experience and what it's about. But what most moved me [was how] he told this story of his own experience of Hajj through the sounds and smells. I had the privilege of hearing it through a person of faith who had the experience so viscerally and through the [sounds] and smells and human, spiritual experiences . . . a Jew will never be at Hajj . . . Can anyone else of another faith ever feel like what I am feeling at this moment: a profound religious connection to my God or the one God? . . . What is somebody getting from that moment of communion when they can be brought to tears in explaining that each time it is literally *life giving* to them? . . . Not everyone experiences it that way I'm sure but I feel privileged to be with people who are willing to share what that ritual is bringing, you know, God, Jesus, somebody closer, *physically*, in their life, that moment, that week. I want to know, how do I get that in my tradition?[37]

This account of another person's testimony emphasizes the bodily nature of religious beliefs. Because this woman first heard about the Hajj from someone who described it in non-dominant sensory forms—through smell and sound, rather than sight—she became particularly attuned to the way humans participate in religious practices *with their full bodies*. In turn, when she listens to Catholics describe their experience of taking communion, she is attentive to the physical closeness with God to which they attest. In both cases, this woman discovers that embodied religious practices lead to and support particular religious beliefs. This became something she desired to find in her own tradition.

The extemporaneous exchanges about belief that seem to be at the very heart of dialogue are, in fact, made more profound when accompanied by a guided *doing*. The Philadelphia women are able to realize this, I argue, precisely because their dialogue privileges epistemological processes (belief formation practices) over products (beliefs).

37. Interview by Mara Brecht, July 20, 2007, Philadelphia, PA, digital recording.

Embodied practices constitute religious belief-formation. Like all practices, practice of religious belief-formation, are shown by the women to be best understood when we try them ourselves—with our own bodies. By paying careful attention to the role of the body in religious practices, on the one hand, and, at the same time, endeavoring to engage in each other's formative religious practices, the women of Philadelphia are able to appreciate the diversity of—and disagreements among—beliefs in their group.

They explore the embodied practices of religious beliefs so as to negotiate any disagreements they face in conversation; in turn, they actively demonstrate how dialogue, when viewed as a site of disagreement, is capable of becoming a well-spring for deeper, richer interreligious encounter. Through embodied interreligious exercises—specifically in the areas of feast, prayer, and pilgrimage—the women of Philadelphia unfold new possibilities for interreligious encounter.

Retrieving and Reimagining Epistemology in Interreligious Dialogue

Understanding dialogue to be more about how one's beliefs are formed and received by others than to be about the degree to which beliefs are justified preserves the premise of this essay—namely, that dialogue involves disagreement. Said another way, dialogue can still be seen as an occasion or site of disagreement although the point of the conversation is to understand *why* there is a disagreement rather than *which side* is right. While dialogue does not demand either that participants cling to their beliefs or otherwise abandon them, it does demand that they, as O'Neill's writes, "open [themselves] to understand how another could believe what [they themselves] could not."[38]

Lorraine Code argues that epistemologies influenced by empiricism, positivism, and evidentialism—in other words, traditional epistemological discourse—delineate a very particular end of knowledge; she writes, "The aim of knowledge seeking is to achieve the capacity to predict, manipulate, and control the behavior of objects known."[39] Not all knowing is about manipulation and the ability to assert control. The

38. O'Neill, *Mending a Torn World*, 108.

39. Lorraine Code, "Taking Subjectivity into Account," in Linda Alcoff and Elizabeth Porter, eds., *Feminist Epistemologies* (New York: Routledge, 1993), 17.

women of Philadelphia provide a paradigmatic example: they seek to understand the way their conversation partners form beliefs not in order to proselytize, disprove, or dismiss their beliefs, but rather because they, in the words of one participant, "have been touched and moved and changed by each other" thus leading their understanding of each other to "deepen in a spiral over time."[40]

Applying epistemological discourse to this example of women's dialogue makes it possible to theorize better about how religious beliefs are formed and held in interreligious settings. The women in dialogue seek to understand the religious processes of their conversation partners. They seek to understand, with deep appreciation, not only the epistemic worth of these beliefs, but, more importantly, what leads someone to those beliefs. The attention that the women of Philadelphia give to the processes of belief formation, through both narrative and embodied exercise, not only necessitates a new epistemological understanding of the *point* of disagreement in dialogue, it also calls for a new religious epistemology and, more to the point, one that privileges narrative and embodiment as primary features in the production of religious beliefs.

Toward a Feminist, Embodied Epistemology

Elizabeth Grosz argues that body has been "disavowed" in traditional epistemologies and sharply criticizes the portrayals of knowledge that are "purely conceptual" and "merely intellectual."[41] In reaction to this pattern, Grosz develops an alterative epistemology based on feminist principles—one that places the body at the center of epistemic activity. She goes on to connect this claim to a broader epistemological theory: "Knowledge is an activity; it is a *practice* and not a contemplative

---

40. Interview by Mara Brecht, July 21, 2007, Philadelphia, PA, notes.

41. Grosz defines two ways that feminist theorists tend to conceptualize the body: one "as the surface of social inscription" and the second "as the locus of lived experience." Feminists using the inscriptive model probe how the "the body is marked, scarred, transformed, and written upon, and constructed by the various regimes of institutional, discursive, and nondiscursive power" and those using the experiential model see the body as a means of knowing the world (Elizabeth Grosz, "Bodies and Knowledges and the Crisis of Reason," in Linda Alcoff and Elizabeth Porter, eds., *Feminist Epistemologies* [New York: Routledge, 1993], 197).

reflection. *It does things.*[42] Another way of articulating Grosz's feminist theory of knowledge is as follows: beliefs are at once *exercised* and *exercises.*[43]

That "beliefs are exercised" means they have real implications in the world and affect the lives of those who hold them. As Grosz puts it, knowledge *does things.* Feminism(s) argue for an intrinsic relationship between knowledge and power, and because knowledge, as the Philadelphia women show, is an activity that involves the body, bodies are necessarily shaped by knowledge.[44] Traditional epistemologies often disregard the role the body plays in the production of knowledge and so obscure the impact that knowledge—and the power connected to it—has on knowers.

The second element of Grosz's critique, captured by the statement "beliefs are exercises," points to the idea that beliefs come about through the actions of people who hold them. In the case of religious beliefs, when one of the faithful says, "God exists," that will guide the believer's actions in the world and shape her self-understanding as a being created to be in relation with God. Traditional epistemologies overlook this type of relationship between what the body does and what a person believes or knows. The embodied epistemology arising out of the testimonies of women in dialogue suggest that it is, in part, *through* the body's actions and practices that believers form religious beliefs.

Accounting for the fact that the lives, the existences, and the bodies of religious believers are all affected by their beliefs opens to a more nuanced understanding of the purpose of belief-forming in the first place.[45] Integrating the body into epistemological models allows for a way to see the effects beliefs have on bodies. This is particularly important when one considers beliefs in an interreligious setting. As

42. Ibid., 203.

43. While I use phrase belief/knowledge, this should not suggest a conflation of these two concepts. In fact, they are distinct. The standard epistemological definition of 'knowledge' is captured by the acronym JTB, which is the abbreviated form of 'justified true belief.' According to the JTB definition, a belief is knowledge if it is both justified and true. In an ideal situation, a justified belief happens to also be true, but justification cannot *make* a belief true: truth is independent of justification. Knowledge exists when justified belief and truth coincide and is thus always dependent on both.

44. Ibid.

45. As this analysis suggests, theorizing about the claim "beliefs are exercised" could be a place where the inscriptive and experiential models for the body noted in footnote 40 intersect.

the Philadelphia women show, their embodied sharing, which builds on communal narration practices, is really what enables true interreligious community and, in turn, constructive negotiation of disagreements. Embodied models for religious belief assist scholars in identifying alternative epistemological ends for dialogue beyond control and manipulation—ends such as those articulated by the Philadelphia women of touching, moving, and changing one another.

4

Dialogue in Times of War

Christian Women's Rescue of Jews in Hitler's Germany

Katharina von Kellenbach

It is widely acknowledged that Jewish–Christian dialogue began in the aftermath of the Holocaust. The shock over the systematic murder of six million Jews in Europe changed the way the Christian churches thought about and related to Jews and Judaism. In February 1946, the World Council of Churches expressed its "deep sense of horror at the unprecedented tragedy that has befallen the Jewish people" and acknowledged "with penitence the failure of the Churches to overcome . . . this evil."[1] By July 1947, international leaders of the Jewish and Christian communities met in Seelisberg, Switzerland for the purpose "of cooperation of all men (sic) without distinction of race or creed. For the purpose of cooperation as equal partners in dealing with this problem, Christians and Jews have joined this International Emergency Conference to combat antisemitism."[2] The International Council of Christians and Jews

---

1. WCC "Resolution on Antisemitism and the Jewish Situation," February 1946, in Franklin Sherman, ed., *Bridges: Documents of the Christian–Jewish Dialogue* (New York: Paulist, 2011), 43.

2. International Council of Christians and Jews, "The Principal Objectives of Jewish–Christian Cooperation in Combating Antisemitism," (July 1947), in Sherman, ed., *Bridges*, 338.

(ICCJ) committed Christian participants to a process of theological re-visioning that was first laid out in the *Ten Points of Seelisberg*.[3]

This essay explores the hidden seeds of the post-war Jewish–Christian dialogue sown amidst the genocide against Jews. There are three reasons why we ought to consider the prehistory of Jewish–Christian dialogue. First, the dialogue in the post-war world was dominated by men, but the first efforts to create channels of communication and networks of support across religious communities were led by women. These women operated clandestinely and faced tremendous pressures not only from the Nazi regime but also from their church hierarchies. Though some of them were theologically trained, most of these women worked in teaching and social welfare offices. Their lack of theological prestige and institutional power may explain their greater willingness to reach across religious boundaries but it also accounts for their failure to mobilize religious leaders against genocide. Second, their resistance was prompted by personal and professional relationships with Jews that created cognitive dissonance to the dominant ideologies of antisemitism and anti-Judaism. It took more than tolerant neighborliness to resist the totalitarian regime and to deconstruct the pervasive vilification of Jews. The vast majority of German Christians remained blind and indifferent to the plight of their Jewish neighbors. Those who risked their lives were motivated by relationships that generated empathy and dialogue. Third, dialogue was initiated by people who lived in the borderlands of the Jewish and Christian communities: Christians with Jewish ancestry, converts, couples living in Jewish–Christian intermarriages, and their interfaith children. The ability to navigate the Jewish and Christian border became a life-saving skill. But in the post-war world, people with complex and complicated religious identities were marginalized and excluded from formal Jewish–Christian dialogue settings. Forth, this prehistory serves as reminder that dialogue occurs in particular political contexts, often of oppression and violence, and sometimes of ethnic cleansing and genocide. Dialogue is more than an academic exercise in instruction. It is fundamentally a moral and political endeavor that demands solidarity with those who endure defamation and harassment. In times of severe abuse and genocidal violence, dialogue is a commitment to care and a pledge to resist efforts to dehumanize the religious other.

---

3. "Ten Points of Seeligsberg," (July 1947), in Sherman, ed., *Bridges*, 341–43.

In the Weimar Republic of the 1920s and 1930s, there were no institutionalized settings for Jewish–Christian dialogue, although the term "dialogue" was coined by Martin Buber in his groundbreaking *I and Thou*, published in 1929. Franz Rosenzweig can be considered a father of dialogue when he laid the philosophical foundations for Jewish–Christian dialogue in *The Star of Redemption*, which grew out of his passionate love of and dialogue with Margit and Eugen Rosenstock-Huessy.[4] But apart from these visionary philosophers, churches and synagogues, Jewish and Christian institutions did not encourage formal interactions and dialogue between Jews and Christians at the congregational, institutional or personal levels.[5] This was notably different in the United States, where the National Council of Christians and Jews (NCCJ) was founded in 1927, and in Great Britain, where the Council of Christians and Jews (CCJ) was constituted at the height of the Holocaust in 1942. But in Berlin of the Roaring Twenties, known for its liberal and cosmopolitan atmosphere, where people mixed and mingled freely, there were few opportunities for religiously active, committed Jews and Christians to befriend each other.[6]

This is particularly striking when we consider that Jewish, Protestant and Catholic women graduated from the same public schools and universities and struggled to open employment opportunities for women within their respective religious communities. For instance, Ilse Jonas and Regina Jonas were born around the turn of the century and belonged to the first generation of women to enter the university, which opened to women between 1900 and 1908. They had more in common than last names: they were educated in public schools and attended public universities. They confronted the religious leadership's disbelief and

4. Ephraim Meir, ed., *Letters of Love: Franz Rosenzweig's Spiritual Biography and Oeuvre in Light of the Gritli Letters* (New York: Lang, 2005).

5. "Dialogue," in Edward Kessler and Neil Wenborn, eds., *A Dictionary of Jewish–Christian Relations* (Cambridge: Cambridge University Press, 2005).

6. This included the women's movement. While the Jewish Women's League (JFB) joined the umbrella of women's organizations BDF (Association of German Women), the Catholic women's organization (with about 220,000 members in 1921) did not join, while the Protestant women's association (of about 200,000 members in 1928) joined in 1906 but withdrew in 1918. They did not formally invite dialogue across religious and denominational lines. Marion Kaplan, "Sisterhood under Siege: Feminism and Anti-Semitism in Germany 1904–1938," in Renate Bridenthal, Atina Grossmann, Marion Kaplan, eds., *When Biology Became Destiny* (New York: Monthly Review Press, 1984), 182 (174–94).

opposition and found creative ways to forge public roles for women in church and synagogue. Ilse Jonas earned a degree in Protestant theology, while Regina Jonas graduated from the *Hochschule für die Wissenschaft des Judentums*. Ilse Jonas was ordained into the newly created office of "vicar" in the Protestant Church, while Regina Jonas received a private ordination in 1935 and became the worldwide first female rabbi. It is ironic that the rise of women in the professional roles in religious communities would coincide with the victory of National Socialism. When Adolf Hitler assumed power in 1933, university-educated ambitious women were poised to break the barriers in church and synagogue. They shared visions of gender equality and religious service with their religious communities. But they apparently found little commonality of purpose and did not engage in Jewish–Christian dialogue.

There is no written evidence that Regina Jonas ever interacted with Christian colleagues as she created a female rabbinic role for herself in Berlin.[7] Her success as a preacher and pastoral counselor (*Seel-sorger*) was overshadowed by tightening antisemitic restrictions and her conscription into forced labor. In the fall of 1942, she was deported to Theresienstadt, and two years later, by the end of 1944, to Auschwitz, where she was sent to the gas chambers upon arrival. Meanwhile, her Roman Catholic peers expanded their professional opportunities as teachers and Catholic social service providers and her Protestant peers filled congregational vacancies when their male colleagues were conscripted into the Wehrmacht after September 1, 1939.[8] By 1939, female vicars were fully responsible for congregations and allowed to perform all ministerial functions "in times of emergency when the message of the Gospel from the mouth of a man has become silent."[9] As a group,

---

7. Katharina von Kellenbach "God Does not Oppress Any Human Being: The Life and Thought of Rabbi Regina Jonas," *Leo Baeck Institute: Yearbook* 39 (1994) 213–25; Katharina von Kellenbach, "Denial and Defiance in the Work of Rabbi Regina Jonas," in Phyllis Mack and Omar Bartov, eds., *In God's Name: Genocide and Religion in the 20th Century* (New York: Berghahn, 2001), 243–59.

8. Jill Stephenson, *Women and Nazi Society* (New York: Barnes & Noble, 1975), 178.

9. This *Notverordnung* reads: "In times of emergency, when the proper sermon of the Gospel from the mouth of a man becomes silent, the church administration may permit that women who are qualified proclaim the Gospel even in congregational service." 11. Bekenntnissynode 1942, quoted in Dagmar Henze, "Die Geschichte der evangelischen Theologin—Ein Überblick," *Rheinische Kirchenzeitung* 3 (1991) 98.

they did not publicly renounce antisemitism or condemn the increasing pace of persecution of their Jewish neighbors.

But there were notable exceptions, and it is to these exemplary women that we now turn to examine the dynamics that drew them into resistance. Despite the absence of institutionalized structures of dialogue between religious representatives of church and synagogue, there were multiple interactions and border-crossings. Under National Socialism, the line between Jew and Christian became a matter of life and death. But there was a sizeable population caught in the interstices of the newly created religio-racial categories developed by the Nazi state: converts, intermarried couples, secularists, children of mixed marriages, and anyone whose grandparents had been members of the synagogue. The church women who staffed agencies charged with the care of those who found themselves caught between the Jewish and Christian communities became proficient smugglers across religious, political, and national borders. As they built support networks and established contacts, they developed the necessary skills to navigate and revise Jewish–Christian relations in dialogue.

The borders between religious and ethnic communities are permeable and fluid as long as societies live in peace. But when ideologies ascend to power that promise to unify and purify the nation, race, or religion, then individuals are forced to choose, sometimes at gunpoint. The threat of violence closes the in-between-spaces and border crossings between communities. Religious and ethnic identities harden, often quite suddenly, and individuals who were used to living in a pluralist and open world, where multiple belonging and hybrid identities were tolerated, can find themselves suddenly exposed. Recently, these dynamics were powerfully at work in such far flung places as the former Yugoslavia, Lebanon, Rwanda, Iraq, Egypt, Syria . . . In each case, the sudden introduction of violence created clear boundaries between communities and forced individuals to declare allegiance. It is in such situations that interreligious dialogue becomes an act of resistance because it creates and maintains channels of communication in the face of forces intent on cutting off relations in order to isolate a minority.

For a variety of reasons, hundreds of thousands of Jews had converted to Christianity since the emancipation of Jews in German-speaking lands in the nineteenth century.[10] In addition to conversion, there

10. Deborah Hertz, *How Jews Became Germans: The History of Conversion and Assimilation in Berlin* (New Haven: Yale University Press, 2007).

was intermarriage. In 1939, the Nazi government registered 19,114 intermarried Jewish–Christian households, almost 6,000 of them living in Berlin alone.[11] Then there were the children of these marriages, who came to be defined as *Mischlinge* (hybrids, crossbreeds) of varying degrees. These border-crossers not only practiced a form of lived Jewish–Christian dialogue within families, but they also confronted Jewish and Christian leaders with the internal Other. When the Nazi state revoked civil rights from anyone whose genealogy included three grandparents who were members of the synagogue, thousands of Protestants and Catholics were suddenly exposed as "Jews." Roman Catholic and Protestant church leaders could not afford to ignore the plight of these "Jews" entirely. Similarly, Jewish leaders were confronted with requests for assistance by non-Aryan Christians and had to accommodate the formation of Christian congregations in ghettos and concentration camps. Under the extreme assault of Nazi antisemitism, the traditional lines of religious communities collapsed and new communities of resistance emerged. On the Christian side, these networks were spearheaded by church women.

There are several reasons why women would assume leadership positions in the rescue and relief efforts for Jews. One factor was the low priority given to antisemitism and assistance to non-Aryan Christians by Roman Catholic and Protestant church leaders. Another reason was that welfare and relief agencies were considered more suitable to women's nature, and academically trained women found employment in social welfare agencies charged with assistance to Jews. Hence, the women found themselves involved and confronted with the growing misery and the outrages inflicted upon the German Jewish minority. They began their work conservatively by merely defending the churches' right to treat all of its Christian members equally, irrespective of ethnicity or national origin. But eventually they expanded their scope and collaborated with Jewish agencies and the synagogue to protect Jewish individuals. Of the four women to be discussed, two were specifically charged to focus on Christians with Jewish ancestry: the Protestant Vicar Katharina Staritz and the Catholic Dr. Margaret Sommer began by upholding the churches' right and authority to define its own borders and clashed with the state over the validity of the sacraments of baptism

---

11. Jana Leichsenring, *Die Katholische Kirche und ihre Juden: Das Hilfswerk beim Bischöflichen Ordinariat Berlin 1938–1945* (Berlin: Metropol, 2007), 15.

and marriage. Vicar Staritz was sent to missionize Jews and ended up in the concentration camp of Ravensbrück for asserting the equality of "Jew and Gentile" in the church. Dr. Margaret Sommer coordinated relief efforts for Roman Catholic "non-Aryans" in the *Bischöfliche Hilfstelle* in Berlin and called for public protests when the state moved to forcibly divorce intermarried couples in order to deport the Jewish partners (mostly men). Both women extended their mandate beyond their official charges and built extensive clandestine support networks reaching deep into the Jewish community. Their resistance began in theological faithfulness to Christian definitions of membership and identity which, out of sheer necessity, pushed them toward greater openness and willingness to reach out to anyone who needed and to anyone who was ready to provide help. Their practice of Jewish–Christian cooperation initiated a process of revision in their Jewish–Christian theology.

On the other hand, the Protestant Dr. Elisabeth Schmitz and the Catholic Dr. Gertrud Luckner seemed to have understood the connection between political antisemitism and theological anti-Judaism from the outset. They not only worked practically and politically on behalf of persecuted Jews but also called on Christian leaders to confront and oppose theological anti-Judaism in theory and practice. Their close personal friendships committed them to a principled opposition against antisemitism and anti-Judaism.

The Protestant women had graduated with academic degrees in theology. While Katharina Staritz aimed for ordination, Elisabeth Schmitz was employed as a teacher in public schools. Depending on the region, the branches of the German Evangelical Church debated legislation to establish a separate and inferior theological office for women. To maintain the essential difference between men and women, the office of the female theologian was given different names.[12] The most common professional title for female theologians was vicar (*Vikarin*), minister's aid (*Pfarrgehilfin*), or assistant minister (*Hilfspfarrerin*).[13] Women were

12. The members of the *Verband evangelischer Theologinnen*, the national association of female evangelical theologians disagreed over the question of ordination. The association split in 1930 into a more radical organization striving for full equality with male ministers and the majority settling for a "separate and different" version of the female theologian.

13. These titles were taken from the magazine of the *Verband evangelischer Theologinnen*, which printed a membership list of 254 names and professional titles. *Mitteilungen* 5/2 (1935) 10–16.

not ordained but 'blessed in'; their ministry was restricted to women, youth and children; women were not to preach to men or have authority over them; only unmarried, celibate women could perform as vicars and their employment ended with marriage; their office was to be support- ive and subordinate to the male and supplement his role as minister.[14] Vicar Katharina Staritz was "blessed in" and assigned to provide con- version instruction and baptism preparation for "Israelite women and men" in Breslau on July 1st, 1933.[15] Technically, her assignment broke two regulations: First, as a female vicar, she was not supposed to teach adult males, which put the instruction of Jewish men beyond her reach. Implicitly, her superiors seemed to have counted Jewish men among women and children. Secondly, baptism of Jews had become pointless after the adoption of the "Aryan paragraph" in Staritz' regional, *German Christian* [i.e. Nazi] dominated, Silesian church. Christian mission to the Jews and baptism education was rooted in the tradition of Christian supersessionism and replacement theology. Her early work with mis- sion to Jews evolved into her appointment to head the Breslau branch of the Büro Grüber, which was created in 1938 to address the dire needs of the approximately 350,000 Protestants of Jewish ancestry. By 1938, five years after the Nuremberg racial laws had stripped German Jews and non-Aryan Christians of civil rights and prohibited their employment and school attendance, many people were left destitute and isolated. The majority of the employees in the Büro Grüber were Jewish converts to Christianity and women.[16]

The marginal position of converts and of female theologians who staffed the Büro Grüber made them both more willing to take risks and

14. Dagmar Henze, "Die Geschichte der evangelischen Theologin—Ein Über- blick," *Reformierte Kirchenzeitung* 3 (1991) 97–99; Ilse Härter, "Persönliche Erfahrun- gen mit der Ordination von Theologinnen in der Bekennenden Kirche des Rheinlands und in Berlin/Brandenburg," in Günther van Norden, ed., *Zwischen Bekenntnis und Anpassung* (Cologne: Rheinland, 1985), 193–209; Heike Köhler, "Neue Ämter für neue Aufgaben," *Reformierte Kirchenzeitung* 5 (1991) 165–69; Konvent Evangelischer Theologinnen in der Bundesrepublik Deutschland und Berlin (West), eds., *Das Weib schweigt nicht mehr* (Göttingen: Kirchenkreisamt Osterhold-Scharmbeck, 1990).

15. "Arbeitsbericht Nr.2 der Vikarin in Breslau Lic Katharina Staritz," reprinted in Gerlind Schwöbel, *Ich aber vertraue: Katharina Staritz eine Theologin im Widerstand* (Frankfurt: Evangelischer Regionalverband, 1990), 100.

16. Hartmut Ludwig, *An der Seite der Entrechteten und Schwachen: Zur Geschichte des "Büro Pfarrer Grüber (1938–1940) und der Ev. Hilfsstelle für ehemals Rasseverfolgte nach 1945* (Berlin: Logos, 2009); Wolfgang Gerlach, *Als die Zeugen schwiegen* (Berlin: Institut Kirche und Judentum 1988), 145 and 256.

more vulnerable to abandonment by church authorities. When Staritz issued a memorandum in 1941 in reaction to the newly passed law that forced non-Aryans to wear the Yellow Star, her superiors in the Silesian church denounced her to the Gestapo. Her letter merely reminded her "brothers in office" that "it is the Christian duty of the congregations, not to exclude these members from church service because of this mark. They have the same rights in the church as all the other members of the congregation and especially require the consolation of the Word of God."[17] She became the target of two propaganda articles in the SS-journal *Der Schwarze Korps*,[18] which vilified her as a "sourpuss" and chastised her for her ignorance and lack of racial pride. When she was sent to the Ravensbrück women's concentration camp without trial, her church administration docked her pay.[19] It took progressive members of the Confessing Church in Berlin more than a year to convince the Silesian church administration to intervene on her behalf and to advocate for her release. While Staritz survived, fourteen of her non-Aryan colleagues at the Büro Grüber in Berlin were killed at the hands of the Nazis, as Hartmut Ludwig painstakingly reconstructed despite the lack of written records.[20]

On the Roman Catholic side, Dr. Margarete Sommer also oversaw a staff of mostly non-Aryan Catholics who worked for her when she took over the Bischöfliches Hilfwerk der Diözese Berlin in 1941 (it was set up in 1938, at the same time as the Büro Grüber). Sommer had completed a doctorate in law and economics. Like Staritz, she was watched warily by some of her superiors who became exasperated by her frequent memoranda and pleas for intercessions and protests. Bishop Bertram, the chair of the Fulda Bishops' Conference, complained: "Repeatedly, I am presented with detailed reports about injustices committed against Mischlinge and non-Aryans by Dr. Margarete Sommer . . . and I am supposed to issue interventions to the highest authorities . . . if I am

---

17. Wolfgang Gerlach, *Als die Zeugen schwiegen* (Berlin: Institut Kirche und Judentum, 1987), 286.

18. Kurt Meier, *Der Evangelische Kirchenkampf* (Göttingen: Vandenhoek & Ruprecht, 1984), 307. Gerda Drewes and Eva Kochanski, *Heimliche Hilfe* (Lahr/Schwarzwald: Kaufmann, 1961), 7–16. Her successor in the Büro Grüber was Vicar Herta Dietze.

19. Gerlind Schwöbel, *Katharina Staritz: Eine Theologin im Widerstand* (Frankfurt: Evangelischer Regionalverband, 1990).

20. Ludwig, *An der Seite der Entrechteten und Schwachen,* 87–139.

supposed to pick out hot coals from of the fire, I expect that her superiors examine and validate her intelligence. I hope that you explain this to Sommer because she is not listening to my exhortations."[21] Sommer created an extensive network of contacts, including to the *Reichsvereinigung of Jews in Germany,*[22] the Quakers, the Büro Grüber, and Protestant church circles, as well as high-ranking government informants. She possessed detailed and accurate knowledge of the plans of the Nazis, including the high-level secretive Wannsee meeting in January 1942, where the final stage of the Final Solution was arranged. By February 5, 1942, Sommer reported the details of the decisions arrived at this meeting to Bishop Berning. By the summer of 1942, she sent comprehensive information about the number and fate of the deportations via courier to Rome.[23] But she failed to convince either the Vatican or the German Bishops' Conference to protest publicly against the accelerating pace of the genocide.

Instead, she focused on the state's violations of Catholic doctrine and practice, especially with respect to marriage and divorce. She assumed that she would be able to gain the bishops' attention when the Nazi government prepared to force intermarried couples to divorce in order to deport the Jewish partner. The bishops intervened in defense of the institution of marriage.[24] But they did so diplomatically and not publicly, as Sommer had urged. Both Sommer and Staritz were confined by their churches' unwillingness to take a position in defense of the Jews and were forced to package their resistance around the sacraments of baptism and marriage.

At the end of February 1943, thousands of Jews and non-Aryans in Berlin were arrested at their work places in the so-called Fabrik-Aktion. Among the arrested were approximately two thousand Jewish men who lived in so-called "privileged mixed marriages." They were transported to the Rosenstrasse and processed for deportation. Immediately and miraculously, hundreds of wives, their children and family members began to gather outside the Rosenstrasse and demanded their release. There are no written documents that would tie Sommer to the organization

---

21. Antonia Leugers, "Widerstand oder pastorale Fürgsorge?" 161.

22. Leichsenring, *Die Katholische Kirche und ihre Juden*, 213.

23. Jana Leichsenring, "Wurde der Protest in der Rosenstrasse organisiert," 91–96.

24. Antonia Leugers, "Der Protest in der Rosenstraße 1943 und die Kirchen," 47–80.

of this protest, as there is written evidence for the involvement of Vicar Dorothea Stutkowski of the Büro Grüber.[25] But it is clear that Sommer had lost patience with quiet diplomacy and wanted to see action against the deportations of Jews to the East, of whose fate she had detailed information. It can no longer be reconstructed how and why hundreds of women showed up so quickly in the Rosenstrasse.[26] But the women succeeded with their week-long, non-violent street vigil and gained the release of all of the incarcerated men and the children who were swept up in the raid.[27] By August 1942, Sommer credited the "loud public protest of the population" for the release of the Jewish men and pleaded with the bishops to pressure the regime publicly rather than by polite pleas in private. But she was ultimately unsuccessful and the Catholic Church never publicly spoke out against the Holocaust.

When the war ended in May 1945, Sommer and Staritz reassigned their offices to provide assistance to survivors returning from the camps and those who emerged from hiding underground. Both joined the newly founded "Gesellschaft für christlich-jüdische Zusammenarbeit," the German branch of the International Conference of Christian and Jews (ICCJ) and became activists of Jewish–Christian dialogue until their deaths.[28]

While Staritz and Sommer were constrained by institutional politics and their superiors' caution and hostility, Elisabeth Schmitz operated from the grassroots and tried to lobby influential individuals in person and in writing. Her employment as a public school teacher allowed her to influence church politics as a theologically educated lay member. Her correspondence and memoranda show her as a prescient political analyst of the Nazi state's antisemitic plans as well as forceful theological voice against theological anti-Judaism. Her indictments of the persecution of the Jews belong to the most unambiguous statements

25. Leichsenring, *Die katholische Kirche und ihre Juden*, 251.

26. Nathan Stoltzfus, *Resistance of the Heart: Intermarriage and the Rosenstrasse Protest in Nazi Germany* (New York: Norton, 1996); Antonia Leugers, "Der Protest in der Rosenstraße 1943 und die Kirchen," in *Rosenstrasse 2-4: Protest in der NS-Diktatur—Neue Forschungen zum Frauenprotest in der Rosenstraße 1943*, ed. Antonia Leugers (Mooshausen: Plöger Medien, 2005), 47–80.

27. Cf. Jana Leichsenring, "Wurde der Protest in der Rosenstrasse Ende Eebruar/ Anfang März 1943 organisiert?" *Rosenstrasse 2-4: Protest in der NS-Diktatur*, 81–114.

28. Sommer died in 1965, Leichsenring, *Die Katholische Kirche und ihre Juden*, 285.

written by any Christian theologian in Nazi Germany. She denounced her male peers' failure to recognize and act against Nazi genocidal antisemitism as early as 1933. By April 1933, Elisabeth Schmitz contacted Karl Barth and suggested that the church issue an unambiguous condemnation of antisemitism. "The flood of ingratitude, injustice, hatred, lies, cruelty that has been breaking over our Jewish and Jewish-descended compatriots is evidence of the terrible sin and guilt of the Christian side, which should ignite mortal fear of the judgment of God in us. But the church celebrates victory ceremonies . . ."[29] In his response on May 2nd, Barth lamented his own vulnerability as a Swiss theologian in Germany and declined to speak out publicly against antisemitism. By 1935, she warned of an impending genocide and demanded unequivocal opposition. Her prophetic voice was fostered by her personal friendship with medical doctor Martha Kassel, who had converted to Protestantism in her youth, and introduced Schmitz to the vibrant intellectual and cultural Jewish life in Berlin. When Martha Kassel lost her license to practice medicine in 1933, she moved in with Schmitz into her apartment. In 1935, Schmitz penned a memorandum "On the situation of German Non-Aryans" which she distributed widely among delegates attending a synod meeting of the Confessing Church in Berlin-Steglitz. She listed the outrages of "two and a half years of grave persecution" and chronicled the effects of relentless antisemitic propaganda, economic boycotts, legal discrimination, the exclusion of Jewish children from schools, and the pressure to divorce intermarried couples. She asked: "Why does the church do nothing? Why does she allow this unspeakable injustice? How can she issue joyous declarations of loyalty to the National Socialist state, which are political statements that are directed against the lives of some of its own members?"[30] She was "gripped by cold fear" that Christian ministers preached that these events were a sign of God's judgment against Jews. "Since when does the perpetrator have the right to present his crime as the will of God? Since when is it anything other than blasphemy if the commission of injustice is proclaimed as the will of God?"[31] Her strong words and clear renunciation

29. Letter, Schmitz to Karl Barth, April 1933, Manfred Gailus, *Mir aber zerriß es das Herz: der stille Widerstand der Elisabeth Schmitz* (Göttingen: Vandenhoeck & Ruprecht, 2010), 84.

30. "Memorandum," in Manfred Gailus, ed., *Elisabeth Schmitz und ihre Denkschrift gegen die Judenverfolgung* (Berlin: Wichern, 2008), 210 (191–223).

31. Ibid., 211.

of Christian collusion in Nazi antisemitism remained unacknowledged. The memorandum was never put on the agenda and no action was taken at the synod.

Her friend Martha Kassel renounced her conversion to Christianity. But she accompanied Schmitz to Sunday services in Dahlem on November 16, 1938 in order to listen to Helmut Gollwitzer's sermon on the Sunday of Penance. Schmitz had earlier met with Gollwitzer and urged him to preach against the outrages committed during the 'Night of Broken Glass' [*Kristallnacht*] on November 8, 1938. Two days before the service, Schmitz warned Gollwitzer in a letter that unless ministers all over Germany spoke out from the pulpits "there will only be Jewish graves by the year 1940."[32] His sermon has since become famous for its uncompromising indictment of the fear and caution that prevented believers from acting in defense and solidarity with the "poor neighbor, who waits outside, suffering, without protection, dishonored, hungry, persecuted, and who is afraid for his very existence."[33] He appealed to deeply rooted Christian obligations toward the neighbor, but he did not explicitly mention Jews. Meanwhile, Schmitz' lobbying efforts behind the scenes remained unknown and unacknowledged until recently. She wrote a letter to Gollwitzer, dated November 24, 1938, in which she thanked him profusely for his words and told him that "your words have helped my friend—desperately trying to emigrate—to move beyond deep bitterness and despair over the attitude of the church."[34] Then she added: "has anyone thought of the idea to write to Dr. Baeck in the name of church, and to the Jewish community whose houses of worship have been burned down and dynamited into the air, and whose rabbis were forced to watch in many places? Where will these congregations hold services in this time of emergency?"[35] Schmitz asserted the fundamental equality of Jewish and Christian services and suggested that Christian congregations support not only their non-Aryan baptized church members, but indeed Jewish congregations. She also predicted that following "the annihilation of property" there could be only one more escalation,

32. Gailus, ed., *Mir aber zerriß es das Herz,* 117.

33. Helmut Gollwitzer, "Bußtagspredigt, gehalten am 16. November 1938," in *Freiburger Rundbrief,* 20.73/76 (1968) 25–26; http://www.freiburger-rundbrief.de/de/?area=Archiv vor 1986.

34. Letter, Schmitz to Gollwitzer, in Gailus, ed., *Elisabeth Schmitz,* 223.

35. Ibid., 224.

namely the killing of human beings. "And no one can doubt that these orders will be followed equally promptly, without second thoughts, stubbornly, maliciously and sadistically."[36] Schmitz bought her friend's house, which allowed Martha Kassel to secure ship passage and the costs for an entry visa to Argentina. She accompanied her friend to the harbor in Hamburg on December 10, 1938 and sat down to write her letter of resignation, submitted on December 31, 1938: "I cannot teach the disciplines of religion, history and German in the manner demanded and expected by the National Socialist state." She requested early retirement for medical reasons caused by "chronic conflicts of conscience."[37] Martha Kassel's house in the suburbs of Berlin became a hiding place for non-Aryans and Jews who survived underground for the duration of the war. Schmitz returned to teaching in 1948 in Hesse, where she worked against a culture of forgetfulness and oblivion. She lived an unobtrusive life as a school teacher and never revealed her authorship of the 1935 memorandum, which became famous as one of the precious few Protestant denunciations of antisemitism. Her authorship was only revealed when a suitcase containing her prodigious body of correspondence with Protestant church leaders was accidentally discovered in a church basement in 2004.

It was her relationship with her friend, the convert and reconvert Martha Kassel that introduced Schmitz into the borderlands between Christianity and Judaism. When this border region became dangerous and contested by escalating genocidal violence, Kassel and Schmitz became *Grenzgänger* and "go-betweens," who smuggled information and people across the religious border. They could blend and cross over between church and synagogue and served as vital translators between communities that were segregated by the force of state.

This ability and willingness to cross borders also characterized Dr. Gertrud Luckner's life. She was born in Great Britain and adopted by German parents. She was raised as a Quaker and converted to Roman Catholicism as an adult in 1934. With her PhD in social work, she was appointed Director of Caritas in Freiburg, the Roman Catholic social welfare agency. She travelled tirelessly and built an extensive network of informants and clandestine helpers in order to smuggle Jews out of the country into Switzerland. She crossed denominational and religious

36. Ibid., 225.
37. Gailus, *Mir aber zerriss es das Herz*, 126.

lines and worked with the Quakers, with Katharina Staritz of the *Büro Grüber*, Margarete Sommer's *Hilfstelle* in Berlin and the Representation of Jews in Germany (Reichsvertretung der Juden in Deutschland).[38] She gained the confidence of Dr. Leo Baeck, who entrusted her with the secret password to visit Jewish communities across Germany. On March 24, 1943, she was arrested on the train from Munich to Berlin, carrying 5000 Reichsmark that she had raised from Cardinal Michael Faulhaber and was supposed to deliver to Leo Baeck. The money was intended to help pay for visas and escape routes into emigration, which had become illegal at this point, as large-scale deportations to "the East" got underway. After weeks of interrogations, she was sent to the concentration camp of Ravensbrück because "her pro-Jewish activity and connections to subversive circles . . . give rise to fear, that on release from custody, she will continue to act to the detriment of the Reich."[39] She nearly died repeatedly during her two-year incarceration in Ravensbrück and was saved by Viennese communist inmates. After her liberation by Soviet troops, she returned to Freiburg and immediately convened a small group of Catholic intellectuals who were charged to discuss the question: "How can a discussion on the question of Christianity and Judaism be started within the church?"[40] She hired Kurt Thieme as theological consultant for the *Freiburger Rundbrief,* a circular publication she founded to facilitate Jewish–Christian dialogue. She was the only German participant who was invited to the Seelisberg conference of the ICCJ in Switzerland in 1947. By 1950, her Freiburg group was cited in a *monitum* by the Holy See and warned against alleged "syncretistic tendencies of Jewish–Christian dialogue" and "indifferentism," which might result from too much religious tolerance. Luckner, undeterred, remained actively involved in the drafting process of *Nostra Aetate* that was adopted at the Second Vatican Council and revolutionized Catholic theological doctrines on Judaism.[41] When she died in 1995, she was the

38. Hans-Jonas Wollasch, *Gertrud Luckner: Botschafterin der Menschlichkeit* (Freiburg: Herder, 2005), 26.

39. Protective Custody Order, Reich Security Main Office, quoted in Elias Füllenbach, "Shock, Renewal, Crisis: Catholic Reflections on the Shoah," in Kevin Spicer, ed., *Antisemitism, Ambivalence and the Holocaust* (Bloomington: Indiana University Press, 2007), 209 (201–34).

40. Füllenbach, "Shock, Renewal, Crisis," 210.

41. John Connelly, *From Enemy to Brother: The Revolution in Catholic Teaching on the Jews, 1933-1965* (Cambridge: Harvard University Press, 2012), 239–72; Thomas

only one of the four women to achieve public recognition for her rescue of Jews. Katharina Staritz, Margarete Sommer, and Elisabeth Schmitz died lonely and bitter deaths, painfully aware of their own failures and inadequacies, and largely unacknowledged by their churches and communities, which were intent to forget, deny, and falsify recent history.[42]

These women, all unmarried, were members of the first generation of female academics who worked tirelessly in institutions of the church. They advanced not only the struggle for equal rights of women but confronted the toxic ideology of nationalism, racism and antisemitism that reached deeply into the churches. For every one person they saved, there were hundreds of thousands who perished. They failed to persuade their leaders to renounce Christian anti-Judaism or to take a public stance against the state's genocidal antisemitism. But they built clandestine networks of trust that became seeds for dialogue in the post-Holocaust world. While historians have now amply documented the wholesale failure of the Protestant and Catholic churches to oppose the persecution and rescue Jewish individuals and communities from deportation and murder, their small voice should not be forgotten.[43]

Schnabel, "Gertrud Luckner—ein Leben für die christlich–jüdische Zusammenarbeit," in Andreas Morgenstern, ed., *Der christlich-jüdische Dialog: Laupheimer Gespräche* (Heidelberg: Universitätsverlag, 2010); Elizabeth Petuchowski, "Gertrud Luckner: Resistance and Assistance: A German Woman Who Defied Nazis and Aided Jews," in *Ministers of Compassion during the Nazi Period: Gertrud Luckner and Raoul Wallenberg* (South Orange, NJ: Institute of Judaeo-Christian Studies, Seton Hall University, 1999).

42. Sommer's experiences "preoccupied her mentally for the rest of her life, tormenting her and keeping her from peace of mind . . . The torment of the Jews became her torment until her death in 1965 at 72 years of age." Michael Phayer and Eva Fleischer, *Cries in the Night: Women Who Challenged the Holocaust* (Kansas City: Sheed & Ward, 1997), 41. When Elisabeth Schmitz was buried in 1977 seven people showed up for her funeral, surely a reflection of her isolation and lack of recognition. Manfred Gailus, "Elisabeth Schmitz was keine Filmschauspielerin," in Manfred Gailus, ed., *Elisabeth Schmitz*, 183–90, op. cit. 183. When Katharina Staritz died in 1955, "she was long forgotten. Only in the memory of her family (i.e., sister) and her friends was there any recollection of her witness to Christian love and willingness to protect her Jewish siblings . . ." Gerlind Schwöbel, *Ich aber vertraue*, 90.

43. See Victoria J. Barnett, *Bystanders: Conscience and Complicity during the Holocaust* (Westport, CT: Praeger, 1999); Christopher Probst, *Demonizing the Jews: Luther and the Protestant Church in Nazi Germany* (Bloomington: Indiana University Press, 2012); Robert P. Ericksen, *Complicity in the Holocaust: Churches and Universities in Nazi Germany* (Cambridge: Cambridge University Press, 2012); Doris L. Bergen, *The German Christian Movement in the Third Reich* (Chapel Hill: University of North Carolina Press, 1996); Manfred Gailus and Armin Nolzen, eds., *Zerstrittene*

Their willingness and ability to shuttle between different communities and to smuggle information, goods, and people across the borders laid the groundwork for more formal settings in which (male) representatives of the church and of the synagogue could meet and engage in Jewish–Christian dialogue.

Dialogue is more than a liberal exchange of knowledge because it entails a moral dimension and demands a political practice. In times of conflict, interreligious dialogue calls for practical assistance and political action on behalf of those who are threatened by defamation, oppression, and persecution. Dialogue exercises people's ability to cross boundaries, a skill that becomes critical at times when bridges are burnt and channels of communication are obstructed. In these times, mere neighborliness is not enough. The tolerance of neighbors, who live side by side for decades or centuries, is often built upon benign indifference. A 'live and let live' attitude makes for good neighbors, but it does not supply a foundation for resistance. Dialogue, on the other hand, is a commitment to the life and well-being of one's partner in dialogue. Dialogue imposes moral obligations that require intervention on behalf of those who are dehumanized.

All four women were either converts themselves (e.g., Luckner was raised Quaker and converted to Catholicism), lived with converts (Schmitz), worked with converts (Staritz) and/or intermarried couples (Sommer). Converts are religious hybrids who play a crucial role in times of war because they become expert guides and smugglers across the border that divides "us" from the "them." As historian John Connelly has shown, Catholic converts from Judaism became leading advocates for a "revolution" in church teaching on the Jews in the post-war world.[44]

"Volksgemeinschaft": Glaube, Konfession und Religion im Nationalsozialismus (Göttingen: Vandenhoeck & Ruprecht, 2011); Björn Mensing, *Pfarrer und Nationalsozialismus: Geschichte einer Verstrickung am Beispiel der Evangelisch-Lutherischen Kirche in Bayern* (Göttingen: Vandenhoeck & Ruprecht, 1998). For the Roman Catholic Church, see: Michael Phayer, *The Catholic Church and the Holocaust: 1930–1965* (Bloomington: Indiana University Press, 2000); Kevin Spicer, CSC, *Hitler's Priests: Catholic Clergy and National Socialism* (Dekalb: Northern Illinois University Press, 2008); Spicer, *Resisting the Third Reich: The Catholic Clergy in Hitler's Berlin* (Dekalb: Northern Illinois University Press, 2004); Spicer, ed., *Antisemitism, Christian Ambivalence, and the Holocaust* (Bloomington: Indiana University Press, 2007); Wolfgang Gerlach, *And the Witnesses Were Silent: The Confessing Church and the Persecution of Jews*, trans. Victoria J. Barnett (Lincoln: University of Nebraska Press, 2000).

44. John Connelly, *From Enemy to Brother: The Revolution in Catholic Teaching on the Jews, 1933–1965* (Cambridge: Harvard University Press, 2012), 287–300.

Yet, ironically, people with complex religious identities, the converts, the intermarried and their interfaith children are often considered less than ideal dialogue partners because they do not live fully acculturated lives within one religious community. They are sometimes excluded by theorists of interreligious dialogue and disqualified from representing their religious communities authoritatively.[45] But the prehistory of dialogue establishes a place of honor for residents of the borderlands at the table because of their expert knowledge that helps to navigate the treacherous fault lines between communities.

We should also critically examine the social location of interreligious dialogue in light of this history. After all, it was not the theologians and religious leaders who reached out in dialogue but the people in charge of social welfare and church relief organizations. It was their direct and practical involvement in the lives of victims of antisemitism that allowed these exceptional women to deconstruct and denounce the demonization of Jews—not their theological studies or theoretical analysis. Hence, interreligious dialogue should be understood primarily as a practice of solidarity. The women's professional appointments in the social service sector of the churches gave them more theological freedom and greater flexibility. They were less invested in maintaining theological consistency and upholding institutional standards, which allowed them to collaborate across boundaries and to break legal and religious conventions. But their lack of theological legitimacy and ecclesial power also undermined their ability to shape public policy and political position of their churches.

In conclusion, we need interreligious dialogues at the highest level of religious authority, where theologies are discussed and doctrines are articulated in light of religious pluralism. But we also need dialogue at the grassroots, where activists resist the defamation and ostracism of religious minorities. Women—despite decades of feminist agitation—continue to be better represented at the grassroots than at the religious leadership level. As feminists involved in interreligious dialogue, we need to remember the nameless and faceless women around the globe who have risked their lives in pursuit of the principles of interreligious dialogue in times of war.

---

45. Karla Suomala, "Complex Religious Identity in the Context of Interfaith Dialogue," *Crosscurrents* 62 (2012) 360–71.

5

Abraham and His Family at the Interfaith Border Edge

Asking the Overlooked Question of Gender

Nancy Fuchs Kreimer

In 2012, The Co-exist Foundation gave a major award to William Ury, the founder of the "Path of Abraham Initiative." The Path of Abraham describes itself as "a venture in cultural tourism." The project's website explains: "Ultimately traversing ten countries, Abraham's Path links many of the most fabled and sacred places on earth. In the very places many of us fear to visit lies . . . a spirit that unites human hearts. As we discover when we walk in his footsteps, Abraham is still very much alive in the hearts of people who live along the Path."[1] When I heard about this effort, I wondered, as I often do when Abraham is invoked as a symbol of interfaith unity, what, in fact, is alive in the hearts of all those people about Abraham. How, precisely, can his spirit unite them? And where are the women?

I have long been fascinated by the stories and practices of the interfaith world. When we come together across faith lines, what stories do we tell from our traditions, in what versions and to what ends? What practices emerge? I have become increasingly curious about the prominence of the symbol of Abraham in projects designed to bring Muslims,

1. Http://www.abrahampath.org/about.php.

Jews and Christians together.[2] The Hebrew Bible does say that Abraham was blessed by God and told that "all peoples on earth will be blessed through you" (Genesis 12:3). But the stories of Abraham and his family, as interpreted within the three traditions that treasure them, represent, as Phyllis Trible put it, "ominous beginnings for a promise of blessing."[3]

When well-meaning Jews, Christians and Muslims gather to celebrate our "Abrahamic" connection it is not accidental that it is the father, and not his family, that we reference. While our common father allegedly unites us as siblings, our not-in-common mothers present a more challenging story. When we raise the question of gender, things get messy very quickly. Hagar and Sarah are "set up" in the story as rivals; embracing one of them can prove to be at the expense of the other. If we imaginatively unite the women as allies, Abraham becomes even more problematic, as the roots of sexism and violence are embedded in his story in troubling ways. Contemporary efforts to repair the stories sometimes only highlight the difficulty. Finally, even if Abraham were an uncomplicated symbol of unity between Jews, Christians and Muslims, we would still be leaving the rest of humanity outside the family circle. When seeking an integrative symbol for interfaith engagement, one must ask if perhaps the entire Abraham cycle should be declared irreparably broken.

Despite the concerns outlined above and detailed below, it seems to me that "Abraham" is arguably a serviceable, if ingenuous, symbol for efforts to write Muslims into the American civic narrative, replacing the "Judeo-Christian" tradition—itself a strategic construct—with the "Judeo–Christian–Islamic" tradition. Moreover, we have much to learn from the stories, especially if we are prepared to confront their most disturbing implications. When creating religious practices, the stories of Abraham and his family require radical reconfiguration to be appropriate to the globalized society in which we live. In fact, such

---

2. See, for examples, organizations such as Daughters of Abraham, Abraham's Vision, Children of Abraham, Abrahamic Family Reunion, Abraham's Vision, Abrahamic Partnerships, She Answers Abraham. Books include: Benjamin Hubbard et al., eds., *The Abraham Connection: A Jew, Christian and Muslim in Dialogue* (Notre Dame, IN: Cross Cultural, 1994); Karl-Josef Kuschel, *Abraham: Sign of Hope for Jews, Christians and Muslims* (New York: Continuum, 1995); and Bruce Feiler's *Abraham: A Journey to the Heart of Three Faiths* (New York: Morrow, 2002).

3. Phyllis Trible, "Ominous Beginnings for a Promise of Blessing," in Phyllis Trible and Letty Russell, eds., *Hagar, Sarah and Their Children: Jewish, Christian and Muslim Perspectives* (Louisville: Westminster John Knox, 2006), 33.

reconfiguration is possible and, I will suggest, holds powerful promise, as I have seen in recent efforts to create new "Abrahamic" practices within Jewish tradition. In my concluding section, I will discuss an emerging integrative religious practice—the Interfaith Peace Walk—to show how memories of Abraham may yet be spiritually life-giving in our time.

I hope that this exploration will be of value not only to participants in the Abrahamic conversation, but also to others who care about how stories and practices respond to the challenges of religious diversity and of gender awareness. These challenges confront us both in particular religious traditions and in the growing number of sites where Americans are engaging one another at the edges of their faith borders.

Abraham and his Family in Judaism, Christianity, and Islam: Source of Unity, Source of Division

As Hebrew Bible scholar Jon Levenson recently argued in a book devoted to the thesis, Jews, Christians and Muslims do not see Abraham in the same way.[4] In fact, we know multiple Abrahams, Sarahs and Hagars. A neutral Abraham does not exist. Levenson states it this way: "The question of who Abraham's heirs are and how they inherit his legacy is internal to each of these three related yet distinct traditions."[5] Indeed, a very brief look at our respective foundational texts reveals that Abraham and his family offer a complex picture of how Jews, Christians and Muslims might understand their connection.

In Genesis, the call to create a new people comes to just one man, Abram, later renamed Abraham. But what begins as one family starts to fragment as early as the first generation. When Abraham's wife Sarah is unable to conceive a child, the two agree to use Sarah's maidservant, Hagar, to provide Abraham with an heir. Hagar complies, willingly or not, and gives birth to Ishmael (Genesis 16). Once Sarah belatedly has her own son, she initiates a plan, approved by Abraham, to exile Hagar and her child, sending them into the desert without enough water to live. They survive and, according to the Torah, Ishmael also becomes the father of a people. After this story concludes in Genesis 21, Hagar

4. Jon D. Levenson, *Inheriting Abraham: The Legacy of the Patriarch in Judaism, Christianity, and Islam*, Library of Jewish Ideas (Princeton: Princeton University Press. 2012).

5. Ibid., 214.

disappears entirely from the Hebrew Bible and Sarah all but disappears. In the main, Jewish tradition judges Sarah and Abraham kindly. It understands the family drama as part of God's plan.

The early Christian community explicitly saw itself as part of the family of Abraham. The first book of the New Testament begins with the claim that Jesus was descended from Abraham (Matthew 1:1) and goes on to elaborate the genealogy for 16 additional verses. Luke even knows a story about Abraham that does not appear in the Hebrew Bible (Luke 16:19–31). Although neither Sarah nor Hagar are mentioned in the Gospels, the two women do make an appearance in Paul's writings, Hagar by name and Sarah as "the other woman." Paul uses the story of the rival women as an allegory to address an issue of his own time (Galatians 4:21–31). He suggests that Christians ought to see themselves as the children of promise, the children of Sarah. The Judaizers or Jewish Christians, still part of the nascent Christian church at the time, are enslaving themselves to the law. They are the "children of Hagar" and should be driven out of the community.

While this was an intra-Christian dispute, once the Pauline option triumphed, Christians understood that allegory differently. It came to symbolize Christians and Jews, two distinct communities with different roles in God's vision. Although Jews see themselves as children of Sarah, the Christian church coded them as the children of Hagar. By continuing the divisions of the original story, imagining themselves as the children of blessing, the Christian understanding of the story developed on a parallel but contradictory track to the Jewish one. As in the Jewish tradition, the two women in the story represent the beginnings of division. The traditions are similar in that both see the children of Sarah as the elect, but they differ in who they understand to be elected.

In Islam, the importance of Abraham can hardly be overstated. For the Qur'an, Abraham is second only to Mohammad. The text mentions Abraham over 200 times, including the longest single narrative about him which recounts the near sacrifice of his son (37:100–113). Islam is deemed the true religion of Abraham who was, according to the normative understanding, the first Muslim. In the Muslim retelling of the story of Abraham, Sarah and Hagar, aspects of both chapter 16 and chapter 21 of Genesis appear. Although Hagar is not mentioned by name in the scripture, later versions of the story give her a prominent role as the mother of monotheism, alongside Abraham. Riffat Hassan explains the power of the practices that have developed from Hagar's story, particularly her role in "the most significant as well as the most spectacular social ritual of the Muslim world: the hajj, or pilgrimage."[6]

The Qur'an wrote the Muslim community into the story of Abraham in a different way than the New Testament wrote in the Christians. Mohammad understood himself and all Arabs to be blood descendents of Ishmael, a rare point of agreement between Jews, Christians, and Muslims. In the Muslim understanding, however, no one needs to be banished forever. The Muslim narrative is not concerned with making one of the mothers good and the other bad. In a repair of the Torah's story, Abraham returns and builds the Kaba with Ishmael. In the traditional Islamic view, Abraham provides a bond that ties these three traditions together in a way that makes them more like one another than they are like any other religious group. Neither Judaism nor Christianity, in their classic formulations, shares this view.

For Jon Levenson, the problem with calling all three faiths "Abrahamic" is two-fold. First, it is simply not the case that there is a single figure, Abraham, to whom we all refer. Although Islam comes closest, none of our traditions teaches that we are co-equal "children of Abraham." Second, from within Jewish tradition, Levenson does not want the claim of "elective monotheism"—referred to in Judaism as chosenness—to be blurred in a haze of admirably motivated humanistic efforts to connect. It is precisely that blurring, however, that is the goal of some contemporary appropriations of Abraham. Just as Abraham varies across traditions, he also varies across eras, and, as we will see, the elective monotheism that is a core value for Levenson is, for some contemporary interpreters, part of the Abrahamic story they actively want to revise.

Sexism and Violence

Although barely mentioned by Levenson in his book length treatment of the patriarch, Abraham is also a questionable symbol because his family saga is so deeply sexist. Aysha Hidayatullah and Judith Plaskow suggest we move "beyond Sarah and Hagar," women "whose lives are arguably intertwined less through a notion of sisterhood than . . . jealousy, rivalry,

6. Rifat Hassan, "Islamic Hagar and Her Family," in Trible and Russell, eds., *Hagar, Sarah and Their Children*, 156.

blame, victimhood and violent exclusion."[7] Pim Valkenberg writes, "The stories about Abraham and his children . . . seem to imply that one's dedication to God may be at the expense of one's human relations."[8] Valkenberg minces no words in stating what he finds so disturbing in Abraham's story. In addition to the submission to God's command to kill his son, he also points to the "sexual violence exerted by Abraham on his wives."[9]

Carol Delaney has shown how the roots of patriarchy are imbedded in Abraham's role as a husband and father. Delaney puts the biblical story of Abraham on trial and finds it guilty. For her, a father who is willing to kill his son is not the story we need or want today. She asks, "Why is the willingness to sacrifice [a] child at the foundation of faith?"[10] As an anthropologist, Delaney is aware that the biblical myths are not the only ones by which human beings have shaped their lives. She challenges us to imagine "a new moral vision, a new myth to live by, one that will change the course of history as profoundly as the Abraham story."[11]

Regina Schwartz suggests another path. She views the Abraham story as one of the many places where the Torah promotes violence by envisioning a world of scarcity. She asks, along with Esau, "Have you but one blessing?" The Bible enshrines a system in which "identity is conferred at the cost of the (br)other."[12] She concludes by recalling that the Bible also includes a vision, albeit in a softer voice, of "plenitude and its corollary ethical imperative of generosity."[13] And she suggests that we take that approach to life and also to our reading of the Bible.

---

7. Aaron Hahn-Tapper and Reza Aslan, *Muslims and Jews in America: Commonalities, Contentions and Complexities* (New York: Palgrave Macmillan, 2011), 163.

8. Pim Valkenberg, "Abraham: Conflicting Interpretations and Symbol of Peaceful Cooperation," Laato and Lindqvist, eds., *Encounters of the Children of Abraham from Ancient to Modern Times*, Studies on the Children of Abraham 1 (Leiden: Brill, 2010), 319 (313–26).

9. Ibid.

10. Carol Delaney, *Abraham on Trial: The Social Legacy of Biblical Myth* (Princeton University, 1998), 251. See also Bruce Chilton, *Abraham's Curse: The Roots of Violence in Judaism, Christianity and Islam* (New York: Doubleday, 2008).

11. Ibid., 251.

12. Regina M. Schwartz, *The Curse of Cain: The Violent Legacy of Monotheism* (Chicago: University of Chicago Press, 1997), 80.

13. Ibid., 176.

"Memories need not be in short supply." [14] Schwartz's admonishment will be important later as we explore the creation of "Abrahamic" ritual.

Contemporary Efforts to "Repair" the Story

The traditional Jewish practice of reading Genesis 21 on the first day of Rosh HaShana has the strange effect of placing women, often absent from the Jewish story, in the lead roles. [15] Even stranger, the story focuses on the Egyptian woman rather than the Israelite. Most amazingly, for a community that is now embroiled in conflict with Arabs, understood to be the children of Hagar, we read aloud how once our ancestors banished Hagar and her son, how they tried—evidently without success—to send them out of our story. We begin the New Year by reviewing how interreligious division began in the very first generation of God's call. While much of the tradition (although not all), sees this as part of God's plan, some contemporary Jews are troubled by this story and, depending upon what seems most troubling, attempt to repair it.

Troubled by the interfaith implications of the story as well as by the near sacrifice of Isaac, read on the second day of the Jewish New Year, Rabbi Arthur Waskow created a new practice for the synagogue, an additional Torah reading for the High Holidays. Since we read Genesis 21 and 22 on the two days of Rosh HaShana, he suggests that on the afternoon of Yom Kippur, as the high holidays draw to a close, we read Genesis 24:7–18, the "reconciliation" of Isaac and Ishmael at Abraham's burial. That passage refers to them together for the first time as "his sons." Waskow writes, "Whether this be taken as a vision of reconciliation at the level of our families and friends or at the level of Israelis and Palestinians, Jews and Muslims, I think it bears great value as a healing . . . from the previous traumatic texts." [16]

Rabbi Dalia Marx, a professor at Hebrew Union College in Jerusalem, also sees a dimension of repair within the biblical text itself. "Two boys, both sons of Abraham, sons to mothers who were at odds with

14. Ibid.

15. This was not the intention. Rosh Hashana is a two day holiday and the second day's reading is Genesis 22, the Binding of Isaac. The first day's reading, Genesis 21, serves as prelude. Since Reform Jews usually observe only one day of the holiday, Genesis 21 is usually dropped for the holiday, replaced by Genesis 22 or by Genesis 1.

16. Http://theshalomcenter.org/node/249. The synagogue I attend follows this custom.

each other, sons, each of whom had stood on the edge of violent death, join together to make the effort to bring their father to a proper burial ... Perhaps because of this, the Torah mentions that Abraham died well-satisfied and at a good old age. Isaac and Ishmael knew how to get over the past, over the hatred that lasted a generation, and cooperate in the care of their beloved father."[17]

Ironically, for it is far from Rabbi Waskow's or Rabbi Marx's intention, this repair requires the women to be, once again, "missing in action." By the time of this alleged reconciliation, Sarah is dead, Hagar is elsewhere. There has been no healing for them. If the problem of this text is ethnic and religious diversity, the burial scene provides some solace. But if the problem is the gender implications of the text, it is far from satisfying. As Valkenberg put it, "Women are victims of violence in these stories: this violence is repeated when men keep talking about the God of Abraham, Isaac, and Ishmael without mentioning the God of Sarah and Hagar."[18]

I recently asked a Christian who is a leader in "Abrahamic" peace work how he felt about using the symbol of Abraham in his work. He replied that the symbol was powerful. After all, he said, Abraham's two sons came to bury him in the end. What better image of reconciliation could one want? I pointed out that the two boys do not appear to have had a conflict to begin with. It is the women who struggled, and their conflict never does get resolved. He waved that detail off as unimportant.

Yehezkel Landau attempts to address this problem in his own version of a repair of the story. A long time Israeli American peace activist, Landau considers it important that the telling of the Abraham story involve more than just the boys getting together for a funeral. He does not want to leave Hagar out in the wilderness, and happily reports that he can find a repair in an early version of the tradition itself. Landau appreciates that the great medieval Bible commentator Rashi records a midrash (*Genesis Rabbah* 61:4) in which Keturah, the woman Abraham marries after Sarah's death (Genesis 25:1–2), turns out to be none other than Hagar.[19] Rashi comments on the verse "Isaac had just come back

---

17. Dalia Marx and Ursula Rudnick, "The Shared Testament: Sara and Hagar A Jewish–Christian and a Christian–Jewish Reading," 02/01/2012, http://www.jc relations.net/The_Shared_Testament__Sara_and_Hagar.3679.0.html.

18. Valkenberg, "Abraham," 319.

19. Http://www.jewishchronicle.org/article.php?article_id=13419.

from the vicinity of Beer-lahai-roi" (Genesis 24:61) to explain that Isaac had gone to that spot after Sarah died in order to bring Hagar to Abraham to wed. The place name Lahai-roi provides the textual hook, as Lahai-roi, according to the Torah, is the spot to which Hagar wandered after being cast out.

Through a feminist lens, however, this midrash is less than helpful. In fact, it actually compounds the problem. Hagar was Sarah's servant, turned over to Abraham to serve sexually. We have no reason to believe she ever wanted to be Abraham's wife in the first place. The fact that the son of her mistress has located her and once again turned her over to Abraham, does not, from a 21st century perspective, make for anything like a redemptive ending.

This repair also flies directly in the face of the many Christian interpretations, particularly by women of color, who see Hagar as a proud and defiant single mother. Having to once again share Abraham's bed, whether as concubine or as wife, hardly seems like a good solution, for her or those who cherish her model of strong womanhood.

The powerful role Hagar comes to play for some Christians throws in sharp relief the difficulty we face in repairing this story. Feminists like Phyllis Trible see Hagar as an important symbol, a three-fold victim of oppression by gender, class, and race. Trible writes of Hagar:

> She is the first person in the Bible to flee oppression; the first runaway slave; the first person whom a messenger of God visits; the first woman to receive an annunciation; the only woman to receive a divine promise of descendants; the only person to name God; the first woman in the ancestor stories to bear a child; the first surrogate mother; the first slave to be freed; the first divorced wife; the first single parent; and the first person to weep. Given all these distinctions, Hagar haunts the biblical narrative and its afterlife in ways that the other characters do not.[20]

This is particularly true for the womanist tradition. As Diana Hayes explains, "Hagar has 'spoken' to generation after generation of black women because her story has been validated as true by suffering black people. She and Ishmael together, as family, model many black American families . . . Hagar, like many black women, goes into the wide world to make a living for herself and her child, with only God by her side."[21]

20. Trible & Russell, 61.

21. Diana Hayes, *Hagar's Daughters: Womanist Ways of Being in the World*

Trible and others see in Hagar's suffering a possible connection to the suffering of Jesus on the cross. For some Jewish readers, this way of embracing the story feels potentially problematic. As Amy-Jill Levine puts it, if Hagar is a suffering servant, what does that make Sarah? [22]

Contemporary renderings of this story—Jewish, Christian, and Muslim—try to escape the sorry implications of the setup. If Hagar is a heroine, than Sarah is a villain. John of Damascus, in the early days of Islam, referred to it as the "religion/superstition of the Ishmaelites." He mentioned that they are also called Hagarenes and Saracens. He offers the following derivation for the latter term, "made destitute by Sara."[23] Whether or not the etymology is correct, our Jewish matriarch has a less than glorious reputation. The story appears to need more radical remaking.

Imaging Alternatives

With the exception of the Book of Ruth, the Hebrew Bible rarely depicts women as collaborators or even friends. [24] While it is in the interest of men to imagine women as divided one from the other, it is in the interest of women to refuse to be split. One way to do that is through fantasy, rewriting the story to enshrine one's own values. What if, as Rabbi Phyllis Berman, suggests, women have secretly handed down a different version of Abraham's household to their daughters, one that the men have suppressed? In Berman's version, Sarai and Hagar met in Pharaoh's harem where they became such good friends that Sarai insisted on bringing Hagar with her when she left Egypt. Sarai, Hagar and Avram were a happy family of three, with Hagar and Avram coming to love one another as well, and the three caring for Yishmael together. The trouble started when Sarai, now named Sarah and a mother herself, had a dream in which she learned that God had told her husband to take his first-born son to a nearby mountain. Clearly, Yishmael was in danger. It

(Mahwah, NJ: Paulist, 1995), 58.

22. Amy-Jill Levine, "Settling at Beer-lachai-Roi," in Yvonne Yazbeck Haddad and John L. Esposito, eds., *Daughters of Abraham: Feminist Thought in Judaism, Christianity and Islam* (Gainesville: University Press of Florida, 2001), 12–34.

23. J. M. Gaudeul, *Encounters and Clashes: Islam and Christianity in History* (Rome: PISAI 1984), 1:29.

24. Lori Hope Lefkovitz, *In Scripture: The First Stories of Jewish Sexual Identities* (Lanham, MD: Rowman & Littlefield, 2010), 153.

was then that Sarah and Hagar hatched a plan to keep Yishmael out of his father's reach.[25] Like many contemporary feminist writers, Berman makes the women allies. We no longer have to blame either Sarah or Hagar, but the story now leaves us with doubts about Abraham and, indeed, about the God he obeys.

Two poets, Rabbi Lynn Gottlieb and Muslim scholar Mohja Kahf, both choose to project Sarah and Hagar into a not yet realized future. In her 1987 song, "Sarah and Hagar." Linda Hirschhorn adapts Gottlieb's poem.

> I am calling you, oh Sarah;
> This is your sister, Hagar,
> calling through the centuries
> to reach you from afar . . .

Sarah responds,

> It was I who cast you out, in fear and jealousy;
> Yet your vision survived the wilderness
> to reach your destiny.
> But it wasn't till my Isaac lay under the knife
> that I recognized your peril,
> the danger to your life.

In the end, they know that their only real future is together.

> We will not survive as strangers;
> We must speak each other's name.
> We must tell each others' stories,
> make each other strong,
> and sing the dream of ancient lands
> where both of us belong.[26]

Mohja Kahf shares the Jewish poet's reluctance to see Hagar and Sarah as models of sisterhood, at least not in this dimension, at least not yet.

25. Rabbi Yehuda Shaviv, from the faculty of Bar Ilan University, wants us to consider the possibility that Abraham had three wives: Sarah, Hagar and Ketura. He finds this an appealing idea. The three can represent Abraham's connection with the "three families of the earth." He notes that it was through the three sons of Noah—Shem, Ham, and Japheth—that humanity was re-established after the flood. Rabbi Shaviv brings a traditional midrash, *Yalkut Shimoni* for Job (903) to show the connection of each of these women to one of the sons.

26. The poem by Lynn Gottlieb can be found at http://www.broadsidemagazine .com/Broadside pdf/159.pdf. This poem was originally published in *Menorah* in January-February 1983.

But, like Gottlieb and Hirshhorn, Kahf uses poetry to imagine a different future, approaching us from a dimension where it is "all good." Kahf goes further, by daring to imagine that reconciled future.

> Out in the blue infinitude
> that reaches and touches us
> sometimes, Hagar and Sarah
> and Abraham work together
> to dismantle the house of fear, brick
> by back-breaking brick.
> Ismaïl and Isaac come around shyly,
> new and unlikely companions.
> knowing there will be no more rams,
> no more blood sacrifice.
> a Hamas sniper, a Mosad assassin fall
> to their knees, rocking; each one cries,
> "I was only defending my—my—"
> Into the arms of each,
> Hajar and Sarah place a wailing
> orphaned infant. Slow moaning
> fills the air: Atone, atone.
> Everyone, this time
> around, can recognize
> in the eyes of every other,
> the flickering light of the Divine . . .[27]

For her poetic rewrite of Torah, Eleanor Wilner prefers to go back into the story and imagine a different turn of events. In doing so, she makes a statement not only about the issue of gender, but also about the vision of exclusivist faith. She begins the poem with a section entitled, "the testing of Sarah." In the opening, Sarah is approached by God with the very same words the Torah reports were said to Abraham, "Take your son . . . etc." But unlike Abraham, Sarah does not comply.

> "No," said Sarah to the Voice.
> "I will not be chosen. Nor shall my son—"

She then tries to convince Isaac to join her in leaving Abraham and the Voice behind. Her plan is to go out and find her rival Hagar and her son Ishmael, whom she now regrets having cast out. Isaac is not so sure he wants to follow.

---

27. Unpublished manuscript, courtesy of the author.

> If we were not God's chosen people, what then should we be?
> I am afraid of being nothing.

Sarah's only answer is to laugh. And she insists that he decide if he is coming with her or not.

> You can be chosen or you can choose.

The poem ends without a decision on Isaac's part, although Sarah's last words hint at what we already know Isaac will do.

> "But what will happen if we go?"
> Isaac asked.
> I don't know, Sarah said,
> "But it is written what will happen if you stay."

At the same time as she is adding Sarah's voice, the poet is rejecting the exclusivist vision of the text, the Jewish idea of election, the very claim Levenson is reluctant to see lost in our rush to interfaith amity. For Wilner, this is part of the goal.

A Sobering Story

In the end, perhaps it is the unvarnished story of Abraham's family that can impart the most important lessons. Pim Valkenberg suggests that in an interfaith encounter, we can use the Abrahamic stories to stimulate reflection on the shadow side of our traditions.[28] In a Jewish context, Tamara Cohen proposes letting the story retain its original harshness, and seeing what we can learn. In her essay "Returning to Sarah,"[29] Cohen points out that the account of Sarah and Hagar is the first time the Torah depicts a relationship between two women. When we meet Sarah, we know little about her, only that she is Abraham's wife, that she has no children and that she has a maidservant named Hagar. These women are not allies. Nor is it a story with a positive model for repentance. Sarah does the wrong thing to Hagar, not once, but twice. While many traditional commentators tried to apologize for our matriarch, Nachmanides, for one, saw Sarah as a sinner and the Israelites' slavery in Egypt as punishment for Sarah's treatment of Hagar. When Cohen wrote

---

28. Valkenberg, "Abraham," 321.

29. Gail Twersky Reimer and Judith A. Kates, eds., *Beginning Anew: A Woman's Companion to the High Holy Days* (New York: Simon & Schuster, 1997).

a feminist Haggadah, she brought the story of Sarah and Hagar into the ritual of Peach by observing the use of the word "oppressed" in two places in Torah.

> Sarah our mother oppressed her Egyptian maidservant Hagar.
>
> "V'ta'aneiha Sarai v'tivrach mipaneyha" (Genesis 16:6)
>
> Sarah oppressed her and Hagar ran away
>
> Go forth and learn: Pharaoh the Egyptian oppressed our people when they dwelled in Egypt.
>
> "Vayarei'u otanu mamitzvrim va'y'anunu va'yitnu aleinu avoda kasha." (Deuteronomy 26:6)
>
> And the Egyptians treated us harshly and oppressed us; they imposed hard labor on us.
>
> This you should never forget: the same word used for Hagar's oppression at the hands of Sarah is used for the Israelites' oppression at the hands of the Egyptians.[30]

Cohen suggests that this story of women at odds with one another in the context of a system of oppressive racial, class and gender structures has something to teach us, just as it is. She asks women to consider their own rivalry with other women, to move from judging Sarah to recognizing the ways in which we can easily become like her. As an oppressed woman, Sarah also ends up oppressing her maidservant. While this reflection may begin with the conflict between Sarah and Hagar, it ends with a larger, more profound observation. Jews, understanding themselves as history's victims, may also become oppressors themselves. The Ma'yan Haggadah teaches, "Go forth and learn. All who have been oppressed can also oppress."

Abraham and His Family in Religious Practice

Given the difficulties with the Abraham narratives, how do we move from sacred stories to religious practices, from myth to ritual? In the early days of the feminist transformation of Judaism, we faced just such a challenge, one with immediate practical implications. While Abraham in the Torah does not appear to know of most of Jewish ritual law, for

---

30. *The Mayan Haggadah*, unpublished.

example, Sabbath and dietary laws, it is Abraham who is first commanded to circumcise his son (Genesis 17:10). Ever since, the time-honored
tale goes, Jewish fathers have brought their sons into the covenant
through *brit milah,* the ancient, exclusively male and still widely practiced ritual of circumcision. As awareness of gender issues grew, the
alternatives created for baby girls—a naming in the synagogue, a party
with no embodied rite, the giving of symbolic gifts—began to feel increasingly inadequate.

In 1981, a group of women rabbinical students and a few newly
graduated rabbis met at Princeton as part of a short lived Women's'
Rabbinical Alliance. A sub-group of seven women, of whom I was one,
decided to work on that very practical problem: how to initiate female
babies into the covenant of Abraham.[31] It seemed to us that the very
plurality of options for girls made whatever happened feel less significant than the *brit milah.*

Could we come up with something that felt authentic enough for
people to forget that a group of young women made it up on a snowy
day in New Jersey? After much discussion of all possible body parts and
acts, we decided upon a ritual of foot washing. We saw it as a gentle
gesture of hospitality, welcoming the new child into the covenant, much
like—as we recalled—Abraham and Sarah washed the feet of the three
visitors/angels.[32] While we saw no way to adapt the act of circumcision
to a girl, we were unwilling to give up a connection to Abraham and
his story. To our surprise, our reconfiguration actually took root. Even
today I meet people who have attended some version of a *brit rechitzah*
(covenant of washing), and believe it to be, if not ancient, at least more
than one generation old. We had begun by asking only the question of
gender, but as is the case in reconfigurations, more things changed than
we anticipated. In substituting a different part of Abraham's story, new
meanings, different from those of the circumcision of the flesh, arose,
new understandings of who the child is in relationship to the family.
While the covenant of circumcision emphasizes the biological connec-

31. See http://www.myjewishlearning.com/life/Life_Events/Newborn_Ceremo-
nies/Liturgy_Ritual_and_Customs/For_Girls/Planning/new_rituals_for_daughters
.shtml.

32. In fact, Genesis 18:4 reports that Abraham ordered water to be brought so the
visitors could wash their own feet. Rabbi Ruth Sohn, also part of the group, gives her
version of the creation of the ritual in Tamara Cohn Eskenaski and Andrea L. Weiss,
eds., *The Torah: A Woman's Commentary* (New York: URJ Press, 2008), 81.

tion of the child as the "seed of Abraham," this ritual opens the possibility of seeing the child as in some sense a stranger, perhaps having come on a long journey—literally or metaphorically—one who comes with a message from God.[33]

While not banished from the scene, Abraham continues to be present, but his story is transformed into sacred practice in a different way.

Integrative Symbols and Practices in Border-Edge Spaces

In *Interfaith Encounters in America*, Kate McCarthy describes how Americans are encountering one another across faith lines in a growing variety of settings. Intellectual exchanges among scholars, like the one for which I prepared this paper, are just one of many venues. McCarthy discusses professional interfaith coalitions to solve civic problems, activists training the resources of their faiths on local and global problems, grassroots groups focused on relationship building, the Internet and, most recently, our own increasingly diverse families.[34]

The places where we engage inter-religiously can themselves become sites of religious or quasi religious significance. For some of us, they are places we find community, wonder and meaning.[35] As Americans increasingly encounter one another across religious difference in explicit ways, these edge spaces are generating their own spiritual meanings, their own stories and practices. Sometimes these emerge without particular consciousness of the fit between the goals of an encounter and the proposed practices. To the extent that these issues are consciously addressed, the focus has been on the question at hand—navigating religious difference in a newly created border environment. In this way, the question of gender is often overlooked.[36]

Grace Yukich, a sociologist drawing on the work of Richard Sennett, studied what can happen when individuals of different faiths gather in what he calls a border-edge environment. She distinguishes

33. I owe this insight to private correspondence with Rabbi Daniel Swartz, reporting his use of this ritual for his daughter, adopted from India.

34. Kate McCarthy, *Interfaith Encounters in America* (New Brunswick, NJ: Rutgers 2007).

35. Jeannine Hill Fletcher, *Motherhood as Metaphor: Engendering Interreligious Dialogue*, Bordering Religions (New York: Fordham University Press, 2013).

36. Virginia Spatz, "Toward a Gender Aware Approach to Interreligious Dialogue," *Journal of Interreligious Dialogue* 9 (May 2012).

between *aggregative* and *integrative* symbols and practices. Aggregative symbols and practices largely maintain the individual distinctiveness of each religious tradition. They layer various elements from different traditions, while encouraging the recognition of commonalities across traditions. For example, Alon Goshen-Gottstein, an Orthodox Jewish Israeli, has suggested that we should abandon the idea of Abraham, a failed integrative symbol. Rather, Goshen-Gottstein recommends that we replace "Abrahamic," with what Yukich would call an aggregative symbol: Moses, Jesus, and Mohammed.[37]

Integrative symbols and practices do not belong to any particular tradition but rather to all those gathered at the border-edge. Here, one must be alert to the tendency of the majority tradition to simply promote its own practices as if they were integrative ones. Truly integrative symbols and practices emerge from border-edge environments as creative responses to something new. As Richard Sennett puts it, "from these ephemeral spaces of interaction and exchange, new and shared practices emerge."[38]

Sometimes they come from one of the religious traditions. In an organization on whose board I serve, one whose mission focuses on Jews, Christians and Muslims, the Abrahamic metaphors are slowly giving way to new images. A recent caravan on the 10th anniversary of September 11th set out with a picture of Noah's ark as its logo. Under that visual, our new logo will read, "One ark, one humanity. We are all in the same boat."[39] Even so, I have noticed how difficult it is for some people to let go of Abraham. For many raised in Western culture, that image of a common father continues to hold a fascination and power that cannot easily be denied. As the biblical character Jacob said, in a different context, "I will not let you go until you bless me" (Genesis 32:26).

37. Alon Goshen-Gottstein, "Abraham and 'Abrahamic Religions' in Contemporary Interreligious Discourse: Reflections of an Implicated Jewish Bystander," *Studies in Interreligious Dialogue* 12/2 (2002) 165–83.

38. Grace Yukich and Ruth Braunstein, "Encounters at the Religious Edge: Interfaith Activism as a Space for Religious Cooperation and Construction," 16. This paper is currently unpublished and not for distribution. It reports on field work with the New Sanctuary Movement.

39. Http://www.clergybeyondborders.org.

An "Abrahamic" Practice: The Philadelphia Interfaith Walk for Peace

Since 2004, on a Sunday in late spring, rain or shine, hundreds of Philadelphians (500–1,000) from a staggering variety of traditions spend the afternoon walking together through the streets of the city from one religious institution to the next. At each stop they listen: to a Sufi telling a story, to a rabbi offering a prayer, to a Seikh youth choir chanting a hymn, to a leader from the Lakota Nation sharing stories. Each year, an interreligious group made up entirely of volunteers plans the Philadelphia Interfaith Walk for Peace and Reconciliation.

Like many grassroots interfaith projects, the walk began as a response to the events of September 11, 2001. Rabbi Lynn Gottlieb of Albuquerque picked up the phone and called across town to a mosque where she reached Abdul Rauf Campos-Marquetti. That April, the two led an Interfaith Walk for Jewish-Muslim Reconciliation through their city. Vic Compher, an active lay person in his Philadelphia church, met Lynn on a trip to Israel and Palestine. The following fall, Vic, along with a Jewish and a Muslim friend, gathered a small group of Jews, Christians, and Muslims to create a Philadelphia version of the walk.

On the way, the peace walkers talk, sometimes spontaneously, sometimes according to design. For several years, we gave instructions to turn to fellow walkers and ask "What brought you to this walk today? How do you keep your hope for peace alive? What would you most like me to know about your religion?" The last few years, we have distributed "bingo cards." Each square has a question: Why do Seikh men wear turbans? What do Jews do on Yom Kippur? Walkers wander among their fellow walkers quizzing one another to find the answers. The dress code is to wear all white. No political signs are permitted. We repeat, almost as a mantra, that the walk is neither a protest nor a demonstration, but rather a "spiritual practice."

The stops along the way are examples of aggregative practices and provide occasion to respect particularistic religious practices as we enter churches, synagogues or mosques. At the same time, the walk itself serves as an integrative practice, using old symbols in a new way. Rather than simply waving the image of a shared father figure and hoping no one will interrogate too closely, the walk takes seriously a piece of the Abraham story that speaks in our setting. It brings to the foreground a trope within the traditions of Abraham that is rich with potential. In doing so, it offers space for many other traditions to join the conversation.

The first peace walk explicitly mentioned the name of Abraham. It spoke of the walk as "a ritual of pilgrimage."[40] Pilgrimage is a powerful aspect of religious life across many faith traditions. In the Torah's telling, Abraham represents the first pilgrim, that is, he is first one to set out on a journey that is not a punishment. Unlike his predecessors in travel (Adam and Eve, Cain, the dispersed generation of Babel), Abraham goes freely, in response to a call.[41] Abraham must walk away from what is familiar toward something new, toward a blessing that is awaiting. Meaning resides in the walking forward, in the journey. Travel becomes a sacred act.

In the call to Abraham, the usually terse Hebrew sounds almost redundant. *Lech l'cha*, the emphatic command, translates as "Go!" The words can also be read, hyper-literally, as "Go to yourself." The Jewish mystical tradition, beginning in the Zohar and continuing through Levi Yitzhak of Berditchev, understands the command to go forward on the physical plane and also the spiritual.

The Imrei Shammai cites an incident regarding Reb Nahum of Chernobyl. He explains the Hebrew of the terse command *lech l'cha*. God sent Abraham on his travels as a mission outward, but also as a mission inward, to improve himself. In order for Abraham to become an exemplar of the mitzvah of hospitality, he needed to know what it felt like to be a guest.[42]

Richard Niebuhr writes, "Pilgrims are persons in motion, passing through territories not their own, seeking something we might call completion . . . a goal to which only the spirit's compass points the way."[43] Medieval pilgrimage routes such as the Camino de Santiago in Spain have enjoyed contemporary revivals. In 1985, 620 pilgrims checked in to a particular destination on the pilgrimage trail. In 2010, the number was over 270,000.

---

40. Http://peacewalk.blogspot.com/.

41. Aviva Gottlieb Zornberg, *The Genesis of Desire: Reflections on Genesis* (New York: Doubleday, 1995), 74.

42. Http://torah.org/learning/ravfrand/5764/lechlecha.html.

43. Quoted in Phil Cousineau, *The Art of Pilgrimage: The Seeker's Guide to Making Travel Sacred* (Berkeley: Conari, 1998), 14.

The practice of the interfaith walk obviously resonates powerfully with Muslims for whom the importance of the hajj is difficult to overstate. Mohammad considered the restoration of the Hajj, a custom that pre-dated Islam, to be the capstone of his prophecy. It is based, as we have noted, on the life of Abraham. God had commanded Abraham to proclaim the first pilgrimage (22:26–29). In addition to the Qur'an itself, the Hajj has attracted interpreters to draw out philosophical as well as mystical meanings, seeing the practice as a rich "symbolic universe."[44]

An important modernist thinker of Islam, Muhammed Iqbal, interprets leaving home for the Hajj as an opportunity to break from habit, routine and repetition. It re-enacts Muhammad's, and before him Abraham's, choice to break with the parochial birthplace and go off to establish something new. The "principle of movement," in Iqbal's view, refutes the myth of "eternal return" . . . a dangerous negation of self and life . . . in this world.[45]

The peace walk succeeds by invoking these resonances—and countless more—through telling a piece of Abraham's story while keeping him and his fractious family decidedly in the background. Thomas Michel wrote, "Dialogue is a new terrain on which we must live our respective religious commitments."[46] Indeed, it is precisely that aspect of the stories of Abraham, Sarah and Hagar that may now serve us well. Sarah, Abraham, and Hagar, each in their own way, had the faith and courage to walk into something new. We can embrace them as model travelers into new terrain, rather than as ancestors who allegedly make us into one family. We can honor something powerful about their legacy and, at the same time, invite others—fully half of humanity—to join us on the journey.

44. Robert R. Bianchi, *Guest of God: Pilgrimage and Politics in the Islamic World* (New York: Oxford University Press, 2004), 23.

45. Ibid., 27.

46. Michel Thomas, "Where to Now? Ways Forward for Interreligious Dialogue: Images of Abraham as Models of Interreligious Encounter," 3. Http://www.acu.edu.au/__data/assets/pdf_file/0005/194216/Public_lecture_-_Gulen_Chair_conference_Thomas_Michel.pdf.

6

Meeting at the Well of Spiritual Direction

A Jewish Feminist Perspective

Sue Levi Elwell

"The personal is political" was a clarion call of the feminist movement that was revived and revitalized in the last quarter of the twentieth century. Women identified with spiritual traditions expanded that call to "the personal is religious" as we demanded equal rites, worked to "depatriarchalize" sacred texts, and challenged the educational institutes that had kept women from taking their rightful places alongside men as religious leaders and teachers. Jewish women developed an emerging Jewish feminism, which we hoped would transform both Judaism and Jewish life. As we look back on nearly forty years of Jewish feminist expression, we ask, "How is Jewish feminism continuing to challenge and change Judaism, Jewish practice, and Jewish identity?"

This essay explores the developing phenomenon of Jewish Spiritual Direction as one realization of Jewish feminist practice, from its interfaith origins to its evolution as a durable tool that both empowers women as spiritual leaders and prepares seekers for transformative social justice work.

Roots of Jewish Feminism

Beginning in the late 1960s, the American Jewish community experienced social and cultural changes that challenged all American secular and religious institutions and organizations. The children of Jews who had experienced quotas and significant barriers to admission into schools, colleges, professions and social clubs found open doors and often surprising degrees of welcome from the same institutions that had barred their parents. Some Jews were stunned to experience themselves as "white," as race was acknowledged as a primary cultural division.[1] The civil rights movement was followed by the anti-establishment movements of the late 1960s and early1970s, and singing the songs of the disaffected Jew Bob Dylan, Jews organized and marched in protests against the Vietnam War. Young Jews were finding their voices as Americans and as activists.

And some young Jews were challenging the institutions in which they had grown up. In the late 1960s, a group of Jewish students, all men, founded Havurat Shalom Community Seminary in Somerville, Massachusetts as an intentional Jewish community where members would live, pray, and study together.[2] In 1972, a group of women, several of whom were colleagues and friends of the founders of Havurat Shalom, came together as "Ezrat Nashim," demanding equal rites and rights in the Conservative Jewish movement. (Their name was a wordplay on the traditional synagogue section where women sat separated from men.)[3] That same year, Sally Priesand became the first woman ordained as a rabbi by a seminary, Hebrew Union College in Cincinnati.[4] Yet it took nearly two decades for the impact of women's religious leadership to be felt in American Jewish life.[5]

1. Karen Brodkin, *How Jews Became White Folks and What It Says about Race in America* (New Brunswick, NJ: Rutgers University Press, 1994).

2. Many of the founders of "the Havurah," as it was known, came together to procure theological student deferments from serving in the US military during the Vietnam War. See Jonathan D. Sarna, *American Judaism* (New Haven: Yale University Press, 2004), 318ff.

3. Shuly Rubin Schwartz, "Conservative Judaism," in Paula E. Hyman and Deborah Dash Moore, eds., *Jewish Women in America: An Historical Encyclopedia* (New York: Routledge, 1997), 1:267–70.

4. See Pamela S. Nadell, *Women Who Would be Rabbis: A History of Women's Ordination, 1889–1985* (Boston: Beacon, 1998).

5. There was a virtual explosion of intelligent writing on the topic, in mainstream

The 1990s saw the development of two parallel movements: the Jewish healing movement and the creation of centers for Jewish feminist exploration. Rabbi Rachel Cowan describes the beginnings of what became the Jewish Healing Movement:

> A small group of women created the Jewish Healing movement in 1990 to expand the normative definitions of Jewish practice to include providing spiritual resources for Jews facing serious illness and their families and caregivers. Five of us—three rabbis (Nancy Flam, Susan Friedman and myself), a breast cancer survivor (Ellen Hermanson z"l who later died of that cancer), and Nessa Rapoport, a novelist who had sustained deep family losses—came together to speak of an enormous absence we had each experienced in our Jewish lives. The Jewish wisdom and practice that help people deal with the suffering that surrounds personal loss and serious illness were not readily available when we needed them.
>
> We were soon joined by Rabbi Amy Eilberg, who formed the Bay Area Jewish Healing Center with Nancy Flam. The healing movement, though not directed at issues unique to women, models the impact of women rabbis on Jewish life. I believe that it took a group of women—including rabbis—to break through the Jewish cultural barrier that saw medical treatment as the only response to illness. We understood that even though illness might not be curable, there were many ways to relieve the suffering. Rituals could restore a sense of calm and order to the emotional and physical chaos of the experience of illness. We knew that relationships and community were the key to healing. So we devised healing services, wrote prayers for patients and doctors alike, created *mikveh* (ritual bath) rituals, and ran support groups. We helped revitalize synagogue *bikkur holim* (visiting the sick) groups.

Jewish periodicals, in newly established feminist periodicals, and in books. Susan Weidman Schneider, editor and founding mother of *Lilith* Magazine wrote a comprehensive compendium, that while dated, remains an important source: *Jewish and Female: Choices and Changes in Our Lives Today* (New York: Simon & Schuster, 1984). See also Karla Goldman, *Beyond the Synagogue Gallery: Finding a Place for Women in American Judaism* (Cambridge: Harvard University Press, 2000); Pamela S. Nadell and Jonathan D. Sarna, eds., *Women and American Judaism: Historical Perspectives*, Brandeis Series in American Jewish History, Culture, and Life (Hanover, NH: University of New England Press, 2001); and Riv-Ellen Prell, ed., *Women Remaking American Judaism* (Detroit: Wayne State University Press, 2007).

Cowan continues: "And then, from working with the spirituality of brokenness, women took the lead in understanding more deeply the spirituality of wholeness, *shlemut*. Amy Eilberg went on to co-create the Yedidya Center for Jewish Spiritual Direction (www.yedidyacenter.org), and Nancy Flam and I helped to found the Institute for Jewish Spirituality (www.ijs-online.org)."[6]

In 1990, I was fortunate to co-found with Rabbi Laura Geller, the Los Angeles Jewish Feminist Center.[7] Within several years, there were several such centers across the country. In addition, academic institutions, both Jewish and secular, began implementing Jewish feminist courses and study programs.[8] These programs and classes brought individuals together for study, celebration, and growth in woman-affirming environments; as in many women's studies classes, conversations that sparked change began but did not end at the door of the classroom.

In 2009, Rabbi Elyse Goldstein wrote in her acknowledgments to her anthology *New Jewish Feminism*, "do we still need the 'F word'? Haven't we done it all? What's left to be done?"[9] Goldstein's collection invites a new generation into the conversation about creating an inclusive Judaism. Susan Weidman Schneider's earlier book began with a section called, "Beyond the Patriarchal Premise," with subsections entitled, "Women as Disabled Jews: Seeking Equal Access," "The Consequences of Women's Exclusion from Religious Obligations," and "Struggling Against Women's Exclusion from Jewish Studies." Goldstein's work, published a quarter of a century later, assumes and reflects a landscape of Jewish life that has profoundly changed. The thirty-seven essays are all penned by Jewish women leaders and change agents: rabbis, scholars, teachers, and writers. It is clear from their essays that the feminist transformation of Judaism and Jewish life has indeed begun.

Goldstein's book, however, has a number of blind spots. There is no reflection on the role of male feminists in the transformation of

---

6. Http://jwa.org/feminism/_html/JWA016.htm.

7. See http://jwa.org/feminism/_html/JWA021.htm.

8. By the conclusion of that decade, the condition of Jewish women's studies was "precarious." See Tobin Belzer, "The Status of Jewish Women's Studies in the United States and Canada: A Survey of University and College Courses as of 1999." The Hadassah Research Institute on Jewish Women, Brandeis University; http://www.brandeis.edu/hbi/pubs/Belzerworkingpaper.pdf.

9. Elyse Goldstein, ed., *New Jewish Feminism: Probing the Past, Forging the Future* (Woodstock, VT: Jewish Lights, 2009), xvii.

Judaism.[10] And none of the thirty-seven essays in Goldstein's book address either a feminist assessment or analysis of the meditative and contemplative practices that are being reclaimed and introduced into many mainstream Jewish contexts. Jewish spiritual direction, for example, reveals deep feminist roots, and serves as a powerful tool for the creation, exploration, expression and expansion of feminist Judaism.

Jewish Spiritual Direction

Spiritual Direction is the intentional practice of entering into contemplative conversation with a trained, nonjudgmental listener to share one's spiritual/religious journey. Rabbi Jacob Staub writes, "ultimately, the goal of this practice is for the seeker to develop the habit of discernment in all aspects of his life."[11]

The origin stories of Jewish Spiritual Direction are rich, varied and contradictory. Some claim that the practice is ancient, and that one individual inviting another to "pour out your heart like water" (Lamentations 2:19) is the beginning of all religious conversation. *Pirkei Avot*, a third century text, instructs the seeker to find both a teacher and a spiritual companion (1:6). For the last two centuries, the *mashgiach*, or spiritual supervisor was a fixture of the yeshiva, the primary institution of Jewish learning. "The *mashgiach* is responsible for the personal and religious development of the . . . students, interacting with them in the hall of study . . . and offering public talks on . . . Jewish observance and the Holy Days."[12] The Hasidic movement, which was founded in the nineteenth century in Central Europe and today exists in many forms in communities across the world, offers a mystical/spiritual approach to tradition. The primary teacher in Hasidic world is the *rebbe* or teacher.

---

10. The single essay in the book written by a man addresses an important, but not the only issue where male voices could challenge the reader. See Joseph B. Meszler, "Where Are the Jewish Men? The Absence of Men from Liberal Synagogue Life," in Goldstein, ed., *New Jewish Feminism*, 165–74.

11. Jacob Staub, "Jewish Theologies and Jewish Spiritual Direction," in Howard Avruhm Addison and Barbara E. Breitman, eds., *Jewish Spiritual Direction: An Innovative Guide from Traditional and Contemporary Sources* (Woodstock, VT: Jewish Lights, 2006), 5.

12. Addison and Breitman, "Introduction: To Revitalize the Spirit of God: Toward a Contemporary Practice of Jewish Spiritual Direction," in *Jewish Spiritual Direction*, xvii.

He is often assisted by *mashpi'im*, "spiritual prompters, (who) offer guidance and instruction."[13]

The practice of spiritual guidance did not survive the challenges of the Enlightenment to traditional Jewish life and educational system. Those trained in European non-Hasidic settings brought Judaisms to America that promoted the study of philosophy, history, and traditional texts. The spiritual development of the individual was not a priority of those who founded and developed the Reform, Conservative, or Modern Orthodox strains of Judaism.

So it is not surprising that spiritual direction had to be re-introduced to contemporary non-traditional Jews. Beginning less than twenty years ago, Jews seeking to deepen their own spirituality and connection with God learned about programs and practices in contemplative Christian communities, and eagerly explored this area of practice and inquiry. Among the first Jews to realize the power of spiritual companionship were Drs. Carol Ochs, Linda Rabinowitch Thal, and Barbara Breitman, and Rabbis Amy Eilberg, Burt Jacobson, Jacob Staub, Zari Weiss, and Shohama Harris Wiener. Of these, some became students at Mercy Center in Burlingame, California; others studied at the Shalem Institute in Washington, DC, and at Fordham University. Each of these individuals experienced powerful and formative guidance with spiritual directors of other faiths.

Several of these pioneers went on, not only to become themselves spiritual guides and directors, but also to develop and oversee programs of spiritual direction that integrate the insights and teachings of Judaism with the wisdom of the contemplative practice of Christian spiritual direction. In 2001, Rabbis Howard Avruhm Addison and Zari Weiss, with Dr. Barbara Eve Breitman, developed *Lev Shomea*, the first program to offer spiritual direction training in the Jewish tradition. Two years later, Rabbi Amy Eilberg and Dr. Linda Rabinowitch Thal inaugurated *Morei Derech*, a similar program under the aegis of the Yedidya Institute for Jewish spiritual direction. In 2001, Dr. Barbara Breitman and Rabbi Jacob Staub initiated the first program in spiritual direction at an American rabbinical seminary at the Reconstructionist Rabbinical College. Programs of spiritual direction were subsequently initiated for rabbis in training at Hebrew College (2005), at ALEPH (2006), and at the Hebrew Union College–Jewish Institute of Religion (2011). All of

13. Ibid., xviii.

those programs continue to evolve, even as the practice of Jewish spiritual direction continues to develop.[14]

Feminism and Spiritual Direction: The Personal Is Spiritual

Among the first Jews to explore the world of Spiritual Direction were several individuals who had distinguished themselves as Jewish feminist teachers and writers. As Howard Avruhm Addison and Barbara Eve Breitman point out in the introduction to their anthology, *Jewish Spiritual Direction: An Innovative Guide from Traditional and Contemporary Sources*, the journey of Dr. Carol Ochs began as a feminist quest.[15] These are Ochs' words: "When I graduated from college, rabbinic seminaries had no place for women, so I studied to enter the profession that seemed closest to the rabbinate—teaching philosophy at the college level."[16] Ochs developed her approach and philosophy of spiritual guidance after seeking her own guides and based upon her own independent study. She then created and maintained a rich practice, working with a wide range of adults. For Ochs, "The spiritual guide's gift has nothing to do with cleverness and the ability to make insightful connections. The gift is to 'get out of the way,' because ultimately the relationship at stake is not that between the guide and the guidee, but between the guidee and God."[17] Her insistence on "getting out of the way" is a radical invitation to the seeker or learner. Like Kathleen Fischer, the author of the only book-length exploration of feminism and spiritual direction, Ochs emphasizes the importance of affirming the agency of the seeker, and of welcoming the seeker into a realm of discovery.[18]

---

14. Ibid, xxvi; and "An Appreciation: Rabbi Shohama Harris Wiener," in Goldie Milgram, ed., *Seeking and Soaring: Jewish Approaches to Spiritual Direction* (New Rochelle, NY: Reclaiming Judaism Press, 2009), xvi–xvii; and conversation with Barbara Breitman, August 2012.

15. Addison and Breitman, "Introduction," xxiii.

16. Carol Ochs and Kerry M. Olitzky, *Jewish Spiritual Guidance: Finding Our Way to God*, Jossey-Bass Religion-in-Practice Series (San Francisco: Jossey-Bass, 1997), ix.

17. Carol Ochs, *Reaching Godward: Voices from Jewish Spiritual Guidance* (New York: URJ Press, 2004), 2.

18. Kathleen Fischer, *Women at the Well: Feminist Perspectives on Spiritual Direction* (New York: Paulist, 1988).

Ochs articulates a deep feminist understanding of this spiritual practice. Most women throughout history who have wanted to engage in serious study, enter into conversations about concepts and ideas, or exercise their own intellectual capabilities have encountered stumbling blocks and locked doors, prejudice, and crushing patriarchy. Illiterate and physically, emotionally, and financially dependent upon men, too many women have been kept from fully contributing to most of the world's cultures. Jewish women like Ochs were kept out of the study halls, sanctuaries and seminaries that were the primary loci of Jewish communal, intellectual, and religious life.

Spiritual direction takes place between two people (individual spiritual direction), or between members of a small and intentional group (group spiritual direction). Meetings, by definition and design, are held in a "safe space," a physical space that is prepared for this particular encounter. The meeting space offers privacy and a sense of spaciousness to the seeker so that s/he may speak freely, sharing words, silence, and more without being heard by, or interrupted by the comings and goings of others. A safe space offers both access and easy egress. Meetings do not take place in an isolated building or in an unused or empty space. The physical space mirrors the spiritual promise of containment that is crucial to establishing, managing, and concluding a safe encounter. So too does creating clear and dependable parameters of time serve both director and directee. Having a fixed time acts as an additional container for the spiritual direction encounter.

The creation of a trusting relationship with a Jewish role model, guide, or teacher with the intent of creating a space for spiritual intimacy may be an unfamiliar quest for many Jews. Because most Jewish life happens in community, the individual encounter may be suspect, charged or frightening. Women's intimate friendships, understood by feminists to be models of spiritual sharing, can help to establish an atmosphere of trust that is a prerequisite for the kind of sharing that can occur in spiritual direction.

Most Jews first encounter teachers, rabbis, and Jewish leaders when they are in a group. The first individual meeting with a Jewish teacher that many Jews remember may be an experience of preparation for their bar or bat mitzvah at age 12 (for girls) or 13 (for boys and some girls).[19] Too often, bar or bat mitzvah preparation has been so

19. Bat mitzvah for girls was not widely practiced in North America until the

focused on mastering a set curriculum that little attention has been paid to the child's situation in life, his or her readiness, or the child's spiritual development.[20] For some students, this encounter, rather than being a positive experience, evokes a sense of invisibility, disconnection, or the irrelevance of their studies. Others carry negative memories of tutors who berated or belittled or even physically or sexually abused them.[21]

Spiritual direction demands the establishment of a physical space where a seeker is welcomed by a guide with appropriate boundaries and a clear sense of the holiness of the enterprise at hand. The daily morning service, as Jews prepare to recite the *Sh'ma*, contains this petition to God: "Enlighten our eyes with your Torah and draw our minds near to You . . . that we will never be shamed." For some Jews, both men and women, a Jewish place where they will not be shamed becomes a space of healing and liberation.[22]

Sanctity of Women's Experience

In 1981, several Jewish feminists established an annual retreat and named the gathering B'not Esh.[23] One of our members, Barbara E. Breitman, has written about the power of sharing our stories in that safe space:

> As we shared the stories of our spiritual journeys, . . . we could sense a palpable presence in the group during and after such sharing. It was a presence of life and energy, of passion and honesty. It was a presence that empowered and emboldened. It was creative and erotic. We felt filled with knowledge and vision. We experienced healing and were pointed toward justice. We sensed that, collectively and in extended community with other

1970s, so this concern only applies to women born after the late 1950s.

20. A reparative, transformative approach is described in Hanna Tiferet Siegel, "Opening the Dialogue with God in B'nai Mitzvah Preparation," in Milgram, ed., *Seeking and Soaring*, 92–112.

21. Tragically, I have met women who were sexually abused by Jewish teachers. One survivor shared with me how she continues to attempt to learn Hebrew but has been deeply and perhaps irrevocably damaged by her memories of abuse by her Hebrew tutor.

22. Meszler writes about men's hesitancy to engage in synagogue classes that might reveal their lack of background. "Ignorance laid open is painful." How much the more so fear of being shamed. Meszler, "Where Are the Jewish Men?," 169.

23. Http://jwa.org/feminism/_html/JWA057.htm.

women engaged in similar endeavors, we were giving birth to
a new vitality, creative and conscious, that had not manifested
before in the long history of our people. We tried to name it
. . . mostly we could not . . . But we felt the presence and held our
experiences with reverence.

She continues, "I came to believe that our stories were sacred text,
that the narratives of our lives were part of an ongoing textual history
of Judaism. The stories we told as we heard each other into speech were
Torah."[24] Breitman's training as an acute and intentional listener of life
stories led her to name how women were discovering the importance,
worth, and meaning of their own life stories by sharing them, particularly in the context of B'not Esh, the Jewish feminist community she,
Alpert, and I had developed.[25] Breitman understood that we women
were sharing the sacred "texts of our lives," a phrase that came to describe the larger Jewish feminist project. This story telling became the
basis for the transformation of the text-based tradition of Judaism as
we crafted new texts, fashioned new life-cycle rituals, and created new
prayers.[26] As we wrestled with claiming a tradition that had marginalized or erased women's stories and contributions, we discovered that
our own journeys offered rich material for understanding inherited text,
and for constructing new sacred stories.

This understanding is at the core of Jewish spiritual direction. In
every tradition, sacred text has been lovingly handed down from generation to generation, and, in most cases, has been honed and shaped by
each individual who "handles" the text. Jews debate about what is considered oral and what is considered written tradition, for although after
the second century, all of Jewish text was preserved in written form,
the long tradition of oral transmission continued to be valorized. The
spiritual director honors the complexity and mystery of each speaker's
telling, and invites the seeker to return to the narrative again and again

24. Barbara E. Breitman, "Holy Listening: Cultivating a Hearing Heart," in Addison and Breitman, eds., *Jewish Spiritual Direction*, 73–74.

25. Kathleen Fischer writes, "The skill of listening is the basis for spiritual companionship with both men and women; but in the case of women the quality of this
listening is crucial. Women have long lived in the intervals between their inchoate
experiences and the definitions given to experience by the stories of men . . ." *Women
at the Well*, 7.

26. Rebecca Alpert, "Our Lives ARE the Text: Exploring Jewish Women's Rituals,"
Bridges 2/1 (Spring 1991/5751) 80.

in hopes of discovering new material or different perspectives that will lead back and forward, illuminating greater patches of the evolving life text the seeker is revealing to him/herself with the help, support, and urging of the other. Kathleen Fischer quotes Madonna Kolbenschlag here: "Women today are . . . creating a new 'wisdom literature' out of the alchemy of their own lives."[27]

The search for the holy is essential to the practice of spiritual direction. For many Jews, like others, the journey towards God language, and towards God, may be circuitous and challenging. And, as Judith Plaskow writes, there is a dominant trope in modern Jewish thought that "Jews don't do theology."[28] The Jewish feminist project both contradicts and challenges this mistaken understanding.

Early on, Jewish feminist thinkers and writers took on what seemed to be an impediment to establishing a connection with God: the exclusively masculine language of Jewish liturgy and traditional Jewish texts. During the ten-day period of the Days of Awe, from Rosh HaShana to Yom Kippur, the primary moniker for God is *Avinu Malkenu*, Our Father, Our King. For many of us, this image of an awesome, forbidding, transcendent Deity was dominant throughout the cycle of the year, and in our mind's eye, when we imagined God, we saw Michelangelo's white haired and bearded patriarch enthroned in the heavens. Thus, Barbara Breitman writes, "It is not uncommon in spiritual direction to encounter people who are troubled because they cannot relate to God as described in traditional anthropomorphic and masculine language and are freed when asked, 'how do you actually experience God or the holy in your life?'"[29]

Jewish spiritual directors have been assisted by the work of theologians Judith Plaskow, Rachel Adler and Rebecca Alpert whose scholarship deconstructs limiting images and expands our theological vocabularies. Their work also challenges us to examine rigid dichotomous images of an either/or Deity, enabling us to consider a God who is transcendent and immanent, disinterested and engaged with the details of our lives, a God who is good and also capricious, angry and

27. Fischer, *Women at the Well*, 13, from Kolbenschlag, in "Feminist, the Frog Princess, and the New Frontier of Spirituality," *New Catholic World* 225 (July/August, 1892) 160.

28. Judith Plaskow, "Calling All Theologians," in Goldstein, ed., *New Jewish Feminism*.

29. Personal correspondence, 27 August 2012.

gracious.[30] The Jewish feminist theological project has been extended and expanded by a powerful cadre of poets, including Marcia Falk and Merle Feld; liturgists, including Karyn Kedar and Naomi Levy; and composers including Debbie Friedman and Shefa Gold. These gifted women helped many find a new language for speaking about and with the holy.[31]

Spiritual direction begins by quieting down the noise in our heads and making space for the still small voice of the spirit. As we become more and more adept at listening, and at hearing ourselves and one another into speech, we discover that finding new language for God is only the beginning. Breitman observes: "Changing God language is revolutionary precisely because it opens up our minds, hearts and public spaces to new ways of imaging power dynamics in relationships between self and other, human beings and the earth, peoples of different faiths and cultures, and expanding roles of spiritual leadership beyond ordained clergy."[32] God, unbound, invites new possibilities and expanded relationships. The feminist theological project, expanded through the process of Jewish spiritual direction, opens doors and windows to seekers to discover holiness in every moment, in every word, in every silence.[33]

---

30. See Donna Berman, "Major Trends in Jewish Feminist Theology," in Goldstein, ed., *New Jewish Feminism*; and the two primary works of Jewish feminist theology, Judith Plaskow's *Standing Again at Sinai* (New York: HarperCollins, 1991); and Rachel Adler's *Engendering Judaism* (Boston: Beacon, 1999).

31. Marcia Falk, *The Book of Blessings* (HarperSanFrancisco, 1996); Merle Feld, *A Spiritual Life: Exploring the Heart and Jewish Tradition*, SUNY Series in Modern Jewish Literature and Culture (Albany: SUNY Press, 2007); Feld, *Finding Words* (New York: URJ Press, 2011); Karyn Kedar, *God Whispers*, *Dance of the Dolphin*, and *The Bridge to Forgiveness* (Woodstock, VT: Jewish Lights, 1999, 2001, 2007); Naomi Levy, *To Begin Again: The Journey toward Comfort, Strength, and Faith in Difficult Times* (New York: Knopf, 1998); Levy, *Talking to God: Personal Prayers for Times of Joy, Sadness, Struggle, and Celebration* (New York: Knopf, 2002); and Levy, *Hope Will Find You: My Search for the Wisdom to Stop Waiting and Start Living* (New York: Harmony, 2010). For the music of Shefa Gold: http://www.rabbishefagold.com/. The music of Debbie Friedman, who died in 2011, is widely available.

32. Personal correspondence, August 27, 2012.

33. See here Jacob Staub's "Relating Personally to a Non Personal God," in his "Jewish Theologies and Jewish Spiritual Direction," in Addison and Breitman, eds., *Jewish Spiritual Direction*, 13ff. Breitman, in "Holy Listening: Cultivating a Hearing Heart," in Addison and Breitman, *Jewish Spiritual Direction*, 82–83, suggests that Tilden Edwards' expansive understandings of God can be especially helpful in opening directee's minds to the range of ways God can be imaged and imagined.

Communal and Individual Practices in Judaism

Historically, Jewish religious expression is primarily communal. However, Linda R. Thal pointedly describes the relationship between the cacophonous communal experience of the synagogue service and the quiet, contemplative and dialogic exchange of Jewish spiritual direction: "Given the communal nature of Jewish spirituality, being able to reflect on personal spiritual experience in the shared religious language may be the linchpin of a specifically Jewish spiritual direction. Perhaps rather than limiting Jewish spiritual direction to 'holy listening,' and 'mirroring,' the director may sometimes refract the directee's speech and experience through a specifically Jewish prism, breaking the speech of generic spirituality into the more nuanced speech of a specific tradition—in this case, Judaism."[34] Thal suggests that Jewish spiritual direction can help the seeker or directee to recognize both the power and the place of Jewish communal engagement. Spiritual direction provides a longed-for opening for the seeker, both those who have never ventured into Jewish communal spaces and those who have fled. Emmanuel Levinas observes, "among those who have left the synagogue and been blown across the world there are many great souls in love with the absolute."[35]

In spiritual direction, the intimate exchange away from the recitation and singing of the synagogue service can serve as a preparation for, and an accompaniment to, the experience of communal prayer. Following the Talmudic tradition of praying in preparation for prayer, one could interpret the soulful exchange of spiritual direction as a sacred entry into a central chamber of attention.[36] Shefa Gold's powerful, repeated, haunting chants of single lines from the liturgy and from psalms slow down the mind and open the heart, and deepen spiritual direction, meditation, and the prayer experience. Amy Eilberg's guide to the prayerbook creates a bridge between the avalanche of words that threaten to bury the uninitiated and the few words that will open new

34. Thal, "Creating Jewish Spiritual Direction: More Than an Act of Translation," in Addison and Breitman, *Jewish Spiritual Direction*, 43.

35. "Education and Prayer," in Emmanuel Levinas, *Difficult Freedom: Essays on Judaism*, trans. Sean Hand (Baltimore: Johns Hopkins University Press, 1990), 272. This is further reflected in the spiritual search at the core of many contemporary Israeli novels, including the works of A. B. Yehoshua and others.

36. Jewish tradition teaches that the pious would meditate for a full hour before entering into the act of prayer.

pathways to discover the divine.[37] These feminist innovations invite every seeker to find her or his own words in the right time, and to begin creating a connection between the intensity of Jewish communal prayer experiences and the very different intensity of spiritual direction.

Jews call ourselves "The People of the Book," which usually reflects the Jewish passion for the Hebrew Bible. By extension, this appellation refers to learning as a life-long enterprise.[38] However, this very descriptor is problematic for Jews who were not given access to Jewish learning from childhood. Jewish men, now in their seventies, eighties, and nineties who grew up in war-ravaged Europe or in crushing poverty may have been denied access to essential Jewish education. Others may not have been introduced to Jewish learning if their parents were committed Communists, or were those who internalized the virulent anti-Semitism of the 1930s–1960s, or were raised in families who assimilated into American or European culture. Until very recently, few Jewish girls, regardless of their socio-economic or cultural background, had access to anything beyond the most basic and introductory Jewish education. And with limited Hebrew skills, it has been until very recently almost impossible to enter into serious Jewish study or what we might call serious Jewish conversation.

Thankfully, the last few decades have been a time of increased access to Jewish learning. *The First Jewish Catalogue*, published in 1973, called itself a "do-it-yourself kit" for Jewish living and opened up the rich options for creating a Jewish life whatever one's Jewish background or geography. The Catalogue hoped to follow the "access to tools" model of the *Whole Earth Catalogue*, serving the "Jewish Counterculture," the emerging generation of Jewish baby boomers who, like their counterparts in the American counter culture, were challenging their parents, their teachers, and the social and cultural institutions of their time.[39] In the last quarter of the twentieth century, Jewish publishing houses began publishing translations of texts and sources that had hitherto

37. "The Siddur: A Guide to Jewish Spiritual Direction," in Addison and Breitman, eds., *Jewish Spiritual Direction*, 197–208.

38. Muslims refer to non-Muslims who follow a revealed scripture as "People of the Book," or *Ahl al-Kitab*. Jews use this term to refer exclusively to themselves.

39. *The First Jewish Catalogue*, compiled and edited by Richard Siegel, Michael Strassfeld and Sharon Strassfeld (Philadelphia: Jewish Publication Society, 1973). I was among the contributors to this first of three volumes; I co-authored a chapter on challah baking. See also http://www.wholeearth.com/index.php.

been accessible only to scholars. And colleges and universities began welcoming trained Jewish scholars as professors into departments of religion, philosophy, theology, literature, history, and more, expanding students' resources.

But for some, this increased access to the Jewish conversation was too little, too late or simply out of reach. Denied Jewish education as children, exposed only to bland and uninspiring role models, or scarred by negative or shaming experiences, some Jews have distanced themselves from Jewish life and Jewish community. For such souls who find their way to spiritual direction, the practice welcomes them onto a very different path of Jewish exploration than they might previously been able to imagine. The intimate, safe, and non-judgmental exchange that characterizes the process and practice of spiritual direction welcomes the seeker where s/he is, and encourages spiritual growth. The director accompanies the seeker on his/her journey, but the goal is set by the seeker, not the director. While the director may offer guiding questions during sessions, or proffer suggestions for consideration between meetings, the process of growth differs from almost any other Jewish learning, practice or activity. Jewish spiritual direction may actually be a powerful source for healing for Jews for whom traditional modes of learning, or participation in communal life, have not worked. Jewish spiritual direction thus expands the Jewish conversation in mode and context.

Building on the work of Jewish feminist scholars and teachers, Jewish spiritual directors welcome directees into the exploration of traditional Jewish tropes, the language of exodus and journey, of *tshuvah/* return and forgiveness, the language of hope and renewal. The cycle and texts of the Jewish year provide rich and natural frameworks for spiritual direction. By inviting the seeker to deeply explore spirituality with distinctly Jewish tropes and language may name one's sense of brokenness, and subsequently serve as a powerful tool for creating wholeness.[40]

Judaism has a long history of self-care, attention to the physical and psychological well-being of the individual as a reflection of each human being created in God's image. An oft-cited Talmudic story tells of Hillel's regular attendance at the public bath as his interpretation of fulfilling his obligation to maintain his body as God's gift. Additionally, there is

---

40. See Section III: The Jewish Path, in Addison and Breitman, eds., *Jewish Spiritual Direction*; and Milgram, *Seeking and Soaring*.

a long history in Judaism of equating physical and mental health, the well-being of the body with the well-being of the mind and spirit.[41]

Here, once more, both Feminism and Judaism point to the self-care that is an aspect of the spiritual direction encounter. The once-monthly hour devoted by the directee to his/her own spiritual exploration is a powerful investment in his/her spiritual health. Different than time spent in exercise, on a solitary walk, or in seated meditation, the exchange of words and silence that occurs between a trained spiritual director and her/his directee serves to re-invigorate, challenge, renew, and support both the seeker and the director. And the acknowledgement that both are part of a larger system of supportive exchanges further strengthens sharing and growth.

Rethinking Models of Jewish Leadership

Every religious tradition has a tradition of contemplative and wise teachers, schooled in life and reflection, who share their gifts with those fortunate to find them. However, too often these leaders, particularly if they have been female, have been unrecognized or marginalized by the larger, established religious community. Women can now pursue studies that lead them toward serving the Jewish people as rabbis and cantors, as university professors and administrators and directors of Jewish schools and camps. One of the gifts from the contemporary Christian contemplative movement to Jewish spiritual direction is the recognition that expert spiritual guides may have many paths to this unique work. Just as the intimate space of spiritual direction offers an alternative to the intensity of Jewish communal experience, and the quiet of shared meditation opens paths to different modes of spiritual discovery, spiritual direction also welcomes new generations of spiritual teachers into the Jewish ranks.

Spiritual direction invites a different model of sharing Jewish wisdom. The spiritual hunger of the feminists who opened this field for deepening Jewish life and practice did not seek recognition or acclaim, nor did they want to set up an alternative path to Jewish leadership. Like all spiritual seekers, they were discovering ways to grow closer to God

41. Http://www.shma.com/2011/06/training-for-caring-communities-a-roundtable/.

and to the pulse of the world. Their open-hearted exploration has made the way for other gifted individuals to follow.

Those who follow them include a rich array of individuals who are serving as a new cohort of Jewish teachers. The diversity of these guides reflects the rapidly changing and richly heterogeneous makeup of many evolving Jewish communities, including sexual minorities, racial diversity, Jews by choice, and many who make homes with Jews: partners, children, and others. This diversity is a source of great strength, and is enriching Jewish communities across the globe.[42]

Spiritual Companionship and Social Change

The Jewish feminist agenda began with the intention of exposing and removing barriers to Jewish study and practice, and raising up new generations of Jews who would fill libraries with Jewish texts, both traditional texts read and interpreted through new eyes and new work exploring topics and issues that we could not yet imagine. And the Jewish Feminist Agenda was always and continues to be focused on the active and passionate pursuit of social justice.[43]

Spiritual direction offers a powerful image to Jews, for the encounter at the heart of spiritual direction realizes Martin Buber's dialogic model of the I–Thou exchange, where the relationship itself establishes a world. These are Buber's words: "the relation is wrapped in a cloud but reveals itself, it lacks but creates language. We hear no You and yet feel addressed; we answer—creating, thinking, acting . . . In every sphere, through everything that becomes present to us, we gaze toward the train of the eternal You; in each we perceive a breath of it; in every You we address the eternal You."[44] The relationship that is established between the director and the directee reflects, mirrors, models and opens the way to a relationship with God. Howard Avruhm Addison writes, "To be a *mashgiach* (spiritual director) means that just as God is attentive

---

42. Some of the organizations that celebrate such diversity include: http://www.jewsinallhues.org/; http://bechollashon.org/about/jewish_diversity.php; and http://www.jewishmultiracialnetwork.org/. There is also a growing body of scholarly work in this area, including Melanie Kaye Kantrowitz, *The Colors of Jews: Racial Politics and Radical Diasporism* (Bloomington: Indiana University Press, 2007).

43. The five final essays in Goldstein's *New Jewish Feminism* explore this issue.

44. Buber, *I and Thou*, trans. Walter Kauffman (New York: Scribners, 1970), 57.

and present, so must we be attentive and present."[45] By being present for and with one another, we set a standard for engagement not only with another human being, but with all human beings. Thus the relationship that is at the core of spiritual direction points not only "in," but "out," not only towards the inner life of the directee, but to her place and her responsibility in the world.

Sheila Weinberg writes eloquently about how spiritual direction, by design and essence, leads to engagement in the world by re-energizing us and re-igniting our passion for justice. She suggests that it is the very act of partnering another on the spiritual journey that provides us, finally, with the strength we need to live in a world of great pain.[46]

Ann Kline also suggests that "All spiritual direction has a prophetic edge. It is a process that calls us to truths at odds with the norms and temptations of the culture we live in. It asks that we claim a love greater than our own desire and make hard choices in the name of that love."[47]

Like Judaism and feminism, the process of spiritual direction "calls us to truths at odds with . . . the culture we live in," reminding us of the biblical challenge to "pursue justice, love mercy, and walk humbly with God" (Micah 6:8). Like both Judaism and feminism, a goal of spiritual direction is for individuals to see themselves as part of something larger than themselves, to see themselves as beings with power and agency in the context of their immediate circles of family and friends, in their communities, and as individuals who can make a difference in the world.

Judaism has survived for five thousand years because of Jews' fierce sense of otherness, or as some would say, Jews' sense of chosenness. Contemporary Jews who choose to examine the particularism that is at the core of Jewish identity and identification face a considerable challenge. The very act of interfaith conversation remains, for many Jews, a leap, a risk, a journey through forbidding territory towards a totally unknown destination.[48] The practice of spiritual direction, which

45. Addison, "Reciprocal Grace: The Vocabulary of Jewish Spiritual Direction," in Addison and Breitman, eds., *Jewish Spiritual Direction*, 59.

46. Weinberg, "Spiritual Direction: No Inside, No Outside," in Addison and Breitman, eds., *Jewish Spiritual Direction*, 131–53.

47. Ann Kline, "Widening the Lens: The Gift of Group Spiritual Direction," *Presence* 10/2 (2004) 41.

48. Blu Greenberg addresses this issue in her essay, "The Blessings and Challenges of Interfaith Friendship," in Sue Levi Elwell and Nancy Fuchs Kreimer, eds., *Chapters of the Heart: Jewish Women Sharing the Torah of Our Lives* (Eugene, OR: Cascade Books, 2013), 115–26.

grew from Christian roots, offers a significant and exciting challenge to Jews. While Jews may be accustomed to challenging the dominant culture, the practice of spiritual direction challenges Jewish culture. The emerging practice of Jewish spiritual direction offers a path of religious inquiry that may seem to be at odds with communal norms of Jewish behavior, for it challenges theological assumptions, questions the place of silence and speech in religious exploration, and empowers new leaders as directors and guides. Jewish spiritual direction invites each individual who engages in this practice to claim, perhaps for the first time, a relationship with the Source of all, a connection that can lead to a new or renewed sense of responsibility for magnifying God's presence in the world. As Judaism sowed the seeds of Christianity, the Christian practice of contemplation and action that is known as spiritual direction is opening the way to a developing Jewish practice that has the power to deepen, enhance, extend and expand the religious lives of contemporary Jewish seekers.

7

Constructive Interreligious Dialogue Concerning Muslim Women

Zayn Kassam

Considering the ways in which Muslim women have become the target of political and religious rhetoric in the Afghan war as well as in discussions on multiculturalism, this essay will focus on the question how we might engage in constructive interreligious dialogue concerning Muslim women. I would like to suggest that there are three myths that need to be identified, examined and overcome in order to be clear-eyed about the challenges that face perhaps not just Muslim women, but many women worldwide, challenges that need to be addressed through feminist activism that could be undertaken through interfaith and transnational networks. Currently, these three myths about Muslim women derail such dialogue before it even gets off the ground. First, the myth that "we are at war to eradicate terrorists and liberate Muslim women." Second, the myth that "capitalism is a good thing, and will improve life for (Muslim) women." Third, the myth that "Islam is a misogynist religion and without secularism, Muslim women will not be able to improve their condition." I would like to examine each of these myths in turn.

We Are at War to Eradicate Terrorists and Liberate Muslim Women

Chandra Talpade Mohanty's landmark essay, first published in 1984, drew attention to the terrible power of representation in her discussion of the "third world woman," who appears as a singular monolithic subject in some Western feminist texts. She writes:

> An analysis of "sexual difference" in the form of a cross-culturally singular, monolithic notion of patriarchy or male dominance leads to the construction of a similarly reductive and homogeneous notion of what I call the "third world difference"—that stable, ahistorical something that apparently oppresses most if not all women in these countries. And it is in the production of this "third world difference" that Western feminisms appropriate and colonize the constitutive complexities which characterize the lives of women in these countries. . . . While feminist writing in the U.S. is still marginalized (except from the point of view of women of color addressing privileged white women), Western feminist writing on women in the third world must be considered in the context of the global hegemony of Western scholarship—i.e., the production, publication, distribution, and consumption of information and ideas.[1]

The cooptation of Western feminists in the larger agendas of U.S. hegemonic imperialism was noted during the Western feminist support for the war on Afghanistan, made famous by Laura Bush's plea to save Afghan women from the fates imposed on them by the Taliban. Both lenses—the one that flattens all Muslim women to their religion rather than looking at the cultural, economic, social, and legal differences operating among them depending on where they are located, and the lens that views all third world women as subject to "male domination and female exploitation"[2] obscure the agency and autonomy of these women, and leads to the prevalent idea, not just in Western feminist discourse

1. Chandra Talpade Mohanty, "Under Western Eyes: Feminist Scholarship and Colonial Discourses" in Chandra Talpade Mohanty, Ann Russo, and Lourdes Torres, eds., *Third World Women and the Politics of Feminism* (Bloomington: Indiana University Press, 1991), 53–55. This essay was first published in 1984, updated for this volume, and subsequently revisited in "'Under Western Eyes' Revisited: Feminist Solidarity through Anticapitalist Struggles," in Chandra Talpade Mohanty, *Feminism without Borders: Decolonizing Theory, Practicing Solidarity* (Durham: Duke University Press, 2003).

2. Mohanty, *Feminism without Borders*, 66.

but in popular media representations as well, that "the third world just has not evolved to the extent that the West has."[3] The superiority of the West then sets the stage for a renewed round of economic and cultural colonization of the non-Western world,[4] arguably already well underway. Mohanty observes: "For in the context of a first/third world balance of power, feminist analyses which perpetrate and sustain the hegemony of the idea of the superiority of the West produce a corresponding set of universal images of the 'third world woman,' images such as the veiled woman, the powerful mother, the chaste virgin, the obedient wife, etc. These images exist in universal, ahistoric splendor, setting in motion a colonialist discourse which exercises a very specific power in defining, coding, and maintaining existing first/third world connections."[5]

History appears doomed to repeat itself as Muslim women continue to be the subject needing our help in Afghanistan, Iran, Iraq, and many other Muslim-majority nations. Indeed, as Jasmine Zine notes, "Discourses of race, gender and religion have scripted the terms of engagement in the war on terror. As a result, Muslim feminists and activists must engage with the dual oppressions of 'gendered Islamophobia' (Zine, 2004a), that has re-vitalized Orientalist tropes and representations of backward, oppressed and politically immature women in need of liberation and rescue through imperialist interventions as well as the challenge of religious extremism and puritan discourses that authorize equally limiting narratives of Islamic womanhood and compromise their human rights and liberty."[6]

Further, Muslims living in Europe are increasingly of concern as the battle over the veil spreads from France to Belgium to Germany to Italy to the Netherlands. As Asma Barlas observes,[7] the *burqa* (body veil) has been used to constitute both the Muslim Other and the non-Muslim Anglo-European self. She argues that the representation of the *burqa* is "about the cultural representation of the West to *itself* by way of

3. Ibid., 72.

4. Ibid., 74.

5. Ibid., 73.

6. Jasmine Zine, "Between Orientalism and Fundamentalism: The Politics of Muslim Women's Feminist Engagement," *Muslim World Journal of Human Rights* 3/1 (2006) article 5, 1.

7. Asma Barlas, "Does the Qur'an Support Gender Equality? Or, Do I Have the Autonomy to Answer This Question?," keynote delivered at the University of Groningen, Nov. 24, 2006; http://asmabarlas.com/PAPERS/Groningen_Keynote.pdf.

a detour through the other."[8] And the other pays a price for this detour since it requires that she be "made lacking what the subject has [but also made] . . . threatening to the stable world of the subject by her radical difference." The Other is thus always already "born accused."[9] Both in the United States and in Europe, we find evidence of the production of images and rhetoric leveled against Muslims to drive home in the public mind the notion that Muslims are a threat. We see such frames at work when Muslim female schoolchildren may no longer wear the veil at school or Muslim women wear the *niqāb* (face veil) in public in France. Under cover of upholding secularism or laïcité lurks the larger fear of the threat of militant Islamist fundamentalism marching into France posing as veiled girls and women, reminiscent of the days when the Battle of Algiers was fought with weapons concealed under the all-enveloping Algerian Muslim women's garb. The reality undergirding a woman's decision to veil might in fact be quite different. Here we might invoke Trinh T. Minh-ha's observation: "If the act of unveiling has a liberating potential, so does the act of veiling. It all depends on the context in which such an act is carried out, or more precisely, on how and where women see dominance. Difference should neither be defined by the dominant sex nor by the dominant culture. So when women decide to lift the veil one can say that they do so in defiance of their men's oppressive right to their bodies. But when they decide to keep or put on the veil they once took off they might do so to re-appropriate their space or to claim a new difference in defiance of genderless, hegemonic, centered standardization."[10]

The rising tide of Islamophobia in Europe includes in its discourse and representation the figure of a veiled woman. A striking example is a veiled Muslim woman accompanied by missile-like minarets in the posters circulated in Switzerland as the country moved to outlaw the building of minarets.[11]

8. Meyda Yegenoglu, *Colonial Fantasies: towards a Feminist Reading of Orientalism*, Cambridge Cultural Social Studies (Cambridge: Cambridge University Press, 1998), 39.

9. Ibid., 6.

10. Http://www2.ucsc.edu/culturalstudies/PUBS/Inscriptions/vol_3-4/minh-ha.html.

11. Http://www.dailymail.co.uk/news/article-1219048/Zurich-approves-poster-racist-image-Islam-ahead-Swiss-vote-allowing-minarets-mosques; html; http://www.msnbc.msn.com/id/34191036/ns/world_news-europe/t/

Even more disturbing is the well-funded campaign within the USA to "manufacture, produce, distribute, and mainstream an irrational fear of Islam and Muslims" detailed in a report produced by the Center for American Progress titled, *Fear, Inc: The Roots of the Islamophobia Network in America.*[12] Forty-one so-called "anti-Sharia" bills have been introduced in 22 states across the country.[13]

swiss-approve-ban-new-minarets/#.Ty1UM5jWb6E).

12. Wajahat Ali, Eli Clifton, Matthew Duss, Lee Fang, Scott Keyes, and Faid Shakir, *Fear, Inc: The Roots of the Islamophobia Network in America* (Washington, DC: Center for American Progress, 2011), 9.

13. Http://gaveltogavel.us/site/2012/05/14/bans-on-court-use-of-shariainternational-law-killed-in-alabama-legislatively-approved-in-kansas-withdrawn-in-new-jersey-sent-to-study-committee-in-new-hamsphire/.

Thus, we must approach feminist or popular calls to save Muslim women with some caution. As noted above, western feminism as such has historically sometimes been co-opted, first by colonial regimes, and subsequently by imperialist ambitions to justify incursions—economic, cultural, and military—into Muslim societies, under the rationale of bringing civilization under colonization, bringing trade and neo-liberal economic globalization under modernization, and bringing democracy under the War on Terror. Such interactions make the use of the term feminism, or ideas associated with it, such as autonomy, empowerment, and the like suspect to those critical of Western interventions. To use the term is also a highly political act for Muslim women, as it has come to suggest that those who use it agree both with the Western agendas operating in Muslim societies and with the secularist ideologies under-pinning much feminist thought.

And yet, Muslim gender scholar activists share with their Western, often white feminist counterparts, as well as with gender activists in other religious traditions, the desire to reclaim women's agency and par-ticipation in discourse production and social institutions. The concerns of Muslim scholar activists who re-examine the Qur'ān for purposes of gender justice are certainly feminist from the point of view of acknowl-edging the full and autonomous subjectivity of Muslim women, and of struggling for gender justice through examining foundational texts in Islam to determine Muslim women's status before God and in society. Their work attempts, as with feminists in other religious traditions, to move beyond patriarchal constructs by examining and interrogating androcentric interpretations of sacred texts and the inscription of such interpretations into social institutions such as legal regimes, especially as they relate to family law, spatial organization, and mosque participa-tion. Like other feminists, they also propose alternative interpretations as liberatory mediums through which to attain gender justice. Sartorial conventions are perhaps among the least of their concerns.

Capitalism Is a Good Thing, and Will Improve Life for Muslim Women

The disintegration of the European colonial empires created nation states accompanied by the Euro-American strategy of employing neo-liberal economic policies to facilitate the growth of global capitalism.

The post-colonial state was expected to adhere to Enlightenment principles and liberalism inherited from the colonial powers in promising liberty and equality to all its citizens, articulated in documents such as Thomas Paine's 1791 book titled *The Rights of Man* and the 1789 French pre-constitution document titled "The Declaration of the Rights of Man and of the Citizen." Upon garnering independence from colonial regimes, the postcolonial state was engaged in creating subjects that would participate in the increasingly growing transnational corporate regimes facilitated by the Bretton Woods institutions, a process we now call economic globalization. Valentine M. Moghadam, a sociologist who is also Chief of the Gender Equality and Development Section at UNESCO, defines globalization as "a complex economic, political, cultural, and geographic process in which the mobility of capital, organizations, ideas, discourses, and peoples has taken on an increasingly global or transnational form."[14] Joseph E. Stiglitz, a former World Bank chief economist and winner of the Nobel Prize in Economics, identifies the economic aspect of globalization as "the removal of barriers to free trade and the closer integration of national economies."[15] Pamela K. Brubaker, a Christian ethicist, sees present-day globalization as capitalist, whose distinctive feature is to utilize the means of production to produce goods that will generate profit, which in turn is reinvested to generate more production to produce more profit, resulting in the accumulation of capital.[16] She details how the Bretton Woods institutions were originally set up in 1944 to globalize the world's economies. Currently constituted by bodies such as the World Bank, the International Monetary Fund, and the World Trade Organization (added in 1995 to set and enforce the rules of trade), these institutions have adopted the economic policy of neo-liberalism and a free market, which Brubaker pithily summarizes thus: "The market is to make major social and political decisions. The state should voluntarily reduce its role in the economy. Corporations are to have complete freedom. Unions are to be restrained and citizens given much less rather than more social

14. Valentine M. Moghadam, *Globalizing Women: Transnational Feminist Networks* (Baltimore: Johns Hopkins University Press, 2005), 35.

15. Joseph E. Stiglitz, *Globalization and Its Discontents* (New York: Norton, 2003), ix.

16. Pamela K. Brubaker, *Globalization at What Price? Economic Change and Daily Life* (Cleveland: Pilgrim, 2001), 18.

protection."[17] As Brubaker explains, three policies followed from the adoption of neo-liberalism: deregulation, privatization, and liberalization, that were packaged together with structural adjustment programs and an emphasis on export-led growth as conditions for International Monetary Fund and World Bank loans. The idea behind this neo-liberal market capitalism, as it has come to be known, was that it would lift the world out of poverty by enabling all people to participate in the creation of wealth. What this means is that deregulation eliminates the control of the state over economic and financial transactions, allowing the market to function freely. Doing so allows the forces of supply and demand to regulate production and increase economic prosperity, and thereby, in the words of Adam Smith, "lift all boats," that is, raise the fortunes of the rich and the poor alike. Privatization shifts the control of public enterprises to the private sector, sometimes to ill effect, as witnessed in California in 2001 when Enron was allowed to take over the energy sector. Liberalization calls for countries to dismantle protective tariffs, giving up domestic control over trade and finance, and allowing foreign banks to own key economic institutions such as national banks, thus taking away any barriers to foreign investment. It should also be noted, in Stiglitz's words, that Western countries "pushed poorer countries to eliminate trade barriers, but kept up their own barriers, preventing developing countries from exporting their agricultural products and so depriving them of desperately needed export income."[18] Countries that resist such policies are simply disciplined through the removal of aid and foreign investment and the refusal to trade with them, in other words, they face economic ostracization. The alternative to such ostracization is, to put it somewhat bluntly, economic exploitation of the poorer countries by the richer countries.

However, instead of eradicating poverty as the Bretton Woods institutions were meant to do through their systems of loans and their policies on trade, the effects on non-first world nations have been somewhat mixed. Industrial and corporate elites have accumulated capital while the middle class has been handicapped through a shrinking economy and the poor have grown exponentially poorer through dispossession and labor exploitation. This holds for countries as well as individuals. A study released in 2006 based on incomes for the year 2000 asserts

17. Ibid., 27.

18. Stiglitz, *Globalization and Its Discontents*, 6.

that the richest 1% of the 3.7 billion adults in the world owned 40% of global wealth; the richest 2% owned 51%; and the richest 10% owned 85% of global wealth—and these rich are to be found primarily in the United States, Europe, and high-income Asian countries such as Japan (and now, in the rapidly growing economies of China and India). The bottom half of adults in the world earned barely 10% of global income in 2000, whereas the top 10% earned 50%.[19] To put this another way, 3 billion people live on less than 2 dollars a day, and the GDP of the 48 poorest countries is less than the wealth of the three richest people in the world. Not surprisingly, 51% of the world's 100 wealthiest bodies are corporations.[20] Moreover, countries that apply for loans from the World Bank and the International Monetary Fund are often subjected to structural adjustment programs (SAPs). The stated aims of such "adjustments" are to enhance a country's economic security by increasing the privatization of key governmental sectors, including social services, and to increase foreign investment by reducing trade barriers and providing a more malleable workforce, all the while reducing public expenditures. Such measures are intended to lead to a decline in state-supported services associated with a welfare state. In this respect, a form of political globalization is underway as the state's autonomy is undermined by the ideologies underpinning economic globalization. Cultural globalization, aptly termed McDonaldization, accompanies both economic and political globalization as homogenous goods become identified internationally as objects of consumption, and move into becoming symbols of power, offering a cosmopolitan, pluralistic, and hybridized cultural diversity as cultural exchanges are made.

The question that needs to be asked is how economic globalization affects women, and how globalization in its multiple facets—economic, political, and cultural—connects to religion. Valentine M. Moghadam observes that economic globalization has generated jobs for women in production arenas, enabling "women in many developing countries to earn and control income and to break away from the hold of patriarchal structures, including traditional household and familial relations."[21]

19. Duangkamon Chotikapanich, D. S. Prasada Rao, William E. Griffiths, and Vicar Valencia, "Global Inequality: Recent Evidence and Trends," Research Paper No. 2007/01, UNU-WIDER, World Institute for Development Economics Research, United Nations University, 15.

20. Http://www.globalissues.org/TradeRelated/Facts.asp.

21. Moghadam, *Globalizing Women*, 37.

However, these benefits are far outweighed by the disadvantages that accrue to women. Apart from the low wages, poor working conditions, and the lack of security and benefits that accompany many of the production-sector jobs opened up for women, especially in export processing zones, unemployment figures for women are still higher than those of men. Meanwhile, women's participation in informal sectors is increasing, as is trafficking in women and the feminization of poverty. In addition, countries that face structural adjustment programs (SAPs) are forced to cut government expenditure on social, health, and educational programs as these are privatized, leaving such programs to the mercy of the market and out of reach of the poor. Such SAPs have been shown to have an adverse effect on women as both men and women lose jobs in a declining economy, leaving women "to bear most of the responsibility of coping with increased prices and shrinking incomes, as women were the ones largely responsible for household budgeting and maintenance . . . the policies [of SAPs] contained an implicit and unspoken assumption of the elasticity of women's labor time, or the idea that women would always fill the gap created by public expenditure cuts in health and social services."[22] Arguably, SAPs have increased unequal gender relations between men and women, as they tend to favor men and income-earning adults.

The effects of economic globalization are further compounded by cultural globalization that, homogenizing even as it hybridizes, elicits nativist resistance to what is often perceived as the powerful onslaught of Westernization that threatens to destroy indigenous culture and identity. As Bayes and Tohidi observe, ". . . thanks in part to globalization, women's movements for equal rights and feminists from different parts of the world have brought their forces together through international and global forums like the UN conferences and growing transnational NGO networking. At the same time, the various conservative religious forces have formed united blocks against the implementation of equal rights . . . Women, whether feminist or not, face neopatriarchal conservative forces that operate through religious states or new religio-political movements known as communalism, fundamentalism, and Islamism."[23] The universalizing discourse of emerging states, seen as "the central site

22. Ibid., 39.

23. Jane H. Bayes and Nayereh Tohidi, eds., *Globalization, Gender, and Religion* (New York: Palgrave, 2001), 7–8.

of 'hegemonic masculinity,'"[24] has, according to Etienne Balibar, suffered from the "practical and ideological sexism (sic) as a structure of interior exclusion generalized to the whole society."[25] As Kaplan et al point out, however, "the woman/feminine signifier continues to serve as an alibi or figure of resistance in the fraternal struggles for control of the nation state and the national project. . . ."[26] Such an "'essential woman' (raced or not) becomes the national iconic signifier for the material, the passive, and the corporeal, to be worshipped, protected, and controlled by those with the power to remember and to forget, to guard, to define, and re-define. . . ."[27] In the case of Muslim post-colonial states women's equality has not been guaranteed by the state despite its universalizing language concerning the rights and protections afforded to all citizens. On the other hand, women have been identified as symbolizing and embodying the values of the nation both by the state and by fundamentalist political groups regardless of whether they align with or, in various degrees, challenge the state for political hegemony.

Fundamentalism is on the rise in every religious tradition despite the global perception that it is solely an Islamic issue. However, religious fundamentalism is not alone in mounting simultaneously a resistance to globalization while re-inscribing patriarchal control over women. In his book titled *Jihad vs. McWorld*, Benjamin Barber uses the term *jihad* as shorthand to describe religious fundamentalism, disintegrative tribalism, ethnic nationalisms, and similar kinds of identity politics carried out by local peoples "to sustain solidarity and tradition against the nation-state's legalistic and pluralistic abstractions as well as against the new commercial imperialism of McWorld."[28] Islamist movements deliver social services where local or state governments are unwilling or unable to do so. Either they are unwilling because the marketization of social services dictates that citizens pay for social services, or local and state governments are rendered unable to do so through Structural Adjustment Policies imposed as conditionalities accompanying World Bank or International Monetary Fund loans. Additionally, such loan interest

24. Quoting Connell 1987, in Carin Kaplan et al., eds., *Between Woman and Nation: Nationalisms, Transnational Feminisms, and the State*, 1.

25. Quoting Balibar 1994, 57, in Kaplan et al., eds., *Between Woman and Nation*, 1.

26. Kaplan et al., eds., *Between Woman and Nation*, 6.

27. Ibid., 10.

28. Benjamin Barber, *Jihad vs. McWorld* (New York: Times Books, 2001), 232.

repayment structures draw away from resources for job creation and so-cial services including health and education. Often, Islamist movements are the only viable instrument for articulating political opposition to the country's established government. In this counter-narrative, Islamist political parties accuse the state of being co-opted by Western economic policies and thereby failing to create a sound and healthy society, which they argue must be one based on Islamic principles.

Unfortunately, rather than formulating alternative economic policies that would address the inequities brought about by free-market capitalism and transnational corporations' assault on labor, or seeking to uphold and facilitate genuine democratic principles and practices, nativist resistance movements such as Islamic fundamentalism, more accurately described as Islamist movements, tend to focus their energies on providing social safety net services and on undermining their local governments by campaigning on a platform that asserts that "Islam is the solution," that is, governance according to Islamic law, popularly known as *shari'ah* (more accurately, *fiqh*). Such governance seems to be heavily weighted in favor of concern with "identity, morality, and the family. This preoccupation places a heavy burden on women, who are seen as the bearers of tradition, religiosity, and morality, and as the re-producers of the faithful. Such views have profound effects on women's legal status and social positions, especially when fundamentalist views are successfully inscribed in constitutions, family laws, penal codes, and other public policies."[29]

However, a positive result of the privations brought about by neo-liberal economic policies and structural adjustment programs on women has been the formation of feminist or women's organizations. These have increasingly become transnational in their concerns, col-laboration, and resulting strategies aimed at achieving social, gender, and environmental justice. Aptly termed "globalization from below," Moghadam points to social organizations created by labor, feminists, and environmentalists as the key agents of anti-capitalist protest op-position to the "globalization from above."[30] Such organizations have also sought to critique the "patriarchal nationalistic" or the "patriarchal religious" ideologies and practices of their politicians.[31]

29. Moghadam, *Globalizing Women*, 47.
30. Ibid., 30–32.
31. Ibid., 102.

The foregoing brief remarks on globalization and its impact on women are offered by way of contextualizing the effects of globalization on women, including Muslim women. Their responses to it, whether expressed in religious terms or not, offer an arena for constructive interfaith work. It is clear that globalization has brought with it many benefits "from above" with respect to opening up employment and trade opportunities on a massive scale, and facilitated in some cases a generation of wealth that has trickled down to ordinary citizens, thereby enabling greater freedom of choice raising the standard of living. However, by and large, such small gains have come at a tremendous cost to those who do not constitute the elite, especially in developing countries (often termed countries at the periphery).

Islam is a Misogynist Religion/Secularism is Essential for Achieving Feminist Goals

One of the debates in Feminist Studies centers around the question of whether it is possible to be religious and a feminist. In part this is so because religions have, by and large, authorized the subjugation of women in the name of God and of the head of the household. As a result, Western feminism has adopted secularism as an underlying philosophy and approach both in its critique of ideological formations that relegate women to a lesser place in the human spectrum, and in its struggle for women's rights across the globe. The issue is further exacerbated in our current climate, where anxieties over the growth of Muslim populations in Western countries and the rise in Islamist ideologies, coupled with a post-9/11 fear of what radical Muslims can do infects any analysis of the situation of Muslim women.

By contrast, some examples follow to illustrate that although the Islamic cultural and legal legacy may provide some impediments to the full realization of women's potential or to gender justice, Muslim women themselves are in fact turning to their religious tradition to argue, on its own terms, that gender inequity is by no means Islamic. For instance, the noted legal scholar, the late Louise Halper, engages a discussion of Islamic law in the context of Iranian women's activism to determine whether democratic change is possible within Islamic law. Interrogating the widely held view that Muslim women "benefit from a regime of secular law and suffer under religious law,"[32] Halper points out that the situation of women under Islamic law in Iran is quite comparable to that of Turkish women under secular Turkish law and not at all like that of women under Taliban-inflected Islamic law in Afghanistan. Rather, she argues, a more compelling determinant of women's status may, in fact, be "the salience of women to the political process and their active involvement in it,"[33] a hypothesis that is tested in conjunction with laws on marriage and divorce in Iran. Noting the strides that have been made in Iranian women's literacy rates, school and university enrollments, fertility decreases, and employment increases in the two decades between 1980 and 2000, Halper asks how such data are compatible with the reinstitution of Islamic law, and what role women have played therein.

Since the law of marriage and divorce exercises a huge impact on the lives of women, Halper focuses on two legislative innovations occurring in 1993 and 1996 to the Divorce Reform Law of 1989, between Ayatollah Khomeini's death in 1989 and Mohammad Khatami's inception as president of the Republic of Iran in 1997. A rich historical summary of the law of marriage and divorce pre- and post-Revolution illustrates the strategies women began to utilize once Khomeini reinstituted Islamic family law. Often they used the *mahr*, a predetermined sum to be paid to the wife in the eventuality of the husband's death or divorce, to negotiate a more favorable situation than they were entitled to under the law. The indigence into which newly divorced women were placed in cases where the *mahr* was practically worthless also motivated attempts by the women's press and women's organizations to draw attention to the issue. In response to such realities, Khomeini added in 1982 a provision in the marriage contract that a wife should receive half her husband's wealth upon divorce. Halper traces the new interpretive moves made by clerics attempting to reconcile feminism with Islam, whose work was published in such women's magazines as *Zanan*, and by women members of the Majles, the Iranian parliament, who sought to find religiously legal ways to address inequities experienced by women under the Iranian Islamic marital regime.

Halper's examination of the political education and participation of women before, during, and after the Iranian Revolution reveals that

32. Louise A. Halper, "Law and Iranian Women's Activism," in Zayn R. Kassam, ed., *Women and Islam* (Santa Barbara, CA: Praeger ABC-Clio, 2010), 3.

33. Ibid.

Islamist women, although they subscribed to the notion that "women's primary roles were in the family, also supported women who wanted or needed to work outside the home" and "became advocates for interpretations of the *sharī'a* more open to the concerns of modernist women."[34] The participation of women in the war effort during the Iran-Iraq War as well as in the labor force during and after the war led to the call for overt government support for the promotion of women's social participation and to the subsequent formation of institutions establishing a direct connection between the government and women's issues. The successes achieved by women after the Iranian Revolution demonstrate that democratic change is indeed possible under Islamic law. As the Iranian Parliament took up the issue of the lack of support for divorced women, women members and their male allies were able to come up with a religiously acceptable solution that relied on the concept of *mu'amalat*, or the social contract, which can be understood as the duties people owe to one another. Embedded within this notion is the idea of *ujrat al-mithāl*, that people should be fairly compensated for their labor, provided the labor is not coerced but is voluntarily provided. As Halper notes,

> Although the marriage contract commits the wife to compensate her husband with her obedience and sexual and reproductive services in return for his maintenance of her, it does not require her to keep house or nurse children. Yet most women do so. Thus, they are entitled to be compensated for this work, should they demand it, as they might do upon divorce. Such a provision was added to the 1991 divorce law at the end of 1992, as another judicially cognizable claim a divorced woman would have upon her husband. This time, the Majles [Iranian Parliament] not only required that the form contract include the provision that the wife was due her wages in case of divorce but also made it possible for a woman married under the old form of contract to get wages for housework, implied into the old contract judicially, if a court found she had not agreed to contribute her work without pay.[35]

A second example may be found in the research conducted by Azza Basarudin, who examines Malaysian Sunni Muslim women's

34. Ibid., 12.

35. "Determination of Wages for Work Done," *Zan-e Ruz*, Dec. 18, 1993, quoted in Halper, "Law and Iranian Women's Activism," 9.

praxis to determine how women balance their religion with the demands of a rapidly changing world. Taking as her case study the Malaysian Muslim professional women's organization named Sisters in Islam
(SIS), Basarudin argues that "their intellectual activism is a contested
site of alternative knowledge production in (re)claiming their faith to
(re)imagine a transformative Muslim *umma* (community) inclusive of
women's concerns, experiences and realities."[36] The author suggests that
the strategy employed by Sisters in Islam constitutes a faith-centered
intellectual activism, which draws upon the sources of the Islamic tradition as well as the larger human rights discourse to effect a "reform from
within."[37] She invokes and builds upon Abdullahi Ahmed An-Na'im's
concept of cultural mediation to show how Sisters in Islam brings the
local into conversation with the transnational in order to campaign for
women's rights within a specifically postcolonial Malaysian Muslim
public sphere.

The politicization of Islam in the public sphere in response to the
British colonial legacy of "economic divide, ethnic distrust, and political discontent"[38] led to an Islamic revivalism that brought in its wake
the Arabization of Malaysian Islam, including gender relations. Women
have steadily been incorporated into the economy commencing with
Prime Minister Mahathir bin Mohamad's development agenda that
brought educational and economic opportunities to women. However,
increasing Islamization in the form of "the rising trend of the total-
izing discourse of conventional Islam"[39] has increased surveillance of
women's comportment and dress, as well as calling for a return to family
values that promote veiling, gender segregation, the erosion of women's
rights under Islamic family law, and subsuming women's rights under
family and national development. Caught in the larger political struggle
for hegemonic rule, Malay Muslim women have become emblematic of
the purity of Malay culture and Malaysian Islam and are thus subject to

36. Azza Basarudin, "In Search of Faithful Citizens in Postcolonial Malaysia: Islamic Ethics, Muslim Activism, and Feminist Politics," in Zayn R. Kassam, ed., *Women
and Islam*, 104.

37. Ibid., 95.

38. Ibid., 97.

39. Ibid., 99.

intense scrutiny, policing, and legislation with a larger context of "racial, ethnic, and religious tension, factionalist politics, and state repression."[40]

It is in this context that Sisters in Islam was formed to address biases toward women in Islamic family law. Under the guidance of Amina Wadud, a noted Muslim American scholar of gender relations in Islam, a group of professional women went back to the text of the Qur'an to understand how this foundational Islamic scripture understood gender and, moreover, what tools were available from within the Islamic tradition for the realization of gender justice. Basarudin traces the process whereby Sisters in Islam developed various strategies to address gender inequality in the specifically Malaysian context, albeit with a transnational consciousness of gender issues in various Muslim societies. A key strategy has been to develop and draw upon hermeneutical recovery projects aimed at reexamining patriarchal monopolies on religious knowledge and gender constructions. The revival and reform of Islamic knowledge is brought to the public sphere through conferences, workshops, legal clinics, and the like. Doing so creates a more informed and hence responsible and responsive citizenry able to bring faith to bear on the challenges of globalization, especially insofar as these relate to and impact gender and gendered practices. Such efforts are further undergirded by publications ranging from press releases to letters to newspaper editors, legal memoranda, working papers, and scholarly books. In addition, Sisters in Islam has developed an international profile, thereby encouraging a sharing and enriching of resources and strategies beyond the local to the global.

The connection of praxis to theory is nowhere more readily seen than in the legal and sociocultural regimes that govern the lives of women, which in Malaysia, as in most Muslim majority countries, are informed and legitimated by religious interpretations. Thus, Basarudin pays special attention to polygamy-monogamy campaigns and moral policing initiatives and to the role that Sisters in Islam has played and continues to play in bringing gender justice to bear on these issues within the context of Islamic family law. Challenges to Sisters in Islam's legitimacy and authority are to be expected; however, its work must be seen, Basarudin argues, as "fracturing" conventional Islamic hegemony, that it "is seeping through the cracks to rupture the delicate relations of

40. Ibid., 100.

power."[41] Indeed, Sisters in Islam's intellectual activism may be squarely placed within the stream of recovery projects that are grounded in a belief in Islam's inherent gender egalitarianism, given its moral and ethical vision. As a specific example of their success, in 1990, Sisters in Islam published a booklet titled, "Are Muslim Men Allowed to Beat Their Wives?"[42] resulting from five years' worth of conferences and workshops on the issue of domestic violence. They then coordinated with other women's groups to meet with the Federal Government's Religious Department, and eventually proposed a Domestic Violence Act that was prepared for the cabinet in March 1994. Although it passed in the parliament, implementation of the bill kept stalling, but, after 11 years of workshops, campaigns, negotiations, and re-draftings, the Act was implemented on June 1, 1996.

Finally, one may turn to the work of Sherine Hafez. In Hafez's 2003 study of two Islamist women's organizations in Cairo, Egypt, titled *The Terms of Empowerment: Islamic Women Activists in Egypt*, she notes that the women involved in these organizations "were united around the common goal of perfecting themselves as means of gaining proximity to God,"[43] while their activities comprised preaching, giving religious lessons, teaching illiterate girls, and working for philanthropic causes. Her study attempts to show that even though Islamists are perceived as opposing women's liberation in Egypt, Islamic women's activism has produced a movement that redefines women's social roles in placing women in the public sphere. Although they are driven by the desire to be closer to God, their activities "dismantle the myths that have impeded the participation of women in the religious, social and political arenas of the country."[44] The paradox here lies in these women acceding to ritual forms of behavior and male authority in their search for religious perfection, while nonetheless their activities are aimed at welfare for women and society leading to forms of empowerment for the women concerned. Noting that Islamist women activists pose a serious challenge to researchers because they do not subscribe to a feminist agenda,

41. Ibid., 116.

42. Http://sistersinislam.org.my/sismall/product_info.php?products_id=43; the book is currently out of print.

43. Sherine Hafez, *The Terms of Empowerment: Islamic Women Activists in Egypt* (Cairo: American University of Cairo Press, 2003), 3.

44. Ibid., 4.

Hafez found that for these women, "Islam, like feminism is employed as a framework for women who struggle to seek improvements in society [but in this case additionally] as means of gaining higher levels of religiosity and proximity to God."[45]

However, as Hafez notes, "a true understanding of women's position and activism in Muslim societies cannot be reached by focusing solely on Islamic ideology or socioeconomic processes or by employing universalistic feminist theories."[46] Rather, Muslim women's status must be "contextualized within the historical development of anti-colonial nationalism, state building projects, and nationalism."[47] In her examination of these contextual factors in Egypt, Hafez finds that Islamic women are at the forefront of Islamic revival:

> The phenomenon of veiling and the adoption of the Islamic dress code prevail among the majority of urban women. Many women find their calling in an Islamic ideology that promises not only a worldly status of respectability, but also an eternal value to their good deeds in heaven. Islamic activism is to many women the most easily accessible social means to improve themselves, enhance their social status and instate improvements in Egyptian society . . . In short, Islamism acts as an undiscriminating bridge between the spiritual and the social for women, where many Muslim women of all backgrounds find a place.[48]

Indeed, as Hafez notes, "the women's Islamic movement has cut clear across class barriers, and more importantly provides a sense of solidarity and belonging that no other movement has afforded women in Egypt before."[49] Hafez considers how mosques and Private Voluntary Organizations (PVOs) "act as centers of pedagogy to produce Islamically disciplined women,"[50] where sermons and lessons emphasize how women are to interact with others with respect to their dress, greeting, talking, entertaining, all the while "tapping into one's inner resources and strengths to rise above the mundane of metropolitan life."[51] Through

45. Ibid., 17.
46. Ibid., 21.
47. Ibid.
48. Ibid., 32–33.
49. Ibid., 59.
50. Hafez, *Terms of Empowerment*, 67.
51. Ibid.

disciplining the body in order to gain mastery over the self, turning that self into service to others, and thereby hoping to attain perfection of religiosity and piety in order to draw closer to God, such women are empowered:

> Just as prayer disciplines the soul, fasting tames unchecked bodily desires. During Ramadan, Muslims abstain from food, drink, and sexual relations. It is a time that stretches from sunrise to sundown, during which bodily discipline regulates the spirit of the Muslim and his or her control over the body. Once more, this is a practice that disciplines as it empowers . . . By perfecting religious practices such as prayer, fasting and subscribing to Islamically informed social and behavioral models, women reinforce mastery of religion in a society in which Islamism commands attention in the public sphere.[52]

Such empowerment comes, however, through the reinforcing of traditional gender constructions but at the same time undermining them by emphasizing both the equality and the complementarity of the roles of men and women. The growing impact of the Muslim Brotherhood's teachings in various Muslim-majority Arab nations links women's domesticity and social welfare activities to "a love of God."[53] Domesticity and social activism outside the home are not restricted by class, as women of all social strata participate in and attend the activities organized by the PVOs, including sermons. At one such sermon to women from the lower socioeconomic level, women were counseled to be "instrumental in dealing with today's problems of poverty and ignorance" while being told that work "is not just employment for a wage, it can also be voluntary or charity work."[54]

Hafez notes that the "absence of a notion of an agent who pursues a deliberate and conscious attempt at actively seizing opportunities to instigate change and placing this agency instead in the hands of God is a characteristic of Islamic women's activism."[55] Such a displacement of agency was, for instance, employed by women at a PVO who ran into difficulties with the men in the mosque adjacent to their space, who, envious of their success, accused them of embezzling funds and de-

52. Ibid., 68–69.
53. Ibid., 71.
54. Ibid., 73.
55. Ibid., 75.

manded a payment. Utilizing the strategy of articulating that they were "working for God," they were able to bring the men around (making a voluntary contribution to the men's causes also helped) and to carve out a legitimate social space for their activities aimed at helping others, thus fulfilling their self-styled mandate to become better Muslims.[56]

In ably making the case that "Islamic women create alternative forms of empowerment while remaining embedded within structures that appear to support their domination,"[57] Hafez draws upon Foucault's notion of the relational individual—according to which "the subject is not merely subjugated in relations of power, but is also formed by power."[58] While Islamist women "submit themselves to structures of authority that privilege men, they paradoxically empower themselves in dealing with men by acting in accordance with prevalent norms of ideal female behavior."[59] In her more recent work on the activism of Islamist women tackling poverty in Egyptian villages where village women are taught literacy, hygiene, and microfinance, Hafez further develops the point that the Islamist women themselves are formed under the regimes of a secularizing, modernizing and liberalizing state and integrate these values into their Islamic vision of social development:

> In their attempts to introduce the villagers of Mehmeit to sustainable development, the women activists drew on their own desires and ideals . . . [they] regarded these development schemes to improve the villagers' education, independence, and sustainability as a form of Islamic worship . . . The social development project in [the village of] Mehmeit offered a range of possibilities for viewing the concomitance of religion and secularism.[60]

Hafez carefully distinguishes between Western and Middle Eastern understandings of patriarchy, agency, and autonomy to explore and substantiate her argument that women involved in Islamist movements succeed in drawing upon cultural norms—indeed, embodying them through technologies of self—to challenge male domination over society

56. Ibid., 78.

57. Ibid., 80.

58. Ibid.

59. Ibid.

60. Sherine Hafez, *An Islam of Her Own: Reconsidering Religion and Secularism in Women's Islamic Movements* (New York: New York University Press, 2011), 149–50.

and to address conditions that undermine women such as illiteracy, lack of health care, and poverty, and to influence decision making.[61] Hafez' work thereby makes a significant contribution to understanding how the models employed by Western feminist discourse that view Islamist women as subjugated and repressed miss their mark, and instead offers insights into the production of the Islamist woman as subject. Clearly, women-centered activism does not need to reject its cultural and religious norms in order to be effective. Hitherto understood as replicating, reproducing, and reinforcing uneven systems of power through their commitment to male-centric understandings of Islam, Hafez here shows in the manner of Deniz Kandiyoti that women bargain with patriarchy in ways that both uphold unequal power relations and undermine it while substantively empowering women in various social, economic, and legal arenas.

She notes that despite the superficial view that Islamist women are driven solely through religious directives and male-centric cultural codes, these women are, "not caught between the two polarizing forces of a modernizing state and an Islamic return to tradition. Instead, women who participate in Islamic movements normalize these distinctions in their practices . . . Even though their goals and identities are based on an established religious conviction, Islamic women activists also accept secular liberal views that often see the individual as both free and independent but simultaneously acting according to divine will and sovereignty."[62] The value of Hafez' work for gaining a more profound understanding of Islamist women's activities, not to mention for fundamentalist women's activities across religious traditions, is not to be understated.

Concluding Remarks

In conclusion, then, one might ask, how interreligious dialogue involving Muslim women changes in light of the three myths discussed here? How do we navigate between the incessant production of images and rhetoric that continue the trope of saving Muslim women within the context of realpolitik realities of a "war on terror," which in part masks both imperial ambitions and wars to ensure access to resources? How

61. Ibid., 100–101.
62. Ibid., 161.

do we, as feminists and as scholars of religion, undertake dialogues that are mindful of the consequences for women, as well as their societies, of unbridled capitalism in the name of globalization, and couched as an instrument through which to spread democracy? How do we move to positions of resistance to the upward flow of wealth and the depletion of social and environmental safeguards for all? And finally, how do we get past the representations of Islam as misogynist, and the veil and religiosity as anti-feminist, to grapple with the very real issues that Muslim women face, that they have defined for themselves and are evident in the activist work in which they engage? How do we get past the secular/religious divide to consider how women globally draw upon cultural resources available to them to address gender inequities and to foster gender development? Through these three examples, I have attempted to show, as Isobel Coleman in her study of women in Muslim societies (Saudi Arabia, Iraq, Iran, Afghanistan, and Pakistan) notes, that progressive Muslim men and women, whom she terms "quiet revolutionaries,"[63] are drawing upon sources of Islamic authority, discursive institutions, practices such as *ijtihad*, and faith-based activism to change the terms of religious debate, and to fight for women's rights within Islam instead of against it. Getting past these three myths opens up the field for some very rich interreligious dialogue as it would allow for such dialogue to be grounded in an understanding of the very real issues Muslim women face due to our global interconnections.

63. Http://www.isobelcoleman.com/books/ in connection with Isobel Coleman, *Paradise Beneath Her Feet* (New York: Random House, 2010).

8

The Qur'anic Rib-ectomy

Scriptural Purity, Imperial Dangers, and Other Obstacles to the Interfaith Engagement of Feminist Qur'anic Interpretation

Aysha Hidayatullah

The ordinary Muslim believes, as seriously as the ordinary Jew or Christian, that Adam was God's primary creation and that Eve was made from Adam's rib. While this myth has obvious rootage in the Yahwist's account of creation in Genesis 2:18–24, it has no basis whatever in the Qur'an, which in the context of human creation speaks always in completely egalitarian terms.

—Riffat Hassan, "Muslim Women and Post-Patriarchal Islam"[1]

Beginning in the 1990s, pioneering scholars of feminist Qur'anic interpretation re-read the Qur'an's story of Adam and Eve to argue for the full moral and spiritual equality of men and women in Islam. The establishment of this Qur'an-based principle of egalitarianism was significant not only for its role in ushering in a new era of Muslim feminist readings of the Qur'an, but also for another reason rarely discussed: its negative impact upon the possibilities for feminist Qur'anic interpretation's

1. Riffat Hassan, "Muslim Women and Post-Patriarchal Islam," in Paula M. Cooey et al., eds., *After Patriarchy: Feminist Transformations of the World Religions*, Faith Meets Faith (Maryknoll, NY: Orbis, 1991), 44.

engagement with Jewish and Christian feminist theologies. As the passage above indicates, the feminist reading of the Qur'anic Creation story relies in large part on the claim that its sexist interpretations result from the contamination of Qur'anic exegesis by erroneous Biblical traditions. This paper is an attempt to grapple with the hermeneutical strategy of "purifying" the Qur'an from Biblically influenced interpretations in order to yield feminist meanings from the Qur'an, along with other longstanding tensions framing the interaction of Muslim feminist interpretation of the Qur'an with Jewish and Christian feminist theologies.[2]

The decade after 9/11 saw a growing interest in interfaith dialogue among women in the U.S., particularly women of the so-called "Abrahamic" religions, as observed in the organizing of interfaith panels at major conferences such as the American Academy of Religion and in the publication of edited collections of Jewish, Christian, and Muslim women's scholarship.[3] The premise of these interactions was that an examination of the shared experiences of the "daughters of Sarah and Hagar" would yield enriching mutual engagement through a common interest in combating patriarchal dominance in Judaism, Christianity, and Islam. The reality of these interfaith endeavors, however, unfolded quite differently from this vision, in part because of the glossing over of at least three problems which I will touch on briefly: the phantom of colonial feminism that continues to stir Muslim defensiveness; the tokenizing and surface character of a number of multi-faith feminist conversations; and the cooptation of Muslim feminist thought as part of violent state agendas for "democratizing" the Muslim world. Also crucial to our understanding is an examination of Muslims' belief in the Qur'an's ascendency over the Bible, according to which the former

2. There are, of course, important tensions in dialogues between Muslim women and non-Jewish/Christian women, and this is certainly a matter of great concern, but unfortunately beyond the scope of this paper due to time constraints. Since Muslims see Islam as sharing a direct revelatory lineage with Judaism and Christianity, I have chosen to discuss relationships between feminists of the three religious groups.

3. For example, "Hagar, Sarah and Their Children: Jewish, Christian, and Muslim Women in Dialogue," held at the 2006 Annual Meeting of the American Academy of Religion in Washington, DC (sponsored by the Women in Religion Section), featuring Judith Baskin, Francine Cardman, Amina Wadud, Emilie M. Townes, and Phyllis Trible. Edited collections include: Phyllis Trible and Letty M. Russell, eds., *Hagar, Sarah, and their Children: Jewish, Christian, and Muslim Perspectives* (Louisville: Westminster John Knox, 2006); and Victoria Lee Erickson, Susan A. Farrell, eds. *Still Believing: Jewish, Christian, and Muslim Women Affirm Their Faith*, Faith Meets Faith (Maryknoll, NY: Orbis, 2005).

serves as the revelatory corrective and completion of the latter. An overview of these issues will provide the broader context for understanding Muslim feminist hermeneutics of the Qur'an inclined to notions of scriptural purity and apologia.

Qur'anic Ascendancy and Isra'iliyyat

Contemporary historians of the Qur'an have observed an inherent tension at play in the Qur'an's assertion that it is a continuation of God's revelation to Jews and Christians (referred to by the Qur'an as the "People of the Book," where "Book" refers to God's collective scriptural revelation). On the one hand, the Qur'an draws on the established authority and legitimacy of its scriptural precursors and emphasizes its common lineage with the Torah and Bible in order to persuade readers of its genuineness as God's revelation. On the other hand, it professes its unique veracity by claiming distinctive accuracy and ascendancy over previous revelations, which, it suggests, have been changed, distorted, or misinterpreted. The Qur'an thus asserts its authority by simultaneously aligning itself with *and* dissociating itself from the Torah and the Bible. This tension is apparent in numerous Qur'anic verses:

> 6:92 And this is a Book which We have sent down, bringing blessings, and confirming (the revelations) which came before it . . .

> 5:13–15 . . . They [the Children of Israel] change the words from their (right) places and forget a good part of the message that was sent them . . . And also from those who call themselves Christians, did We take a covenant, but they forgot a good part of the message that was sent them . . . O people of the Book! There has come to you our Messenger, revealing to you much that you used to hide in the Book, and passing over much (that is now unnecessary). There has come to you from Allah a (new) light and a perspicuous Book.[4]

This tension was of course translated into the interpretations of classical and medieval commentators of the Qur'an and appeared in a number of ways. As the Qur'an refers to numerous Biblical stories without

4. The translation of these verses is based on Yusuf Ali's translation of the Qur'an. 'Abdullah Yusuf 'Ali, *The Holy Qur'an: Text, Translation, and Commentary*, 4th ed. (Brentwood, MD: Amana, 1989).

supplying a complete narration of them, it assumes the reader's familiarity with those stories; thus an understanding of the Qur'an relies upon a basic knowledge of Biblical narratives. Therefore early commentators commonly employ Biblical sources in elaborating upon the meanings of Qur'anic narratives closely related to the Bible, and they make interpretive decisions about the discrepancies between Biblical and Qur'anic renditions of parallel stories. They often deduce significant doctrinal and theological principles in their readings of the Qur'an's *overt distinctions* from, or *additions* to, Biblical material. When it comes to the Qur'an's *silences* on certain details of parallel stories, commentators have a choice: they may either choose to adopt details and meanings from Biblical sources, or to invest Qur'anic silences with meanings that depart from the Biblical tradition.

According to the findings of recent scholarship, the incorporation of information from Biblical sources into the Islamic tradition was generally the *modus operandi* of the first Islamic century. Historians note the porous boundaries between Islam and its monotheistic precursors, allowing for the copious borrowing and assimilation of Jewish and Christian traditions into Islamic ones to the extent that it is difficult to identify a cohesive "Islam" clearly distinguishable from Judaism and Christianity until at least a century after the time of Muhammad.[5] The term *isra'iliyyat* has been used by Muslims (likely since the 10th century CE) to refer to sources of information directly or indirectly related to the Bible that were drawn upon by authorities of early Islam to elaborate Islamic doctrine and Qur'anic meanings.[6] The term has been used variously over time to refer to one or more of the following: historical accounts by Jews and Christians; material derived from the Hebrew and Christian Bibles; traditions on cosmogony and Biblical figures from Bible-related sources; and folklore on Biblical figures.[7] These materials might derive from translations of the Bible; Jewish and Christian exegesis; folklore and popular stories circulating in the Arabian Peninsula;

5. See for example Fred M. Donner, *Muhammad and the Believers: At the Origins of Islam* (Cambridge, MA: Belknap, 2010).

6. See Roberto Tottoli, "Origin of the term Isra'iliyyat in Muslim literature," *Arabica* 46 (1999) 195.

7. Ibid., 193; Gordon Newby, "Tafsir Isra'liyyat: The Development of Qur'an Commentary in Early Islam in Its Relationship to Judaeo-Christian Traditions of Scriptural Commentary," *Journal of the American Academy of Religion* 47, Thematic Issue S (1980) 686.

and apocryphal versions of Biblical stories.[8] These sources may have been transmitted into the Islamic traditions on the authority of Jewish and Christian converts to Islam, via Muslim inquiries with rabbis and priests, and in general through interactions with Jews and Christians in and around the Arabian peninsula.[9]

The use of *isra'iliyyat*, particularly in Qur'anic commentary, served both the practical purpose of aiding commentators in narrating gaps in the Qur'an's abbreviated text, as well as the symbolic purpose of providing the Islamic tradition with "external confirmation" of its revelatory genealogy.[10] However, in the fourteenth century CE, the term *isra'iliyyat* took on pejorative connotations. In his famous Qur'anic commentary, Ibn Kathir (d. 1373) criticizes the role of non-Islamic sources in corrupting the pure core of Islamic tradition, referring to the *isra'iliyyat* as objectionable sources of information.[11] This attitude toward the *isra'iliyyat* reflected the increasing insularity of the early medieval codification of Islamic doctrine. In coping with Islam's "heterogeneous origins," Islamic scholars selectively attributed authority to a limited number of early trusted Islamic figures from among the successors to the companions of the Prophet. This was an attempt to legitimize and authenticate the Islamic tradition's early borrowings from Jewish and Christian sources,[12] but it ultimately had the effect of drawing stricter boundaries around the properly "Islamic" tradition and casting suspicion upon all other usages of "non-Islamic" sources.

Modern Exegesis and Gender Discourses

In the modern period, anxieties about sources "external" to the Islamic tradition were compounded by Muslim responses to colonialism and modernity. During the era of European colonialism in the Muslim world, Muslims debated the place of rationality, science, and democracy in Islam. In the late nineteenth and early twentieth centuries, an

8. Michael Pregill, "Isra'iliyyat, Myth, and Pseudepigraphy: Wahb b. Munabbih and the Early Islamic Versions of the Fall of Adam and Eve," *Jerusalem Studies in Arabic and Islam* 34 (2008) 227.

9. Ibid., 230.

10. Newby, "Tafsir Isra'liyyat," 694.

11. Tottoli, "Origin of the Term Isra'iliyyat," 193–94.

12. Pregill, "Isra'iliyyat, Myth, and Pseudepigraphy," 220, 240.

intellectual trend known as Islamic modernism emerged whose proponents attempted to reconcile Islam with modern values, calling for modern Islamic reform rooted in Islamic authenticity. Modernists held that Islam was *already inherently* compatible with the trends of the European Enlightenment, particularly with scientific modes of thought, and they advocated "rational" interpretation of Islamic texts, arguing for its precedent in the heritage of authentic Islamic tradition. Such calls for rational interpretation were accompanied by an intensified rejection of *isra'iliyyat* sources.[13] Muhammad Abduh (d. 1905), one of the most influential thinkers of Muslim modernism around the turn of the twentieth century, is credited with reviving an adamantly negative stance on the use of *isra'iliyyat* in Qur'anic exegesis.[14] Abduh and his contemporaries deplored Qur'anic commentators' resort to reading miracles, fantastical legends, and other historically unverifiable information from Biblical sources into the text of the Qur'an, regarding them not only as unscientific, but also as extraneous and alien to the pure heritage of Islam. This position is thought in large part to be responsible for inspiring the widespread and enduring rejection of the *isra'iliyyat* among the majority of Qur'anic interpreters in the twentieth century and today.[15]

Also central to debates about Islam and modernity in the nineteenth and twentieth centuries were questions about the place of women in modern Muslim society. As has been extensively documented by historians of modern Islam,[16] modern discourse on Muslim women cast them as territorial objects in a battle between Western colonizers and reactionary Muslims, both of whom reduced Muslim women to the gatekeepers of Islamic cultural "essence." Colonial administrators and missionaries viewed Muslim practices of sex-segregation as barbaric, pointing to the treatment of Muslim women as evidence for the necessity of European "civilizing" missions in the Muslim world. The justification of colonial projects in the Muslim world using feminist claims evoked defensive responses to feminism among Muslims, who claimed women's place in society as a site for preserving the most sacred

13. Barbara Freyer Stowasser, *Women in the Qur'an, Traditions, and Interpretation* (New York: Oxford University Press, 1994), 24.

14. Tottoli, "Origin of the Term Isra'iliyyat," 208.

15. Ibid., 209.

16. See for example Leila Ahmed, *Women and Gender in Islam: Historical Roots of a Modern Debate* (New Haven: Yale University Press, 1992).

and deeply held values of Muslim culture and morality. The historical memory of feminism's association with colonial agendas in Muslim societies has had the overall effect of tarnishing and delegitimizing the indigenous feminist thought and activism of Muslim women, to the extent that Muslim communities today remain suspicious of calls for gender reform, viewing it as a foreign cultural import used in the service of brutal attacks upon Muslims. This history continues to hamper the widespread acceptance of feminist perspectives on the Qur'an despite their recent growth and influence, as many Muslims continue to bristle at any notion of feminism because of its violent past. It is in part due to this association with feminism that some Muslim women scholars may be reticent to engage in interfaith feminist conversations that do not account for feminism's violent colonial history in the Muslim world. Such discussions take for granted the benefits of feminism to religious communities, alienating Muslim women scholars with a different experience of feminism, not to mention perhaps further diminishing their credibility with Muslim audiences.

Contemporary Tensions in Dialogue

The problem of feminist encroachments upon Muslim women is also observed, albeit differently, in the context of contemporary women's interfaith dialogue. Many interfaith conversations often proclaim an Abrahamic or multi-faith scope without pursuing the deeper meanings and conflicts inherent in this gesture in the first place. Such gatherings presume that the benefit of interfaith dialogue among women is self-evident, and that the pursuit of feminist conversations across religious boundaries need not be questioned or defended, as if it is somehow naturally mutually beneficial to all its participants and altruistic in its results. Even the most basic metaphorical phrasing used to summon these gatherings fails to name the tensions that animate them. Take, for example, what has almost become cliché in interfaith gatherings of Muslim, Christian, and Jewish women: the invocation of the 'Sarah–Hagar' paradigm, which draws upon the memory of two figures whose stories are ensnared by rivalry rather than linked through some form of female solidarity.[17] And yet, the problem of Sarah and Hagar's dysfunc-

---

17. For further discussion of this topic, see Aysha Hidayatullah and Judith Plaskow, "Beyond Sarah and Hagar: Jewish and Muslim Reflections on Feminist Theology," in ,

tional relationship as a metaphor for coming together is virtually never a subject of conversation. The failure to acknowledge the tensions in this casually-invoked metaphor from the very start is perhaps a symbolic indicator of a larger, unnamed underlying problem: that it is in fact *not* entirely clear that interfaith dialogue in its current manifestations is a productive enterprise for Muslim women, or that it serves their interests without reproducing the same dynamics of power that feminism critiques.

We have all attended more than one multi-faith panel discussion and perused more than one edited volume that includes one Muslim contributor (or at most two) within a group of mostly Christian feminist voices. The *intent* behind the inclusion of Muslim voices is not tokenistic, though I would argue that its *function* almost always is. Indeed, good intentions matter little practically speaking when a persistent ignorance about basic tenets of Islam continues to guide discussions. The product of these conversations is more often than not a surface discussion that fails to seriously engage Muslim contributions, and that effectively (though again, not intentionally) treats Muslim women as placeholders for diversity slots in panels and volumes. It is likely because of such dynamics that Amina Wadud, a pioneering scholar of feminist Qur'anic interpretation, has confessed: "when I want to seriously challenge patriarchy from within my own faith tradition, I do not go to the Woman and Religion section of the AAR [American Academy of Religion]. They accept anything I say in a tokenistic fashion."[18]

Moreover, the power differentials between diverse women in such discussions are almost never confronted. Wadud observes that women's interfaith discussions have "reinforced . . . other hegemonies" such as Christocentrism and white privilege "at the expense of more comprehensive intellectual and political alliances against oppressions."[19] This is of particular concern to Muslim women in the current moment in light of the rampant racialization experienced by Muslim communities in the U.S. Here, it is perhaps helpful to draw a distinction between truly *inter*faith discussion, which readily and critically confronts power dynam-

Reza Aslan and Aaron Hahn Tapper, eds., *Muslims and Jews in America: Commonalities, Contentions, and* Complexities (New York: Palgrave Macmillan, 2011), 163–64.

18. Amina Wadud, "Roundtable Discussion: Feminist Theology and Religious Diversity," *Journal of Feminist Studies in Religion* 16/2 (2000) 94.

19. Amina Wadud, *Inside the Gender Jihad: Women's Reform in Islam* (Oxford: Oneworld, 2006), 122.

ics and disparities *between* women, and simply *multi*-faith discussion, which is characterized by unengaged and merely additive inclusion of Muslim/minority women in cross-religious conversations. In the latter, Muslim women are simply included in an effectively tokenistic manner without being engaged by informed conversation partners. In truly *inter*faith feminist conversations, an understanding of power relationships energizes exchanges, allowing participants to move beyond additive inclusion and shallow understandings.

Post-9/11: Disciplining Islam

For Muslim women, it is not only a lack of fully mutual engagement that has hampered meaningful interfaith exchange; there is also the much more serious problem of Muslim women scholars inadvertently contributing to the violent disciplining of Muslim communities by collaborating with Jewish and Christian feminist scholars, particularly after 9/11. As Kwok Pui-lan has rightly observed, surface interreligious dialogue may function as "a device used by . . . metropolitan centers to manage religious differences."[20] Interfaith dialogue involving Muslims is one such site for the U.S. State to manage and discipline forms of Islam that are not amenable to its global political agendas. Muslims who interact with supposedly less literalist and more woman-friendly religious populations of American Jews and Christians become perfect targets in reforming Islam "from the inside out" according to U.S. interests. Muslim women participating in feminist interfaith dialogue may be "co-opted into the government's political project of identifying 'moderate' and 'liberal' Muslims" in order to promote 'moderate' forms of Islam that do not pose a radical threat to U.S. geopolitical dominance.[21] For example, as Saba Mahmood has argued, the U.S. State has encouraged theological projects among Muslims "along the lines of the Protestant Reformation," endorsing and promoting the perspectives of Muslims employing approaches to the Qur'an that depart from notions of the text being the literal speech of God.[22] The work of Muslim feminist scholars

20. Kwok Pui-lan, *Postcolonial Imagination and Feminist Theology* (Louisville: Westminster John Knox, 2005), 203.

21. Juliane Hammer, "Identity, Authority, and Activism: American Muslim Women Approach the Qur'an," *The Muslim World* 98 (2008) 456.

22. Saba Mahmood, "Secularism, Hermeneutics, and Empire: The Politics of Islamic Reformation," *Public Culture* 18/2 (2006) 329.

is particularly useful in the service of such agendas, supplying the testimony of "insider" voices of "liberated" Muslim women whose treatment of the Qur'an appears to align with state interests. Thus, in participating in interfaith feminist discussions, Muslim women run the risk of inadvertently serving as spokespersons for political projects that violate Muslims' self-determination. In the current climate, Muslim women must proceed cautiously, carefully discerning exactly whose interests are being served in cross-religious conversations.

Feminist Interpretation of the Qur'an and the Creation Story

Thus far it has been my purpose to clarify the overall pressures and challenges faced by Muslim women scholars in engaging in interfaith conversation in order to provide the wider context for understanding feminist Qur'anic interpretation's postures toward Biblical material. Despite the tensions and power dynamics exhibited in their interfaith interactions, Muslim women have in fact steadily (and discreetly) drawn upon the works of Jewish and Christian feminist theologians for the past three decades, though without overtly acknowledging this. Like Jewish and Christian feminist theologies, the goal of feminist Qur'anic interpretation is the criticism of sexism and male normativity in textual exegesis. As I have discussed elsewhere, the bibliographies of Muslim feminist works reveal a knowledge of Christian and Jewish feminist writings, and their contents incorporate arguments and terms similar to those found in Jewish and Christian feminist works, though without drawing attention to those similarities.[23]

Riffat Hassan, the author of this paper's opening epigraph, appears in a number of her writings to have been significantly influenced by her dialogues with Jewish and Christian women beginning in 1979 and calls for the development of "feminist theology" in Islam. She writes: "In my judgment the importance of developing what the West calls feminist theology in the context of the Islamic tradition is paramount today."[24] Her work on the Qur'anic creation story likely inspired her study of Jewish and Christian feminists' readings of the Book of Genesis. She recalls,

23. See chapter 3 in Aysha A. Hidayatullah, *Feminist Edges of the Qur'an* (Oxford: Oxford University Press, forthcoming 2014).

24. Hassan, "Muslim Women," 43.

"As a result of my study and deliberation, I came to perceive that not only in the Islamic, but also in the Jewish and Christian traditions, there are three theological assumptions on which the superstructure of men's alleged superiority to women has been erected."[25] For Hassan, these assumptions are that the first woman (Eve) was created *from* and *for* the first man (Adam), and that woman caused man's fall from grace. The Qur'anic narrative of creation, she argues, contradicts all three assumptions. Here, I will argue that Hassan's engagement with feminist readings of the Bible in fact leads to an impasse rather than a partnership with Jewish and Christian feminist theologies.

The story of Adam and Eve is one of the occasions on which the Qur'an does not supply as many details as the Bible. It also refers to human creation more generally, without naming Adam and Eve, in verse 4:1: "Oh humankind! Reverence your Lord, who created you from a single soul [*nafs*], created from it its mate [*zawj*] and from the two scattered (like seeds) countless men and women."[26] Most of Hassan's argument relies on what this verse positively says about human creation in general terms; the rest of her argument is based on what the Qur'an does *not* say about Adam and Eve specifically. Pointing to verse 4:1, Hassan argues that woman and man are created in egalitarian terms, from a single *nafs*, or soul, at the same time. She asserts that the word *nafs* is conceptually neither male nor female (though grammatically feminine); thus there is no linguistic justification for attributing maleness to the *nafs* from which all of humankind originates (or for assuming that this original *nafs* is Adam).[27] Likewise, the *zawj*, or mate, partnered with the *nafs* is conceptually neither male nor female (though grammatically masculine), which also disrupts the assumption that the *zawj* of *nafs* is female (or Eve).[28] To rule out the possibility of man/Adam being God's first creation anywhere else in the Qur'an, Hassan points out that the word *ādam* "functions generally as a collective noun referring to *the*

25. Riffat Hassan, "Islam," in Arvind Shamra and Katherine K. Young, eds., *Her Voice, Her Faith: Women Speak on World Religions* (Boulder, CO: Westview, 2003), 228.

26. This translation is based on Yusuf Ali's translation of the Qur'an.

27. Riffat Hassan, "The Issue of Woman–Man Equality in the Islamic Tradition," in Leonard Grob et al., eds., *Women's and Men's Liberation: Testimonies of Spirit* (New York: Greenwood, 1991), 74; Hassan, "Muslim Women" 45.

28. Hassan, "The Issue," 72.

human (species) rather than to a male human being."[29] Finding no mention of Eve being created from Adam in the Qur'an, Hassan concludes: "In none of the thirty or so passages that describe the creation of humanity . . . is there any statement that could be interpreted as asserting or suggesting that man was created prior to woman or that woman was created from man."[30] Hassan asserts that according to the Qur'an, "Allah's original creation was undifferentiated humanity and not either man or woman;" in addition, the creatures who were to become man and woman "were made in the same manner, of the same substance, at the same time."[31] Thus, she finds the Qur'an to be contrary to the popular belief among Muslims that Eve was created from and for Adam. Finally, Hassan notes that the Qur'an does not treat Eve as the cause of Adam's temptation or some kind of "fall" of humankind. The text uses the dual form to refer to *both* Adam and Eve eating from the Tree of Knowledge and *both* being tempted by Satan; thus, in Hassan's assessment both bear equal responsibility for committing this sin in the Qur'anic narrative.[32] Moreover, God forgives both Adam and Eve, and the rest of humankind does not suffer for their sin.[33]

Hassan aims to distinguish the Qur'anic story of creation from a number of Hadith accounts (reports attributed to the Prophet and his companions) in which woman/Eve is created from the rib of man/Adam and tempts him to sin through her seductions. She argues that the circulation and popularity of Hadith reports that contradict the Qur'anic creation narrative are responsible for the general belief among Muslims "that women—who are inferior in creation (having been made from a crooked rib) and in righteousness (having helped Shaitan in defeating God's plan for Adam)—have been created mainly to be of use to men who are superior to them."[34] Hassan absolves the Qur'an of responsibility for such notions and instead faults the Hadith; she calls for the rejection of such Hadith reports, since the authority of the Qur'an supersedes

---

29. Hassan, "Muslim Women," 45.
30. Ibid., 44.
31. Hassan, "The Issue," 74, 77.
32. Hassan, "Muslim Women," 47, 49.
33. Ibid., 49–50.
34. Ibid., 54.

that of the Hadith: "Muslim scholars agree on the principle that any Hadith that is inconsistent with the Qur'an cannot be accepted."[35]

Having severed the story of the rib from the Qur'anic text—performing what we might call a "rib-ectomy" on the Qur'an, Hassan wonders how the story of the rib managed to make it into the Islamic tradition: "If the Qur'an makes no distinction between the creation of man and woman . . . why do Muslims believe that Hawwa' was created from the rib of Adam?"[36] Comparing Hadith accounts of the rib story to Genesis 2 and 3, Hassan finds the Bible to be the culprit, claiming that the objectionable Hadith reports exhibit an "obvious correspondence to Genesis 2:18–33 and Genesis 3:20."[37] Providing no explanation for this correspondence, she states as a matter of fact that the rib story "obviously originates in Genesis 2," adding only that the Hadith reports' minor deviations from Genesis are due to "Arab biases" that were "added to the adopted text." [38] Without any further comments on the historical processes or larger implications of this adoption, Hassan concludes that the responsibility for negative attitudes towards women originates not in true Islam as found in the pure Qur'anic text, but rather in outside influences that corrupted the Islamic tradition: "It has been amply demonstrated that the Qur'an, which to Muslims in general is the most authoritative source of Islam, does not discriminate against women despite the sad and bitter fact of history that the cumulative (Jewish, Christian, Hellenistic, Bedouin, and other) biases that existed in the Arab-Islamic culture of the early centuries of Islam infiltrated the Islamic tradition, largely through the Hadith literature, and undermined the intent of the Qur'an to liberate women."[39] In the specific case of the Creation narrative, the rib story "has no basis whatever in the Qur'an."[40] According to Hassan, the fault lies instead with the contaminating influence of Genesis on fabricated Hadith reports which have caused Muslims to misread the Qur'an. Like her modernist predecessors, Hassan rejects the use of *isra'iliyyat* texts to interpret the Qur'anic creation story.

35. Ibid., 46.
36. Ibid., 45.
37. Hassan, "The Issue," 75–76.
38. Ibid., 79, 76.
39. Hassan, "Muslim Women," 59.
40. Ibid., 44.

Though Hassan's argument is echoed in a number of other Muslim feminist works (namely, those of Amina Wadud[41] and Asma Barlas[42]) and has been frequently recognized for its role in recovering an egalitarian notion of creation in the Qur'an, surprisingly little has been said of its problematic invocation of notions of scriptural purity and contamination. In seeking to distance the Qur'anic narrative from Muslim interpretations that are demeaning to women, Muslim feminist scholars have effectively attempted to "purify" the Qur'an from Biblical influences. The claim that sexist readings of the Qur'an originate in the erroneous overlay of Biblical traditions onto the Qur'an rests not only upon an apologetic stance on gender in the Qur'an, but also implies Islam's feminist ascendancy over Judaism and Christianity. It is to these problems that I will now turn my attention more pointedly.

The common Muslim feminist position that *pure* Islam (as found in the *pure* Qur'an, unadulterated by outside influences) is perfectly egalitarian and that sexist scripture is the problem of Christians and Jews has not gone unnoticed by Jewish and Christian feminists. Judith Plaskow, for instance, recalls being in the company of Muslim feminists who "insisted that the Qur'an is perfect and completely supports the liberation of women. The implication—sometimes stated directly, sometimes not—is that we poor Jews and Christians are saddled with sexist Scriptures while Muslims are not."[43] For Jewish feminists in particular, the experience of enduring such insinuations is not new, having been targeted by anti-Jewish tendencies in some early works of Christian feminist theology. A number of those works adopted "traditional Christianity's negative picture of Judaism by attributing sexist attitudes to Christianity's Jewish origins," arguing that sexist tendencies in Christianity originate in Judaism and are contrary to Jesus's actual teachings.[44] The explanation for the appearance of sexist elements in Christian tradition was that "Jesus tried to restore egalitarianism but was foiled by

41. See Amina Wadud, *Qur'an and Woman: Rereading the Sacred Text from a Woman's Perspective* (New York: Oxford University Press, 1999), 20.

42. See Asma Barlas, *"Believing Women" in Islam: Unreading Patriarchal Interpretations of the Qur'ān* (Austin: University of Texas Press, 2002), 138–39.

43. Plaskow's words in Aysha Hidayatullah and Judith Plaskow, "Beyond Sarah and Hagar," 166.

44. Judith Plaskow, "Christian Feminism and Anti-Judaism," in Judith Plaskow and Donna Berman, eds., *The Coming of Lilith: Essays on Feminism, Judaism, and Sexual Ethics, 1972–2003* (Boston: Beacon, 2005), 89.

the persistence of Jewish attitudes within the Christian tradition."[45] In Plaskow's words, such arguments have perpetuated a "patriarchal ethic of projection" onto Judaism.[46] In invoking notions of Qur'anic purity and deflecting the responsibility for sexist Qur'anic interpretation onto the Biblical tradition, Muslim feminist scholars do much of the same by failing to own up to the Islamic roots of sexist interpretation and simply projecting it onto an external source. In pursuing this route, they neglect to fully account for the endurance of contrary readings of the Qur'an and to take stock of the systemic problems of sexism deeply interwoven into Qur'anic interpretation in ways that rule out a simple surgical extraction.

For example, the question of why the rib story is so prominent and persistent in the Islamic tradition remains understudied by Muslim feminists. If the Qur'an is in fact the overriding sacred source of Islam, and Hadith traditions that contradict it are unacceptable, why has the rib story remained so well intact until the twentieth century? Is it to be explained only as an interpretive "error" caused by repeated male bias in reading the Qur'an? Hassan speculates that the rib traditions' "continuing popularity among Muslims in general indicates that they articulate something deeply embedded in Muslim culture—namely that women are derivative creatures who can never be considered equal to men."[47] This is certainly true, and an important part of the answer, but I would argue that there is likely more than that at work. Perhaps there are other reasons why so-called "biblical overlay" has been so successful as an interpretive mode in reading the Qur'anic creation story. Could it be that in some ways the Qur'an is *itself* amenable to the interpretive inheritance of the rib story? The strong evidence Hassan provides in her reading of verse 4:1 is helpful in arguing for the egalitarian sense of the Qur'an's general view of human creation, and her reading of the dual form is persuasive in demonstrating that the Qur'an ultimately holds both Adam and Eve responsible for being swayed by Satan and for eating of the tree. But the rest of Hassan's argument rests on what the Qur'an does *not* say about Adam and Eve. As with other Bible-related stories that appear in the Qur'an, it is left up to commentators to decide what to do with the Qur'an's omissions of details.

45. Ibid.
46. Ibid., 92.
47. Hassan, "Muslim Women," 47.

As I mentioned earlier, in cases of Qur'anic omissions, interpreters may either choose to adopt details and meanings from Biblical sources, or to read the Qur'an as departing from the Biblical tradition. In other words, the Qur'an's silence on certain details of the Adam and Eve story leave it open to the interpreter's choice; the Qur'an simply does not spell out the details of how *exactly* the male body came to be differentiated from the female body or how *exactly* both Adam and Eve came to be tempted by Satan. We may argue that some interpretive choices in filling in the details are more sound than others and that reading against the rib story is the soundest interpretive route. However, if we do so, we must first contend with indicators in the Qur'an itself that suggest otherwise. As Kecia Ali has courageously pointed out, while many verses of the Qur'an align with the ethic of gender egalitarianism espoused by verse 4:1, other portions of the Qur'an suggest male dominance and authority over women.[48] She rightly points out that "modern apologetics and feminist analyses frequently overlook the very clear authority delegated to men over women' bodies."[49] In the end, I agree with Ali's assessment: "It is not simply enough to simply posit that 'the Qur'an is egalitarian and antipatriarchal,' and to blame interpretations that deviate from that perspective entirely on 'misreadings.'"[50] In this case, it is not enough to blame sexist interpretations of the Qur'an on viewpoints supposedly informed by *isra'iliyyat*. In other words, it is not enough to rely on verse 4:1 to inform our feminist readings of the Adam and Eve story and chalk up problematic readings to Biblical 'contamination' no matter how much our feminist interests drive us to do so. While we have the boon of verse 4:1 and others like it (such as 33:35 and 30:21), the truth of the matter is that we also have a number of other verses (such as 4:34 and 2:223) that suggest an attitude toward women that is in fact more congruent with the rib story than we would perhaps like to admit. We cannot simply hold up the former while downplaying the latter; Muslim feminists must account for and contend with both if we are to offer fully convincing feminist re-readings of the Qur'anic Adam and Eve story.

---

48. Kecia Ali, *Sexual Ethics and Islam: Feminist Reflections on Qur'an, Hadith, and Jurisprudence* (Oxford: Oneworld, 2006), 128.

49. Ibid., 126.

50. Ibid., 132.

In addition, I would argue that we must examine more carefully what we are doing when we attempt to purify the Qur'an from Biblical traditions. Are we not inadvertently repeating the same claims to authenticity and primacy as neo-traditional sexist interpreters— replicating the same act of labeling as "un-Islamic" what we do not agree with in the interpretive tradition? In doing so, not only do we as Muslim feminists replay the patriarchal dynamic of interpretive absolutism, but we also end up failing to account for how Biblical influence, as evident in the early history of Islam, is often seamlessly woven into the Islamic tradition. In other words, the rib story cannot be said to be simply be an *isra'iliyyat* problem if it is so prominent and deeply fused into the Islamic tradition; the rib story can no longer be said to be purely Biblical when it is simply *not* neatly separable from the Islamic commentarial tradition. Can something so enduring in the Islamic tradition simply be viewed as external to it? What does it mean for something to be internal or external to Islam? If we were to adopt the logic that things in the Islamic tradition that are traceable to the Biblical tradition are actually "un-Islamic," we are faced with the problem of having to toss an enormous portion of our Islamic heritage into the dustbin of things "un-Islamic." Here, the logic of purity and contamination—in faulting the *isra'iliyyat* and in failing to own up to other factors in the Islamic tradition that buttress the rib story—simply does not hold up. Muslim feminists are certainly not the only ones to employ notions of scriptural purity as an exegetical strategy; indeed, they are in the company of numerous medieval and modern exegetes. However, relying on this interpretive approach ultimately undermines Muslim feminist aims in reading the Qur'an.

As Kecia Ali has asserted, it is imperative that we as Muslim feminists own up to the complexity of our interpretive endeavors and choices instead of resorting to apologetic generalizations about the Qur'an. I argue that we must do so as an alternative to clinging to the false notion of a pure tradition. It is not only that there is no such thing as a "pure" Islamic tradition, but also that even if we attempt to construct one, Muslim feminists will always be playing a losing game. The mantle of pure Islam can always, and likely will, be taken up by anyone else, including the staunchest supporters of sexist interpretation of the Qur'an; and when they do, we find ourselves in the same position we were before all of our hard interpretive work: the pitting of "our" word against "theirs." After all, we end up supporting the primacy of a pure Islamic tradition that is invoked to renounce the credibility of feminist readings. We must be able to come up with ways of arguing for Muslim women's justice other than resorting to the line that "pure" Islam is on our side. We must be willing to move forward confidently in pursuing a theologically-reasoned ethics of women's dignity—regardless of whatever the "pure" meaning of the Qur'an may be.

As the illustrious Audre Lorde once said, "the master's tools will never dismantle the master's house. They may allow us temporarily to beat him at his own game, but they will never enable us to bring about genuine change."[51] Muslim feminists could choose to replay the authoritarian dynamics of Qur'anic interpretation that have enabled male commentators to commit the very epistemological violence against women that we have sought to root out. We could choose to reinvoke the patriarchal ethic of projecting our tradition's sexism onto other traditions. We could opt to achieve a short-term feminist gain for ourselves at the expense of other women, and engage in interpretive maneuvers that confine us to oppositional relationships with the religious Other from whom we separate ourselves through a claim to purity. But what will we have gained in the process? In the end, when we use the master's tools, we must ultimately lose to the master, adopting his rigid and arrogant ways as our own.

51. Audre Lorde, "The Master's Tools Will Never Dismantle the Master's House," in *Sister Outsider: Essays and Speeches*, Crossing Press Feminist Series (Trumansburg, NY: Crossing Press, 1984), 112.

9

Women Negotiating between Religions and Cultures

The Case of Chinese Muslims in Hong Kong

Wai Ching Angela Wong

The conflict between religions and cultures in the world has at times been exaggerated. Emphasis on the irreconcilability of religions and cultures tend to focus mainly on doctrines and institutions overlooking many facets of religious behavior in the specific contexts of everyday practice. In the following, I shall draw on the case of Chinese Muslim women in Hong Kong and examine their practice of living between religions and cultures. I shall contend that while conflicts are often orchestrated by international parties for various political interests, women have often negotiated the delicate balance between religions and cultures. As Pierre Bourdieu would argue, doctrines as theorization and institution as social regulations are only human attempts to objectify lived experience "independent of individual consciousness and wills."[1] However, the very reality of temporality tends to counter the rules of objectification. That is, there is necessarily a time deferral in practice which substitutes "strategy" for the rule and ensures the irreversibility of events and actions. In short, while the structure of a religious tradition (including its

1. Pierre Bourdieu, *Outline of a Theory of Practice* (Cambridge: Cambridge University Press, 1977), 4.

doctrines and institutions) obliges the believer to act in accordance to its rules and regulation, the actor's everyday practice inevitably defies predictability and works instead in many ways toward improvement of one's situation.[2] Temporal deferment as conceived by Bourdieu may thus provide the basis for understanding the act of negotiation between the global discursive construction of a combatant religious identity and the strategic practices of cultural accommodation and reconciliation of the Chinese Muslims in Hong Kong.

With increasing Islamic revivalism around the world, there is a recent return to veiling in the local Muslim community, including the Chinese Muslim community. When the global Islamic community recently reacted strongly against an American anti-Islam video, Chinese Muslims joined their South-Asian and Arab fellow believers in solidarity for a protest in Hong Kong on September 23, 2012. On the one hand, both of these above phenomena—wearing the veil and joining an international Muslim protest—show that, despite the physical and cultural distance between Hong Kong and the Islamic global political front, the identity of the Chinese Muslims in Hong Kong is linked to the international Muslim community. And yet on the other hand, the moderate application of the veil and the low profile of the anti-American rally in Hong Kong also demonstrate a certain distance between Hong Kong and the global movement. How then can Chinese Muslim women, as the designated (gender) bearer of the tradition, meet the present challenge of accommodating their Islamic faith to Hong Kong urbanity, Chinese values and a multicultural community? This case study of women's practice in the small but highly complex Muslim community in Hong Kong will hopefully unmask monolithic representations of Islamic religion and culture and help to reconstruct a discursive space for the meeting of traditions and values in women's practical living.

Chinese Muslims in Hong Kong

The Muslim community in Hong Kong represents a mix of ethnicities and cultures. According to the *Hong Kong Yearbook* 2011, Muslims constitute less than 3 percent (about 220,000) of the total population. This number includes the transient population of about 120,000 Indonesian migrant workers and a mixed population of about 70,000 Indians,

2. Ibid., 9–10.

Pakistanis, Malaysians, Africans, and Middle Eastern people. There are approximately 30,000 Chinese Muslims, only about 0.4 percent of the total population.[3] Nevertheless, these numbers are only estimates, arbitrarily given out by the Secretary of the Incorporated Trustees of the Islamic Community Fund of Hong Kong (the Islamic Fund) every year.[4] Unfortunately, besides these estimated figures, there is very little documentation about the general Hong Kong Muslim community and still less about the Chinese Muslims.

For the sake of political convenience, before 1997 South Asians had constituted the official representatives of the Muslim community in Hong Kong. From the beginning, the Islamic Fund, comprised of mainly South Asian organizations, has been designated as the Muslim representative body overseeing the mosques (and related buildings) and cemeteries in Hong Kong. Except for the Islamic Union of Hong Kong (the Islamic Union) which has grown into a mixed ethnic body comprised of a large percentage of "local boys" (本地仔) and Muslim Chinese by intermarriage,[5] the other three constituent members of the Islamic Fund include the Pakistan Association, the Indian Muslim Association, and the Dawoodi Bohras, all of whom have clear South Asian ethnic affiliations.[6] Due to the Islamic Fund's requirement that constituent members must surrender their organizational properties to the Fund once they became members, the Chinese Muslim Association, the principal coordinating body for social and religious services for Chinese Muslims in Hong Kong, has refused to become an official member.[7]

---

3. *Hong Kong Yearbook* 2011; http://www.yearbook.gov.hk/2011/en/pdf/E18.pdf.

4. Interview on September 10, 2010.

5. The mosque, the Masjid Amar and Osman Ramju Sadick Islamic Center situated in Wan Chai, in which the office of the Islamic Union is based, is also the first mosque initiated to be built by a "local boy," Ramju Sadick, in 1967. Since then it has attracted large numbers of local boys and Chinese Muslims. There is a Chinese restaurant integrated in its eight-storey complex. Cf. Ho Wai-Yip, "Historical Analysis of Islamic Community Development in Hong Kong: Struggle for Recognition in the Post-colonial Era," *Journal of Muslim Affair* 21 (2001) 67.

6. See Joel Thoraval, trans. Zhang Ning, "The Arrangement of Funeral and Prayer: The Historical Outlook of The Incorporated Trustees of the Islamic Community Fund of Hong Kong," (in Chinese) in *Guangdong Minju yanjiu lunzong*, vol. 5 (Guangzhou: Guangdong People's Press, 1991), 221–48; and Pluss, "Hong Kong's Muslim Organization," 19–23.

7. It was established in 1905 and has "quietly" played the role of coordinating social and religious activities for the Chinese Muslim community.

The double marginality of the Chinese Muslims as a small minority in Hong Kong and a shadow of their South Asian fellow believers has, in hindsight, helped them to maintain a relatively comfortable distance from the global Arab community in terms of the latter's tightening position on the international political plane. Chinese women, committed to a minority faith of Islam in Hong Kong, are thus left to explore and practice different possibilities between cultures, sometimes without guidance, and sometimes with unexpected resources and less constraints. Rather than being trapped in the American ideological propagation of the "clash of civilizations," the Chinese Muslim women navigate their way through their religious faith and practice to meet the demand of the modern women in a highly "Westernized" Hong Kong. Through careful steering through the multiplicity of their cultural identities, they have demonstrated the possibility of simultaneously living as a Muslim, a Chinese and an autonomous woman in Hong Kong.

Intermarriages between Indians and Chinese took place as early as the late nineteenth century,[8] in spite of the fact that policemen and prison guards were not allowed to marry local women in the early period.[9] These early migrants mostly married back home and retained familial relations with the subcontinent. When the ban was finally lifted with the Japanese occupation in 1941, and as many Indian Muslims settled down in the colony and began to build their businesses and families in Hong Kong, interracial marriages between Indians and Chinese became more common. When the Indian settlers and the mixed couple raised their children as Hong Kong natives, new generations of "local boys" (本地仔)[10] emerged, who would distinguish themselves from the "visitors," referring to the "home based" South Asians who came to Hong Kong for jobs in the latter years.[11]

This complex ethnic and cultural background of the Muslim community in Hong Kong became quite evident as I visited the Chinese Muslim women in the Islamic Union in 2010. During the summer of that

8. Anita M. Weiss, "South Asian Muslims in Hong Kong: Creation of a 'Local Boy,'" *Modern Asian Studies* 25 (1991) 421, 429 (417–53).

9. Ibid., 431.

10. Indian or Pakistani men who were born in Hong Kong, grew up in Hong Kong, and speak fluent Cantonese, the local dialect. The prior generations of their families have settled in Hong Kong for many years, for different reasons. More details will be explained below.

11. Weiss, "South Asian Muslims in Hong Kong," 417, 433.

year, I interviewed five Chinese women through contacts provided by Basmah Lok, the Manager of the Islamic Union. Most of the interviews took place at the Masjid Ammar and Osman Ramju Sadick Centre at Wan Chai, except for one conducted at the company of the interviewee. The age of the five women ranged from 35 to 73 years old at the time of the interviews. There was one housewife, four full-time workers, two of whom work in an honorary capacity. All of the women have some post-secondary education, and their occupations include school vice-principal, manager, director of an NGO, and self-employed company owner. All five got married, with one woman re-married, one widowed, and one considering a divorce. Three of them had children and two did not. All of their families appear to do well economically and should be considered middle to upper middle class. The most impressive finding about them is that while they all defend Islam as a gender egalitarian religion, they also exercise rather broad and flexible interpretations of their faith in their various contexts.

Amazingly, in the family lineages of these five women, there are at least twelve nationalities or ethnicities represented. Among the five women, only Man Kei was married to a Chinese. In the four other families, there are altogether 13 different ethnicities, religions and nationalities represented. With family lineages interwoven through multiple generations of marriages, the five women interviewed had reported cross-fertilization of Muslims across regions and continents, representing families of an unusually complex tapestry of cultural, ethnic and religious identities. In short, the focus on the Chinese Muslim women in Hong Kong serves not only as a microcosm of the complexity of cultural identities in a Muslim community but also as a window to the world of people practicing and living multiculturalism in everyday life.

Chinese Pragmatism and Islamic Law

The rhetoric of squaring Islamic culture with pre-modern and archaic tradition usually measures Islam's discriminatory treatment of women against modern standards. The problems highlighted include Muslim's recognition of a man's legal power over his wife as head of the household, the practice of polygamy, the deprivation of women's right to divorce, and their lack of right to custody of children and maintenance of marital property. Many Islamic feminists inside and outside of Muslim countries advocate for the abolition of these laws because they perpetuate and legitimize violence against women. Surah 4:34 of the Qur'an, which has been widely used to justify wife-beating, is seen as one such example that must either be radically reinterpreted or completely abandoned. The question of whether Islam can square with modern feminist demand for autonomy and freedom is the topic of continuous debate.[12]

The instigation of the conflict in the Middle East gave rise to a global wave of Islamic revivalism that has also affected Hong Kong Muslims. Being a cosmopolitan city, Hong Kong is always open to and in contact with the international Islamic world. Just glancing over the newsletters (*IU-Newsletter*) of the Islamic Union in 2010 and 2012, one can find many references to Islamic communities all over the world. They include fundraising activities on behalf of Muslims in Indonesia, Pakistan and Burma, the organization of *hajj* (pilgrimages) to Mecca, the cooperation with overseas universities and programmes such as Iranian National Day, and the organization of training and lectures by a visiting scholar from Jordan. In short, the Hong Kong Muslims are part of the international Muslim community sharing the life of the global fellowship.

The influence of the international movement for Muslim revivalism on the Chinese Muslim women in Hong Kong is apparent. In the interviews, conservative views of women's roles and place in the family and society are dominant. With the antagonistic atmosphere around Islam on the global level, a defensive rhetoric is generally adopted by the local Muslims. When speaking with me, an outsider, the Chinese Muslim women generally take an apologetic approach, relating eagerly to me the benefits of the Islamic precepts for women in terms of respect and protection. Although two of my interviewees have full-time paid jobs and are in fact heads of their respective offices, many of them support the view that women's primary responsibility lies within the home. The best educated of the five, who serves as the vice-principal of a high school, believes that God created man and woman differently. Women are created gentler and are suited for caring for the family; it would be quite unacceptable for men to be the same. Aleeza who runs her organization on honorary terms also agrees that men should be breadwinners

12. Valentine M. Moghadam, "Islamic Feminism and Its Discontents: Toward a Resolution of the Debate," *Signs: Journal of Women in Culture and Society* 27 (2002) 1135–71.

and women should be homemakers and child-caretakers. It would be wrong for a man to forfeit his responsibility and take care of only small things at home. "It would set a bad example for the children."[13]

All of the women defended Islam as a religion that is meant for their protection. Yamin, who received a degree in Islamic studies in Malaysia and serves frequently as instructor for Islamic induction courses at the Masjid Ammar and Osman Ramju Sadick Centre, gave the following elaboration on Islamic views on women:

> Islam . . . has given us [women] lots of rights, and many of them are not permitted in other religions . . . In respect to the right of inheritance, women are entitled to half of the share of inheritance available to men. Some may say this is unfair, but what women inherit would become their own, what men inherit would only contribute to the whole family. In my view, this is better for women. When the witnesses of two women are equal to only the weight of that of one man, they only have to carry half of the responsibility. Why is this so? This is because women are more sentimental, they may not be able to exercise judgment rationally.[14]

This conservatism in the views toward the role and position of women in Islam can be explained by Bourdieu's conception of the "field" and "habitus" in his theory of practice. The fields are constituted by the habitus of many generations, that is, the ways people grow up and subscribe the values inculcated in the different roles and places assigned to them. They would act the way they are expected and speak the language they learn in the process in order to be "successful." The fields and habitus provide the structure in which the meaning of an action is reproduced. Indeed, Bourdieu argues that there is no way one can understand an isolated action if not placing it within the system where the action is played out.[15] If women have been the venue of contestation between Islamic and "modern" Western values, women in the Hong Kong Muslim community cannot perceive themselves independent of it. The global Islamic defense of its teachings on women serves in this respect as the "field" of their practices. As such, their conservative rhetoric of confining women to the domestic role must be understood in the light

13. Interview on August 8, 2010.

14. Interview on July 17, 2010.

15. Bourdieu, *Outline of a Theory of Practice*, 15.

of the larger political background of the battle for Islamic identity and dignity.

Regarding the most contentious issue of the veil, all women interviewed have either embraced it as an indicator of their commitment to the religion as soon as they were converted, or have revived the practice after many years of negligence as a sign of their re-dedication to Islam. Islam requires both men and women to dress modestly (Qu'ran 24:30–31 and 33:59–60) but the requirement has been turned into a kind of religious dress code imposed only on women. In the West the veil has become a symbol of women's oppression and its banning signals women's liberation. The recent legal stipulations around the veil in France staged openly the battle between Islam and the West over the symbolic meanings of the veil—over the bodies of Muslim women. The anti-West Muslim men and women defend the veil as a sign of modesty and protection for women. Many Islamic feminists campaigning for its banning in public contend that the practice is archaic and the veil can only be an outright sign of women's subjugation. The debate is well documented on both sides, but the Hong Kong Chinese Muslim women chose to side with the veil. Yasmin alluded to the French practice in her conversation and expressed her dismay. "Muhammad did not make [the veil] a compulsion for everyone to obey. Take it or not, that's between you and Allah. Personally I think, the so-called civilization today is in fact more barbarous. Take for instance the case in France, you cannot wear a veil to school . . . Banning [of the veil] is in fact a deprivation of somebody else's right."[16]

There is clearly a general commitment to the veil in the present Muslim community in Hong Kong. There were only a few women who did not wear the veil during the few visits I made at the Islamic center. The increased visibility of veiled Indonesian helpers in public probably provides a source of encouragement; the growing emphasis of the religious significance of the veil in the global discourse on Islamic identity is most likely the main factor. Over the last decade, the veil has emerged as an "essential" identity marker for Muslims to which the Hong Kong Chinese Muslim women also feel obliged.[17] This was about the time Za-

16. Interview on July 17, 2010.

17. The relative freedom for women in the local Muslim community to choose to veil or not is observed during my several visits to the Islamic Union and its restaurant in which there were always a few women who did not wear the veil.

meena started her courtship with her now husband and converted into Islam. She saw the challenge to veil as a test of her faith and she proudly passed it. "People in the mosque said that I was the first one who started to veil immediately after conversion!"[18] For Man Kei, although she was born and married into families of long Muslim ancestry, veiling was not a practice in her daily living until seven years ago. "I started to veil in 2005 only, . . . I didn't know that I have [*sic*] to veil before then. My family never puts on the veil."[19] While Zameena is proud to be acknowledged as one of the first in her mosque to take her religious dress code seriously, Man Kei testifies to the fact that veiling has not been a common practice in Chinese Muslim families. She was only made aware of it in the middle of the 2000s, about four years after the 9/11 attacks in New York. All women interviewed are now wearing their veils on a daily basis despite the veil's invitation of public gaze and disapproval from families and friends.

> There is certainly pressure in veiling . . . With the heat, . . . the women in the neighborhood would say things. (Man Kei)[20]

> My colleagues would say, "it's alright to believe [in Islam], but do you really have to wrap up yourself like this?" . . . They would question me, "why believe in the religion of the 'Ah cha' (阿义)[21]? Aren't you hot wearing it [the veil]?" (Zameena)[22]

While the Islamic global cartography finds its imprints in the Chinese Muslim women, there is also discordance in their practices. Bourdieu's conception of the "field" and "habitus" helps us to understand the forces with which every individual has to live and yet there is also the space for individual strategizing in each situation. While all five Chinese Muslim women strongly defended Islam as an "egalitarian" religion, agreeing that women's role and place are primarily domestic, and that the veil is meant for women's protection, they are not as submissive to these rules and regulations as their rhetoric may sound.

18. Interview on August 14, 2010.

19. Interview on August 31, 2010.

20. Interview on August 31, 2010.

21. Making fun of the common sound "jah" in many Indian names, local Chinese transliterated it into a Cantonese name "Ah Cha" to cover all ethnic South Asians in Hong Kong.

22. Interview on August 14, 2010.

Living the modernity of Hong Kong urban life with its rich Western colonial heritage, these women are faced with many negotiations in their everyday practices. Backed by the marriage law of Hong Kong, they are not hesitant to reject polygamy. Yasmin plainly says that polygamy is against the law and Islamic teachings are adaptable to particular contexts. In the conversation with the three mothers there is also no resistance to the Western style education system, which very often means Christian education, because it represents the best education in Hong Kong. Additionally several of them not only choose to work outside the home, they also enjoy a high degree of autonomy in daily life. Yamin, the school's vice-principal who prioritizes men's rational capacity over women's, is making many decisions in her everyday work. "In general, I don't think the decision I made is of any less quality of that made by a man."[23] She admitted that there is more pressure on a woman than on a man serving in a senior administrative position and it is not easy to take care of both the family and work at the same time. But she believes that, because of her leadership role, she has to take up her duty responsibly regardless of her religious constrictions. There is certainly a gap between what she believes to be the proper gender role performance and what she practices in her workplace every day. Moreover, understanding very well that her daughters would find it difficult to follow their Muslim precepts in a Christian school, she feels relaxed about them not wearing the veil. "Children of the non-Chinese Muslims will wear their veils to school, but [those of] the Chinese will not. . . . I just let my children do as they wish. There is no compulsion in religion."[24] Yasmin interprets her principle of flexibility as one derived of Chinese pragmatism, a kind of flexibility that she thinks Muslims in the Middle East could not afford.

Zameena who took pride in putting on her veil once converted, will not allow herself to be bored by a uniformed headscarf. As someone who followed the latest fashion trends before becoming Muslim, she admits that, "to veil has been some struggle because it looks so different from what I used to be."[25] Then she decided to apply her fashion sense to veiling by buying a great variety of headscarves and spending lots of time wearing them every day to make sure that she has the look desired.

23. Interview on July 17, 2010.
24. Interview on July 17, 2010.
25. Interview on August 14, 2010.

Aleeza who is very firm on men's role as breadwinners, insisted that she would not follow her husband blindly. "If he is wrong but still assumes the commanding tone, if he is impolite and unreasonable and still asks for unconditional submission only because he is my husband, I would refuse to go along."[26]

In short, there are no blind followers of rules in these Hong Kong-Chinese Muslim women but active cultural adapters who do not lose faith in the face of modern challenges. Rather than squaring themselves with the increasingly strict instructions of Islamic teachings on women, they wear the symbol of Islamic faithfulness and adopt Islamic gender "egalitarian" rhetoric while making practical choices to live, work and raise their children. If this is Chinese pragmatism in the way Yasmin explains her attitude of flexibility, it has helped these women adapt their faith to concrete situations that work for them. The usefulness of theory is, as Charlene Haddock Seigfried, a feminist pragmatist, argues, "ultimately answerable to those whose lives are supposed to be bettered by it."[27]

The Role of Family in the Dialogue between Chinese and Muslim Identities

There are very few studies on Islamic women in China and of the few, Keng-Fong Pang's early study of the Muslim women in Hainan Island, the southern coast of China, is one. Her study demonstrates that when given the right circumstances, Chinese Muslim women can be quite autonomous and are leading lives far from the model of oppression.[28] Most important, it is also a case demonstrating how Chinese pragmatism steers religious revivalism away from developing into dogmatic extremism. In dealing with conflicts, the Chinese are often seen to adopt a pragmatic approach. Aleeza, the manager of a religious NGO, quoted the Confucian concept of "the way of the mean" (中庸之道) to describe the moderate way Chinese people prefer, that is, always avoiding go-

26. Interview on August 20, 2010.

27. Charlene Haddock Seigfried, *Pragmatism and Feminism: Reweaving the Social Fabric* (Chicago: University of Chicago Press, 1996), 263.

28. Cf. Keng-Fong Pang, "Islamic 'Fundamentalism' and Female Empowerment among the Muslims of Hainan Island, People's Republic of China," in Judy Brink and Joan Mencher, eds., *Mixed Blessings: Gender and Religious Fundamentalism Cross Culturally* (New York: Routledge, 1997), 41–58.

ing to extremes where possible. When Yasmin explained her attitude of flexibility about not asking her daughters to veil, she referred to it as the Chinese way, that is, not forcing yourself into difficult situation unnecessarily. In times of need, it is believed that principles can be "bended" to fit the needs of the situation. The pragmatic strategizing to hit the "mean" seems to be one of the most helpful approaches in dealing with multicultural living in the families.

The most obvious daily negotiation takes place at home, between the interracial couple, the multicultural marital family members, and the often diverse religious traditions of the women's native Chinese families. As noted in the previous section, the Hong Kong Muslim community is a highly culturally mixed group with members coming from all over Asia and the world. Due to the specific historical context outlined above, interracial marriages between Chinese women and South Asian "local boys" are common. For the women who were born to Hong Kong Chinese families, their family members often have different religious beliefs. They are Christians, including Catholics, Buddhists, practitioners of ancestral worship, and followers of various Chinese deities such as Kuan Yin (Goddess of Mercy) and Wong Tai Sin (a local, syncretic religion combing Confucianism, Daoism and Buddhism). Indeed, living under the same roof with family members of different religions is a common phenomenon in Hong Kong. Yasmin, Zameena, and Aleeza, the Chinese women who were converted to Islam because of their marriages to South Asian Muslims, become a window through which different cultures and traditions come to face one another up close on daily basis. And for Man Kei and Rania, both of whom are Chinese-born Muslims, Chinese culture is, willingly and unwillingly, part of them both in the positive and the negative sense.

Given the minority status of the Chinese Muslims within the Hong Kong Muslim community, comparison of the status and personalities between Chinese and South Asian Muslims happens naturally in our conversation. As observed, the "they (South Asians)-versus-us (Chinese)" axis is very often drawn even among the interracial couples. Indeed, it is within the interracial families that mutual respect and understanding between the two ethnic groups are most intensely tested. For the interracial couple, tensions and differences are often felt after the initial stage of romantic union slips away. Yasmin's marriage with a Pakistani local boy lasted for only three years. She thought they shared similar sense of religiosity until they got married. Cultural differences between the two began to show soon after marriage and loomed larger and larger to the day they decided to separate. Her husband's family blamed their divorce on her Chinese identity. Her former in-laws believed that if she were a South Asian she would have remained married. The gulf between two cultures was even larger for Zameena whose husband from Kashmir had no experience of Hong Kong before they were married. Throughout the last twelve years of marriage, Zameena's short stays with her husband in India or his periodic visits to her in Hong Kong ended in bitter rows and resentment. Neither the life of Kashmir nor that of Hong Kong were bearable to the visitor from the other side. Two different lifestyles—daily habits, personal hygiene, and eating manners—grew increasingly abominable to one another. The initial romantic encounter of two cultures grew into an unbearable clash.

According to Weiss, since marriage became permitted between Indian-Pakistani Muslims and local Chinese women during Japanese occupation, the number of these marriages rose steadily.[29] While Indian-Pakistani women were still most commonly involved in arranged marriages to men back "home," the Indian-Pakistani men living in Hong Kong seemed to have better opportunities of finding local spouses, especially since the local women they decided to marry would eventually convert to Islam. For "local boys," who live and work in Hong Kong within the Chinese community and who are fluent in the local language of Cantonese, courtship and marriages with Chinese women happens as a matter of fact. Loh, the Manager of the Islamic Union, confirms that interracial marriages between South Asian Muslim men and Chinese women converts such as those of Yasmin, Zameena, Aleeza and Rania are quite common in the community. Unfortunately, in her observation, many difficulties have emerged from these intermarriages and not many marriages have resulted in happy endings.

While there are obvious areas of conflict between Chinese and South Asian cultures, it has proven no easier to negotiate difference for the Muslim converts and their Chinese families. As mentioned, Yasmin, Zameena and Aleeza were all born to Chinese families whose members have subscribed to many different religions. According to *Hong Kong Yearbook* 2011, besides the Muslims mentioned, there are probably more than a million Buddhist followers, another million Daoists

---

29. Weiss, "South Asian Muslims in Hong Kong," 432.

(each about 14% of the total population), about 480,000 Protestants and 363,000 Catholics (together almost 12% of the population), about 40,000 Hindus, 10,000 Sikhs, and a number of Jews, Baha'is and Zoro-astrians (together about 0.7% of the population).[30] Due to the absence of systematic member registration for most religions, there must be some who are left out of any institutional calculation above. This includes people practicing ancestral worship, participants of temple and village rituals, and worshippers of various Chinese deities. There is also a common belief that every Han Chinese is a Confucian to some degree. In fact, for the majority, paying respect to the Chinese pantheon is simply part of everyday life.

Except for Man Kei who has a Muslim family genealogy, all four women found the Chinese religions that they grew up with too materialistic and superstitious, "they have deities and Buddha all over heaven" (天神佛). Both Yasmin and Aleeza referred to their parents' religious life as "worshipping just almost any deities." Most interestingly, Rania's natal family who is supposed to be Muslim for generations is also much involved in the worship of various Chinese gods. Rania explains this in terms of their material interests that have led them astray. She is particularly critical of their idol worship, forfeiting the real blessings that should have come from Allah. Alternately, given the colonial privileging and the subsequent dominance of Christian schools, Christian social services and hospitals in Hong Kong, there is hardly a chance for a local born Chinese to grow up without coming into some contacts with Christianity. For example, her Catholic mother baptized Zameena when she was young and she has a younger sister who is still Christian. In fact, her sister once insisted on placing a cross in the middle of the sitting room in the flat that the two sisters shared. Rania, born into a Muslim family that worships many deities, once converted into Christianity as well. Her eldest sister is a Christian and Rania is presently the only remaining Muslim in the family.

Despite much difference between family members in terms of religious affiliations and cultural practices, the common ground for Chinese, South Asians and Muslims to live and relate to one another seems to remain the notion of "family." Despite the fundamental doctrinal

---

30. *Hong Kong Yearbook* 2011; http://www.yearbook.gov.hk/2011/en/pdf/E18.pdf. Just like the numbers of the Muslim population provided in the *Yearbook*, the numbers for each of the religions are only estimates due to lack of official census data.

conflict between monotheistic Islam and pantheistic Chinese religions, their respective teachings on filial piety and the emphasis on "harmonious" relationship are lifted up as the ethical principle for practicing inclusiveness. Recently Yasmin's parents have been quite involved in Buddhism, including the adoption of Buddhist names and taking vegetarian meals for at least two days a week. Despite her firm defense of the Islamic way of life, Yasmin shows much respect for her parents' recent commitment because, according to her understanding, filial piety is what Allah would like her to do. "There are in fact many similarities between Islamic and Chinese traditional teachings on family."[31] After her conversion to Islam, she actually finds her relationship with her parents much improved and notices increasing mutual respect between them. Since filial piety is regarded as the most important foundation to Chinese culture and morality, the perceived similarity between the two traditions in this regard provides an invaluable point of reference to reconcile living between two cultures. The Chinese adoption of the title of Day of Filial Piety (忠孝節) for the Muslim festival of Qurbani (Day of Sacrifice) is, in this respect telling.

Rania particularly dislikes her grandmother whose "immoral" behavior was the source of much pain for her early childhood and who, in her view, fell short of the ideal practices of a devout Muslim. But Rania has no problem with her Christian sister who has never tried to talk her out of Islam. Although in the case of her other sister who follows Kuan Yin, Rania would prefer her to follow Allah instead, believing that her sister's family difficulties would be better resolved if she did. However, in order to maintain a good relationship with one another, members will refrain from the subject of religion whenever they gather. Since she is financially better off, Rania will make sure that each of her siblings will be taken care of. Zameena, too, is committed to the care of all her siblings as she is the "eldest sister" in the family. "The eldest sister" (or the eldest brother if any) is the next most respected position in the Chinese family, which implicates both authority and responsibility over the young ones. For this reason, she doesn't feel offended by her sister's challenge of her faith by placing the Christian cross in the sitting room, but would choose not to take part in family gatherings that are related to Chinese religious festivals. One may argue that Chinese pragmatism is once again at work. Pragmatism as William James sees it is the best

31. Interview on July 17, 2010.

mediator and reconciler in times of conflict because it "unstiffens" theories: "Pragmatism is willing to take anything, to follow either logic or the sense, and to count the humblest and most personal experiences. She will count mystical experiences if they have practical consequences . . . Her only test of probable truth is what works best and combines with the collectivity of experience's demands, nothing being omitted . . . Her manners are as various and flexible, her resources as rich and endless, and her conclusions as friendly as those of mother nature."[32]

Practical reasoning prompts these Chinese Muslim women to conclude that taking care of their family members is their primary responsibility as Chinese but also an important part of their duty as good Muslims. The maintenance of good familial relationships with parents and siblings has been set as a goal above cultural differences and a strategy to work through religious diversity in everyday life.

Faith and Practice: Negotiating Islamic Marriages and Divorce

We have seen how the Chinese Muslim women negotiate their ways through belief and practice for the accommodation of different values, cultures and religions in their everyday life. However, some difficulties of interracial encounter, divergences of life histories, perceptions of meanings and worldviews, habits and lifestyles, and ways and means of communication are much beyond individual capacities to resolve. For two of the interracial married women interviewed, one is already divorced and the other is seriously considering it.

The difficulty for Muslim women to exit from marriages even if they are abusive has been one of the major feminist critiques of Islam. It is generally understood that Muslim husbands can be released from their vows virtually on demand by saying "I divorce you" while their wives have hardly the choice. In some cases, fear of poverty keeps many Muslim women locked in bad marriages, as does the prospect of losing their children. However, as seen from the cases above, divorce is not uncommon in mixed marriages in the Muslim community in Hong Kong. And in the case of Yasmin, the frequent lecturer for Islamic courses, not only did she get divorced, but she also remarried and considered

---

32. William James, *Pragmatism and the Meaning of Truth* (Cambridge: Harvard University Press, 1978), 43–44.

her decision religiously sound. All five interviewees regard divorce as generally permissible by *Qur'an* 4:21. The clause includes some detailed instructions such as a cooling period of three months so that the woman is clear of any pregnancy, that she may collect all her *mahr* (dowry) and keep the custody of her children if divorce is initiated by the man. There is provision for divorce to be initiated independently by women as well.

Yasmin is most definite about the *Qur'an's* permission of divorce and remarriage. "There is restriction to men's initiation only in other religions, women are not allowed to initiate it, but in my case I was the one who initiated it."[33] She is well aware of the *Qur'an's* discouragement of divorce as a general principle, but she is also sure of its permission when necessary. "When something develops to an extent where its disadvantages have outweighed its advantages, it is permissible. The condition is that we have to think through it, not making any decision in haste. The couple also sought the opinion of a third party and did soul searching through prayers. In short, the process was not taken lightly. Indeed, parting amicably is a way of making peace between the two parties. Despite her remarriage, Yasmin and her former husband remain friends and would occasionally meet and dine at the restaurant of the Islamic Union with their daughters. In the process of contemplation for divorce, Zameena is sure that this is not what Allah prefers. "But when you run into marital problem, Muslim brothers and sisters would advise you to bear it until there is no other way than to initiate divorce."[34] With the *Qur'an's* affirmation of divorce as the last resort, Zameena does not need to be forced into choosing between divorce and her faith. Rather, faith legitimizes her choice to divorce.

Having observed many failed marriages, Aleeza argues that the only situation which calls for Muslim women's consideration of divorce is when they discover that their husbands no longer follow the Islamic way. In short, the weight of faith is a determinant in the women's assessments of their marital crises. Indeed, Yasmin has been very serious about her faith and has become a learned teacher through her completion of the Islamic program at the University of Malaysia. Throughout the interview, she seemed to feel basically guiltless as a divorcee and showed no remorse in her decision, either in terms of her religious belief or her social position in the community. She stands firm as she

33. Interview on July 17, 2010.
34. Interview on August 14, 2010.

defends this as the right of a Muslim woman guaranteed by the *Qur'an*. Reasoning in a more sophisticated way, Zameena prefaced her thoughts on divorce with her pride over her recent spiritual ascendance. "Honestly, my husband is not a good follower. As I learn more about my religion, the more distance is felt in my relationship with him."[35] For both Yasmin and Zameena, a divorce is reasoned to be sanctified if it consists of the following three factors: first, that the man is not a "true" follower of Islam; second, that the woman has reached a level of piety much more advanced than that of her husband; and third, as scripturally instructed, it is used as the last resort aiming to achieve reconciliation and peacemaking with one another.

The reasoning of the Chinese Muslim women is not a simple submission of doctrine to action. In fact, just as they take seriously the Islamic teachings on the role and place of women, they reflect on the Qu'ranic verses on divorce with sincerity and care. For them, the truthfulness of the Qu'ranic verse is found not only in its approval of divorce but the practicality implied for the situation. Everyone who has gone through a difficult marriage would know how precious a promise of peaceful separation would be. In this sense, the "supportive" scriptural text does not only resolve the sense of guilt and remorse in the struggling couple but also sets forth the hope of a new beginning for the divorcee. Due to the frequent unfortunate separation of interracial couples in the Hong Kong Muslim community, the Chinese women are not hesitant to take the best chance provided by the Qu'ran to address their marital crisis. Surprisingly in these instances, Islam turns out to be much more lenient than many people would think. In comparison with evangelical Christians in Hong Kong who still see divorce as something violating the divine will, Islam in its contextual application is much more open to siding with the welfare of women, and hence Islam is more equipped than other religious traditions in Hong Kong to address the contemporary issue of marital crisis. Most interestingly, the religion that the world believes to be most oppressive to women turns out to be a more liberating tool for the Hong Kong-Chinese Muslim women in need.

Seigfried reminds us that no theoretical category can contain lived experience.[36] The focus on practice is therefore an essential approach to

35. Interview on August 14, 2010.
36. Seigfried, *Pragmatism and Feminism*, 9.

appreciating fully the seemingly inconsistent reasoning of the Chinese Muslim women in their processing faith in action. For practice is always pluralistic, it allows the meeting of different logics to advance the best result desired. Often caught between the double charges of being not radical enough in terms of theoretical positioning (as compared to the leftist or the socialist) and not being sufficiently grounded with the variations of historical contexts, pragmatist feminists insist on the refusal of subordinating life actions, in all their diversity and contradictions, to theoretical rules and institutional regulations.[37] It is practice, Seigfried contends, that best defends the "legitimacy and irreducibility of multiple perspectives."[38]

Conclusion

There is a great deal of anxiety in doing interreligious dialogue today because of the proliferation of identity politics among different races, classes, genders, and between the East and the West or the First and the Third Worlds. Contradictions abound as different identities continue to diversify and multiply beyond national or geographical boundaries. In his description of religions around the world, Mark Juergensmeyer reminds us of how a map of world religions is colored by patches of one among the others but never tightly distinguished by any regional or national borders. There is scarcely any region that is composed solely of members of a single strand of traditional religion. Indeed, religion has always been part of a fluid process of cultural interaction, expansion, synthesis, borrowing, and change.[39] That is, the boundaries between religious communities and traditions have been permeable and there are very few instances where one religion or culture is not touched by another. In this sense, doing interreligious dialogue cannot be restricted to one tradition talking to another on doctrinal or institutional matters alone as if we are living in entirely different sectors of the world. There is thus limitation in the expression "interreligious dialogue" as it anticipates, and reinforces boundaries as much as it intends to break

37. Ibid., 262–63.

38. Ibid., 10.

39. Mark Juergensmeyer, "Thinking Globally about Religion," in Mark Juergensmeyer, ed., *Global Religions: An Introduction* (Oxford: Oxford University Press, 2003), 4.

them down. Alternately, if people are embedded with many layers of culture and identities, the space of "inter" in dialogue may focus on the "in-between-ness" of traditions which is not so much a condition of "neither-nor" but "both-and." This is a space where active negotiations between principles and values are being tested and cultivated in daily practices. If explanation is constantly attuned to both the institutional authority and individual applications, concrete actions are temporary, revisable, strategic, and directed toward specific ends-in-view.[40] I believe that explorations from this perspective will show that neither is religion nor the experience of women a monolithic entity; rather, the two are always engaged in active negotiation and interaction which implies diversity, adaptation and choice.

40. Seigfried, *Feminism and Pragmatism*, 276.

10

Beyond Beauty

Aesthetics and Emotion in Interreligious Dialogue[1]

Michelle Voss Roberts

Lalita, a Krishna devotee, begins her response to a piece of my research, "I hope this does not offend you in any way," and she concludes, "Please let me know what you think, how you feel about what I said." In my reply, I write, "I am grateful for your comments . . . I value our friendship . . . I worry about . . . I wonder . . . I return the hope that I have not offended you."[2] Our dialogue is full of the language of emotion.

Some observers have posited that women build trust through relationship and consequently bring a greater degree of emotion to interreligious dialogue than men.[3] Others theorize that women express

1. I am grateful to Emily Holmes and Jon Paul Sydnor, who generously offered their insights on earlier drafts of this paper, as well as to Stephanie Corigliano, Francis Clooney, and Zayn Kassam for probing its implications for comparative theology and religious identity.

2. Lalita is a pseudonym.

3. According to Helene Egnell, participants in the Women's Interfaith Journey in 2002 contrasted the "emotional, caring, peace loving, down-to-earth and practical" nature of women with the "rational, theoretical, calculating and . . . violent" tendencies of men, whose dialogue they perceived as dry cerebral exercises. Helene Egnell, "Other Voices: A Study of Christian Feminist Approaches to Religious Plurality East and West" (PhD diss, Uppsala University, 2006), 88, cf. 167.

strong emotion with one another in interfaith settings because they are otherwise silenced or excluded in the official discourses of their own traditions.[4] Indeed, even though I enjoy academic freedom and train Christian ministers, some of my remaining filters may relax when I speak with Lalita. And even when we disagree, her hospitality and consideration of my feelings show that she cares about the integrity of our relationship. We enact a holistic dialogue in which narrative, social situation, and emotion matter as much as ideas.

Lalita and I write about our personal emotions, but we also discuss emotion as a component of our religious traditions. We speak about *bhakti rasa*, devotional sentiment. Our emotions, both in relation to our faith traditions and in relation to one another, are part of a larger aesthetic orientation. In this essay, I explore *rasa* (aesthetic emotion) as an analogue for interreligious dialogue. Theorized as emotion that is both rooted in the body and culturally inflected, *rasa* can help to unpack the under-theorized work that emotion plays in interreligious dialogue. *Rasa* offers a theoretical framework for understanding and incorporating affective responses to religious difference.[5]

In the West, the Enlightenment's fear of the passions as physical drives subordinated emotion to the control of reason. Romantic thinkers accepted the basic distinction of emotion from reason but valued emotion as a primal source of insight. Recent scholarship has turned away from emotion as an essence or thing to be controlled, manipulated, or valued. Today, a lively interdisciplinary conversation centers on how emotions interact with, exhibit, and influence rationality.[6] We recognize that culture shapes the physical and interpretive components of emotion on levels of which we are often unconscious.[7] The old linkage of women

4. Egnell, "Other Voices," 13. See also Maura O'Neill, *Women Speaking, Women Listening: Women in Interreligious Dialogue*, Faith Meets Faith (Maryknoll, NY: Orbis, 2006), 95.

5. In theoretical discourse, "affect" denotes preverbal semiotic states, while "emotion" refers to discrete, discursively identifiable conditions. *Rasa* theory incorporates a broad spectrum of phenomena that includes both.

6. Martha C. Nussbaum, for example, writes of "the intelligence of the emotions" to describe their positive role in ethics. *Upheavals of Thought: The Intelligence of the Emotions* (Cambridge: Cambridge University Press, 2001).

7. For a review of these trends, see John Corrigan, "Introduction: Emotions Research and the Academic Study of Religion," in John Corrigan (ed.), *Religion and Emotion: Approaches and Interpretations* (Oxford: Oxford University Press, 2004). One germinal collection on emotion in India is Owen M. Lynch, ed., *Divine Passions:*

with emotion (which in its positive form romanticizes women's relational aptitude and in its negative form demands that hysterical women be controlled by reasonable men) is beginning to weaken as feminist scholars disentangle these stereotypes from women's actual behavior.[8] The premise of this essay is that emotions (like gender, sexuality, culture, and religions) are not singular or static essences but multiple, produced by discursive means, and continually changing. As such, emotions constitute an important subject of dialogue and comparison for women and men alike.

Hindu traditions inspire me as a comparative theologian to think about the role of aesthetics and emotion in religious experience. Although this essay does not engage in close textual comparison, it is the fruit of a deeper comparison that highlights ethical tensions in Hindu applications of *rasa* and in comparable Christian traditions. A focus on aesthetics honors the affective condition of wonder that arises in the presence of the other. Comparison allows us to move past aesthetics as a study of the beautiful to a holistic interreligious encounter that involves body, mind, and emotion. After introducing the concept of *rasa*, I explore wonder in the context of religious pluralism. Along the way, I invoke *rasa* theory's ideal of the sympathetic spectator (*sahṛdaya*) as a stance for dialogue, and I call upon the notion of the complementary emotional state (*vyabhicāribhāva*) as an analogue for the work of synthesis that occurs in a person who takes up this stance.

Rasa

The Indian theory of *rasa* (aesthetic emotion) highlights the multiple and embodied means through which emotion arises. *Rasa* basically means taste, relishing, or the essence of a thing. It denotes sap, juice, and a special concoction whose flavor is distinct from any of the ingredients.[9] *Rasa*'s use as a technical aesthetic term derives from the Indian tradition

---

The Social Construction of Emotion in India (Berkeley: University of California Press, 1990).

8. Catherine A. Lutz, "Engendered Emotion: Gender, Power, and the Rhetoric of Emotional Control in American Discourse," in Catherine A. Lutz and Lila Abu-Lughod, eds., *Language and the Politics of Emotion* (Cambridge: Cambridge University Press, 1990), 69–91.

9. Susan L. Schwartz, *Rasa: Performing the Divine in India* (New York: Columbia University Press, 2004), 7.

of dance-drama in Bharata's *Nāṭya Śāstra*, where it refers to emotional states savored by spectators of the drama. As in the culinary sense of *rasa*, the process of refining emotion transforms physical and mental elements into an experience that is greater than their sum. Bharata lists eight stable human sentiments (*sthāyibhāvas*) that can be refined into aesthetic sentiment (*rasas*): the erotic (*śṛṅgāra*), the comic (*hāsya*), the pathetic (*karuṇa*), the furious (*raudra*), the heroic (*vīra*), the terrible (*bhayānaka*), the odious (*bībhatsa*), and the marvelous (*adbhuta*). A ninth, peace (*śānta*), was added to the list after later debate. As a work of art balances and blends various components, the audience savors these nine emotional "tastes."

We ordinarily experience emotion in particular, ego-bound ways. Sorrow, terror, and love-in-separation are painful; but in the theatre, according to Bharata and his commentators, when these feelings are refined into *rasa*, they are pure bliss. Ordinary emotion is thus discontinuous from aesthetic emotion. *Rasa* is independent of beauty: pleasant feelings evoke it, but so do the odious and other unpleasant sentiments. In the realm of art, we relish sentiment in its pure, universal, or generalized (*sādhāranīkaraṇa*) form, stripped of the coloring of individual personality and circumstance. For Bharata, a shared human nature accounts for this universality. Over the course of many lives, everyone has had some experience of the basic emotional states, their soliciting factors, and common responses. Art can therefore appeal to spectators from many walks of life.[10]

Commentators on the *Nāṭya Śāstra* frame aesthetic experience in religious terms. A performance parallels the creation of the world: both are *māyā*, artifice. The actor is to the spectator as the supreme spirit (*paramātman*) is to the individual soul (*jīva*): the actor retains her identity but engrosses the person susceptible to the illusion she weaves onstage.[11] Audiences become so engrossed in this world that they fail to notice the technique by which they have been lured there. Because the experience of *rasa* takes the audience beyond the concerns of the ego,

10. Bharata, *Nāṭyaśāstra of Bharatamuni: Text, Commentary of Abhinava Bhāratī by Abhinavaguptācārya and English Translation*, Vol. 1 (Chapters I–XIII), M. M. Ghosh, trans., Pushpendra Kumar, ed. (Delhi: New Bharatiya Book Company, 2006), 278–79 (prose after VII.5 and VII.6).

11. J. L. Masson and M. V. Patwardhan, *Aesthetic Rapture: The Rasādhyāya of the Nāṭyaśāstra*, 2 vols. (Poona: Deccan College Postgraduate and Research Institute, 1970), vol. 1, 36. Cf. Schwartz, *Rasa*, 23.

it offers a fleeting taste of the goal of spiritual discipline. Ascending beyond the ordinary constraints of space, time, and sensory limitation, we savor the bliss of the infinite.[12] In contrast to ordinary emotion (*bhāva*), *rasa* is *alaukika*, non-worldly, transcendent, or sublime.

The great literary theorist Abhinavagupta posits that the taste of *rasa* (*rasāsvāda*) can prepare one for the taste of the ultimate reality (*brahmāsvāda*). For him peace, the emotion of calm contemplation experienced in meditation, is paramount. All other *rasa*s participate in it when they are refined to the point of bliss.[13] By contrast, for Gaudīya Vaiṣṇava worshippers of Krishna, the *rasa* of love takes precedence. Merged with devotional experience as *bhakti rasa*, this sentiment takes the form of five varieties of loving relation to the Lord. Theologians of this tradition explore the nuances of *rasa* theory in great detail. Their major innovation lies in moving away from emotion in general to a personal experience of the contemplative, respectful, friendly, parental, and amorous devotional loves.[14]

In art, *rasa* arises in the audience through "the combination of excitants, consequents, and transitory emotional states."[15] This brief statement, known as the *rasa sūtra*, encapsulates how *rasa* works. Because I turn shortly to the importance of wonder for religious experience, wonder may serve as an example of how this formula functions in an aesthetic context.

Wonder (*adbhuta rasa*) is the aesthetic development of the foundational emotion (*sthāyibhāva*) of astonishment. The first ingredient in *rasa* is the appropriate excitants or contextual markers (*vibhāva*s).

12. Schwartz, *Rasa*, 14, 25. Cf. Kapila Vatsyayan, *Bharata: The Nāṭyaśāstra* (New Delhi: Sahitya Akademi, 1996), chapter 4.

13 Abhinavagupta, *Locana* 2.4 in Daniel H. H. Ingalls, Jeffrey Moussaieff Masson, and M. V. Patwardhan, *The* Dhvanyāloka *of Ānandavardhana with the* Locana *of Abhinavagupta* (Cambridge: Harvard University Press, 1990), 225–26. For a discussion of the importance of the aesthetic sentiment of peace for Abhinavagupta, see J. L. Masson and M. V. Patwardhan, *Śāntarasa and Abhinavagupta's Philosophy of Aesthetics* (Pune: Bhandarkar Oriental Research Institute, 1969).

14. Donna M. Wulff, "Religion in a New Mode: The Convergence of the Aesthetic and the Religious in Medieval India," *Journal of the American Academy of Religion* 54 (1986) 683. The primary theologian of this movement is Rūpa Gosvāmin. See David L. Haberman, trans., *The Bhaktirasāmṛtasindhu of Rūpa Gosvāmin* (Delhi: IGNCA and Motilal Banarsidass, 2003).

15. My translation of the *rasa sūtra*: *tatra vibhāvānubhāvavyabhicārisaṃyogādrasa niṣpattiḥ*. Bharata, *Nāṭya Śāstra*, 227 (prose after VI.31).

These factors include magical illusions, magnificent architecture, and the appearance of divine beings. The second ingredient, *anubhāva*, is the consequent effect of these stimuli: a character communicates wonder through physical indicators such as wide eyes, fixed gaze, goose bumps, tears of joy, and spontaneous utterances of amazement. The third ingredient consists of feeling states that accompany the primary emotion. These are known as *vyabhicāribhāva*s, emotions that move or change, because they are transitory. They are also sometimes called *sañcāribhāva*s because they nurture or complement the main sentiment. To foster the marvelous sentiment in the viewer, an actor exhibits passing states such as paralysis, choked voice, and agitation.[16] *Rasa* is the subjective experience that ideally takes place in audience members when all of these factors come together. As this brief example illustrates, the factors that evoke *rasa* cover a spectrum of sensory and mental states.

Wonder as Religious Orientation

The sight of celestial beings evokes wonder. So do devotional monuments of paint and stone. Mary trembles before the appearance of the angel. Arjuna gasps in astonishment when Krishna, his charioteer, reveals his true divine form. The tourist pauses, awestruck, as she enters the Meenakshi Temple, just as she does when she sets foot in a great cathedral. They cannot take it all in.

Wonder has been seen by some theorists as the synthesis of all *rasa*s, but it is also perhaps one of the fundamental religious orientations.[17] Robert Fuller observes that wonder in the Indian tradition is more than simple interest or curiosity. It is related to the central moment of devotional worship, the moment of seeing and being seen by divinity (*darśana*).[18] Through repetition, rituals such as *pūjā* or the Eucharist encapsulate the experience of wonder; and in turn the experience of

16. Bharata, *Nāṭya Śāstra*, 267 (prose after VI.74).

17. The reasoning goes that wonder assists the emotions of love and heroism, is present in "reversed" form in comedy, and characterizes the blissful climax of any aesthetic experience. Just as a skillful storyteller conceals and reveals details until the plot comes to a thrilling conclusion, an aspect of surprise is essential to art's success. V. Raghavan, *The Number of Rasa-s*, 3rd ed. (Madras: Adyar Library and Research Center, 1975), 203–5.

18. Robert C. Fuller, *Wonder: From Emotion to Spirituality* (Chapel Hill: University of North Carolina Press, 2009), 10.

wonder continually reinvigorates ritual.[19] Practices such as meditation employ sensory stimuli or deprivation to mute our customary modes of perception and deepen awareness of the "ground" or "core" of consciousness.[20] Such insights into the basic wonder or awe of existence have been foundational to the work of Christian theologians from Friedrich Schleiermacher and Rudolf Otto to Paul Tillich.

Wonder at the cosmic order may be at the root of human ethical inclinations. According to Fuller, "Wonder entices us to consider the reality of the unseen, the existence of a more general order of existence from which this world derives its meaning and purpose. It is thus only to be expected that wonder also entices us to believe that our supreme good lies in harmoniously adjusting ourselves thereto."[21] He argues that wonder has important adaptive and cognitive functions: when we put aside exclusive self-interest, we develop higher moral functions of empathy, compassion, and care that are adaptive for our species' long-term relationship with our environment.[22] Feminist philosopher Luce Irigaray also sees wonder as the foundation of ethics, but she locates it in the intimate encounter of sexual difference: "This other, male or female, should *surprise* us again and again, appear to us as *new, very different* from what we knew or what we thought he or she should be."[23] For Irigaray, the wonder of the other precedes evaluation; it prevents the assimilation of the self to the other.

Religious traditions not only ritualize the experience of wonder and mine it for ethics, but they are also objects of wonder in themselves. Interreligious encounters can provoke physiological responses typical of aesthetic experiences. Wonder initiates a subsequent process of accommodation that helps us assimilate new data. "Our natural tendency when viewing visual art is to assimilate its patterns and forms to our existing cognitive schemata. This perceptual activity inherently produces arousal and pleasure. Some works of art, however, are not easily assimilated to existing schemata. They prompt us to learn, to accommodate to new perceptual and cognitive schemata. This experience of

19. Ibid., 68.

20. Ibid., 131.

21. Ibid., 15.

22. Ibid., 14, 60.

23. Luce Irigaray, *An Ethics of Sexual Difference*, trans. Carolyn Burke and Gillian C. Gill (Ithaca, NY: Cornell University Press, 1993), 74.

accommodation . . . is itself often pleasurable."[24] Just as our brains seek out patterns in a complex piece of music, we instinctively seek strategies to manage and comprehend eruptions of the wondrous in the world's religious traditions. After the initial suspension of awe, we begin to encode and evaluate the experience.

Interreligious dialogue often takes its point of departure from the attempt to identify shared beliefs, shared approaches to scripture, or shared projects for collaboration. While the search for theological and ethical common ground is worthwhile, it risks diminishing the irreducibility of religious traditions. It can fail to satisfy the affective dimension of the encounter. Although we may search for familiar patterns of belief and practice, our expectations are often thwarted. Like works of art, religious traditions amaze us with their complexity.

Wonder and Religious Difference

Interreligious encounters affect us at many levels. Whether we read the texts of others, observe their religious practices, or simply attempt to understand our neighbors, we are engaged as whole and complex persons. Intellectually, we may try to reconcile what we already believe with what we have encountered. Spiritually, we may consider how the encounter affects our commitment to our religious tradition. But perhaps the most fundamental response occurs on an emotional or affective level. Stressing the affective aspect of encounter, comparative theologian Francis X. Clooney recommends a process of comparative reading that renders the reader "vulnerable to intellectual, imaginative, and affective transformation" by the texts of other traditions.[25] He notes that by intensifying emotion within the reader, texts can inspire the determination to live according to their reality. They may exert these effects not only on the intended audience, but on outsiders as well.[26] The interreligious reader might emerge from this inspiration with renewed attention to parallel emotional dynamics in her own tradition.

24. Fuller, *Wonder*, 117.

25. Francis X. Clooney, *Beyond Compare: St. Francis de Sales and Śrī Vedānta Deśika on Loving Surrender to God* (Washington, DC: Georgetown University Press, 2008), 208.

26. Francis X. Clooney, "Passionate Comparison: The Intensification of Affect in Interreligious Reading of Hindu and Christian Texts," *Harvard Theological Review* 98 (2005) 371–74.

Beyond the intended emotional impact of texts and practices, the primary emotions they evoke exert an aesthetic force of their own. They become *rasa*s, emotions transmuted into a sense of aesthetic contemplation. The religious reader may experience peace or love as evoked in a text or performance; but when this experience rises to the level of aesthetic rapture (*rasa*), it takes on an additional significance. Abhinavagupta's analogy between aesthetic appreciation and theological wonder highlights how both pull the individual away from ordinary egoic concerns. Immersed in *rasa*, we suspend habitual attachments to identity. In his theological framework, the same suspension occurs when one tastes nondual union with divinity.[27]

The non-utilitarian and other-centered aspects of wonder epitomize *rasa*'s transcendence. If part of what distinguishes *rasa* from ordinary emotion (*bhāva*) is that it transports the viewer away from self-reference, then even in its ordinary manifestation, wonder has an innately rasic function. As Martha Nussbaum describes it, "This emotion responds to the pull of the object, and one might say that in it the subject is maximally aware of the value of the object, and only minimally aware, if at all, of its relationship to her own plans."[28] Even as self-reference is momentarily suspended, this aspect of wonder resists the theory that *rasa* absorbs the viewer with emotion in its most *general* form (the principle of *sādhāraṇīkaraṇa*). Here, the viewer is entranced by the astounding features of a *particular* marvelous object. Rather than transcend difference, wonder attends to it acutely.

Christian theologian Jeannine Hill Fletcher applies these facets of wonder to the experience of religious pluralism. She observes that the postliberal insistence upon religions' distinctiveness can become an obstacle to dialogue. If we do not share a common story or language, how can we engage in conversation? If we cannot fully participate in another religious community, how can we hope to understand it? Hill Fletcher pushes beyond the perceived obstacle of difference to argue that the initial moment of incomprehension is the key to the success of everyday

---

27. Loriliai Biernacki, "Towards a Tantric Nondualist Ethics through Abhinavagupta's Notion of Rasa," *Journal of Hindu Studies* 4 (2011) 265. In place of Bharata's term for the *rasa* of wonder (*adbhuta*), Abhinavagupta employs a technical term in Kashmir Śaivism (*camatkāra*) to denote wonder as the peak of both religious and aesthetic experience.

28. Nussbaum, *Upheavals of Thought*, 54.

points of contact, collaboration, and fruitful conversations that do in fact ensue across religions.

> The experience of unknowing in the encounter with otherness offers an immediate theological wellspring because, prior to the endeavor to learn from other faiths, there can be a moment of profound wonder, a moment that comes *before* understanding. It is a moment more immediate to the encounter. The moment in which I "don't get it" is the moment of encounter when all one's orientations and understandings are no longer useful for making sense of the reality encountered. . . . The moment of wonder in the presence of a tradition one does not understand can be a moment that brings one to the awareness of the incomprehensible mystery of God.[29]

Wonder is theologically instructive. The deep mystery of the other structurally resembles divine mystery. Without becoming an insider to a religious tradition, we cannot experience it in full; yet even as insiders to our own traditions, the mystery of the divine remains. In interreligious encounter as in the encounter with holy mystery, a person should never expect complete understanding; yet in both cases, the mind desires understanding even as it knows this is beyond reach. We still seek to know more. The goal is not "exhaustive comprehension" or vindication of one's own beliefs but "wonder itself."[30]

Wonder, as a *rasa* and as the experiential core of *rasa* itself, opens us to the divine. No universal content to religious experience is necessary to make this claim. The apophatic moment, which cannot comprehend *what it is* that is not comprehended, is the paradoxical *contentless core* that aesthetic, interreligious, and mystical encounters share. In the wondrous encounter, the disorientation of coming face-to-face with the irreducible distinctiveness of another worldview participates in the astonishment aroused by divine mystery.

Hill Fletcher places wonder at the heart of interfaith encounter, and in theorizing this sentiment as *rasa*, I extend the analysis into additional aesthetic dimensions. *Rasa* theory offers a framework for understanding why and how this affective response of wonderment is possible, and why it is theologically significant and beneficial in the

---

29. Jeannine Hill Fletcher, "As Long as We Wonder: Possibilities in the Impossibility of Interreligious Dialogue," *Theological Studies* 68 (2007) 549 (531–54).

30. Ibid., 551.

context of religious pluralism. I lift up two additional components of *rasa* theory as important as analogues for what happens in interreligious dialogue: the sympathetic spectator (*sahṛdaya*) and the complementary emotional state (*vyabhicāribhāva*).

Sympathetic Spectator

As we develop an orientation of wonder in interfaith encounter, we become *sahṛdaya*s, persons whose hearts are attuned to the situation of the other. According to classical Indian aesthetic theory, the discerning viewer's heart (*hṛd*) unites with (*sa*) art experience. Within the sympathetic spectator, the emotions expressed in a drama or other work of art are elevated to their refined state through the combination of evocative situations (*vibhāvas*), physical expressions (*anubhāvas*), and other emotional states compatible with it (*vyabhicāribhāvas*). Immersion in a work of art brings the spectator beyond feeling the emotions of the characters (which, in the case of tragedy, would be painful) to a state of blissful contemplation. The sympathetic viewer savors emotion itself.

The *Nāṭya Śāstra* measures the success of a performance on human (*mānuṣī*) and divine (*daivikī*) levels, depending on the reactions of the spectators.[31] Ordinary spectators might respond to the superficial aspects of a work with applause or murmurs of appreciation. "Divine" success, however, occurs when people who are especially cultured, educated, or prepared encounter a phenomenal performance.[32] The chest expands, tears well in the eyes, and the skin ripples with delight. In the devotional realm, "divine" is more than a metaphor for an exceptionally moving performance. Here, the heights of *rasa* are achieved not only through human effort and preparation but also through a touch of divine grace. For Gauḍīya Vaiṣṇavas, amateur performances of scriptural plays (*rās līlās*), though often technically deficient, are seen as a "manifestation of divinity."[33] The audience's mental immersion in the narratives, characters, and physical setting of Krishna's realm grants them special access to his transcendent divine play.

31. Bharata, *Natya Śāstra*, 225–26 (VI.26).

32. Schwartz, *Rasa*, 25.

33. Margaret H. Case, *Seeing Krishna: The Religious World of a Brahman Family in Vrindaban* (Oxford: Oxford University Press, 2000), 151. See also David V. Mason, *Theatre and Religion on Krishna's Stage: Performing in Vrindavan* (New York: Palgrave Macmillan, 2009).

The spectator is not passive in *rasa* experience. Even if all the appropriate excitants, responses, and accompanying emotions are present in the plot and characters, *rasa* will not appear if audience members are insensate to their magic. They must actively appreciate the unique combination of elements. One performer describes a village festival in which she performed a dance depicting Krishna's mother holding the baby on her lap: "I looked at Krishna—isn't he beautiful? Then I looked towards the audience. They were nodding! Yes, nodding! We were seeing Krishna together! It was as we say *anukirtanam* (a re-creation, making anew). The moment with Krishna, it is a presence at *that point* of time."[34] Such heartfelt absorption is the greatest qualification of the sympathetic spectator.

The *Nātya Śāstra* states confidently that art brings out the best in those who are attentive to it. Drama teaches "duty to the unscrupulous, love to lovers, restraint to the undisciplined, self-control to the disciplined, boldness to cowards, energy to heroes, intelligence to those who lack it, and wisdom to the learned."[35] Abhinavagupta elaborates that drama interrupts the pain of those who are ill, delights the tired and sorrowful, and instructs happy persons in the four ends of life.[36] Art burnishes the virtues we already display, and it unearths those we have allowed to lie dormant.

The appreciation of a faith tradition other than one's own resembles an attentive and informed audience's appreciation of *rasa*. *Rasa* theory stipulates that despite the active element in the audience's participation, *rasa* occurs in spectators, not actors. The emotions of performers are ordinary feelings (*bhāva*), not sentiment savored in its pure form (*rasa*). Thus, although some Christian theologians have pursued acting, theatre, and mimesis as models of the Christian life,[37] and David

---

34. Uttara Asha Coorlawala, "It Matters For Whom You Dance: Audience Participation in Rasa Theory," in Susan Kattwinkel, ed., *Audience Participation: Essays on Inclusion in Performance* (Westport, CT: Praeger, 2003), 48.

35. *dharmo 'dharmapravṛttānāṃ kāmaḥ kāmopasevinām /*
nigraho durvinītānāṃ vinītānāṃ damakriyā //
klīvānāṃ dhārṣṭyakaraṇamutsāhaḥ śūramāninām /
abudhānāṃ vibodhaśca vaiduṣyaṃ viduśāmapi //

My translation. Cf. Bharata, *Nātya Śāstra*, 31 (I.108–9).

36. Masson and Patwardhan, *Śāntarasa*, 56–67.

37. See, e.g., Todd Johnson and Dale Savidge, *Performing the Sacred: Theology and Theatre in Dialogue* (Grand Rapids: Baker Academic, 2009).

Haberman reads the Gauḍīya Vaiṣṇavas tradition in terms of acting,[38] I propose that in relation to other faith traditions, persons of faith take the stance of audience members. The enticing, disorienting experience of religious otherness encourages us to become *sahṛdayas*, appreciative viewers who care enough about others to learn to savor their distinctive qualities. The combination of preparation and divine grace that is the mark of the *sahṛdaya's* aesthetic experience also occurs as persons of faith encounter one another. If we want to appreciate the distinct contours of our neighbor's faith, we must learn the idioms, images, and narratives that evoke devotional sentiment for them. In the process, we prepare to receive a taste of the divine that enhances our own devotion and virtue.

Rasa and Interreligious Complementarity

The *sahṛdaya* cannot permanently dwell in the ecstasy of wonder. The rapture slips away and everyday life resumes. Nevertheless, we may emerge transformed to test perceptions awakened in a wondrous glimpse of possibility. In the natural world, this is how scientific discovery is born: "Wonder . . . encourages the construction of hypothetical or possible orders of existence that might causally account for unexpected perceptions. Wonder is thus one of the major sources of our capacity to entertain the possible."[39] So too with theological discovery. Although we might not respond immediately with assessment when we encounter religious others, we do eventually make decisions about the alternative worldviews they represent. We enact a theology of religious pluralism when we order these perspectives within a life of faith.

The category of "transitory" or "nurturing" emotions (*vyabhicāri-bhāva*s, *sañcāribhāva*s), allows the *sahṛdaya* to return from wonder and reflect upon how the interfaith encounter affects her own faith. I approach this theology of religious pluralism from a Christian perspective but invite readers consider its possibilities for other traditions.

As a whole, an excellent work of art will evoke one primary *rasa*: a tragedy will raise feelings of compassion (*karuṇa*), whereas a romance will develop the sentiment of love (*śṛṅgāra*). But according to the *rasa*

38. David L. Haberman, *Acting as a Way of Salvation: A Study of Rāgānugā Bhakti Sādhana* (Delhi: Motilal Banarsidass, 1988).

39. Fuller, *Wonder*, 86.

sūtra, this primary *rasa* arises not only through the combination of eliciting factors (*vibhāvas*) and appropriate responses (*anubhāvas*), but through transitory emotions (*vyabhicāribhāvas*) that foster the main sentiment. These emotions arise temporarily throughout a drama to give fresh perspectives on the main emotional theme. For example, a love story can be enhanced by feelings of jealousy, bashfulness, anxiety, anger in the lovers' quarrels, despondency in the beloved's absence, humor in flirtatious pranks, and so on. Indian devotional traditions surrounding Krishna modify the theme of the *vyabhicāribhāva* to suggest that every human emotion has a place in developing the ultimate affective goal of devotion (*bhakti*).[40] All *rasa*s become *vyabhicāribhāva*s in relation to *bhakti rasa*. Every emotion, when related to the primary religious narrative, enhances devotion.

Christian devotion is similarly enhanced through appreciation of other religious expressions. In other words, just as the overall mood of love can incorporate bashfulness, anxiety, or jealousy, the appreciation of other religious modalities can enrich one's primary mode of piety. Christian devotion, contemplation, or action may remain one's central or stable emotion (*sthāyibhāva*), yet these will be enriched or expanded on account of a deep diversity of experience.

This enrichment is a process of religious formation. For the person who pursues the wonder of encounter toward greater understanding, Clooney recommends a "necessary interim stage of detached objectivity."[41] The reader should undertake the discipline of setting aside normative and evaluative questions. Over time, however, the texts, practices, and performances of the other tradition exercise rhetorical appeal. "Engaged in the reading to fill in the gaps, she or he becomes increasingly affected by it," Clooney writes, "Attentive readers revise and improvise their own ongoing projects of self-formation."[42] Readers may not ultimately be persuaded to accept the texts' view of reality, but in the traverse between their own view of reality and another, they may be transformed in subtle ways.

There is nothing predictable about this interplay. Some Christian readers will enhance their peaceful contemplation as they immerse themselves in Hindu texts; others might reinforce their heartfelt love

40. Rūpa Gosvāmin, *Bhaktirasāmṛtasindhu*, 365 (2.5.45).

41. Clooney, *Beyond Compare*, 208.

42. Clooney, "Passionate Comparison," 383.

of God or find fuel for their prophetic zeal. Without appropriating the other, one's affective responses might also be modified through the encounter. Activism might become grounded in a practice of meditation. Love of Christ might find new dimensions of friendship, affection, or eros. Prayer might develop shades of emotions that would otherwise go unnoticed. The point here is not to prescribe or discipline the emotions but to "stay with the particularities of the reading process across religious boundaries and the affective states generated in this process."[43] Amid ongoing encounter, wonder unfolds into manifold affective tastes.

The ability to contemplate two visions of reality at the same time may be an essentially aesthetic skill. Jon Paul Sydnor illustrates how viewing religious works of art together deepens understanding, even as this understanding eludes words: "vision and speech are not hegemonized or prioritized one over the other but instead exist in complementary relation, each reliant on the other for its own fullness of being."[44] In reflecting on interreligious encounter, as when we discuss art, our language does not take the place of the work of art but always refers back to the work itself: "The same relationship to language can safely be assumed for the other non-discursive manifestations of religion: ritual, ethics, statuary, music, dance, painting and architecture. In each, language must maintain an other-referential discipline in order to prevent self-inflation into a mistaken autonomy. In each, language must point away from itself and toward its subject in order to avoid accidental and distorting dominance."[45] This "other-referential discipline" is the stance of the connoisseur as *sahṛdaya*. I submit that this stance is appropriate, at least as an initial gasp of wonder in the presence of otherness, for the discursive as well as non-discursive forms of religions. The complexity and inner coherence of a theological system are astonishing to behold.

Because religious traditions seem to demand total commitment, logic and language often fail the appreciative spectator who holds commitment to her own faith tradition alongside commitment to understanding another tradition.[46] The notion of complementary emotional

---

43. Ibid., 389.

44. Jon Paul Sydnor, "Shaivism's *Nataraja* and Picasso's *Crucifixion*: An Essay in Comparative Visual Theology," *Studies in Interreligious Dialogue* 15/1 (2005) 93.

45. Sydnor, "Shaivism's *Nataraja* and Picasso's *Crucifixion*," 98–99.

46. See Clooney, "Passionate Comparison"; and Catherine Cornille, ed., *Many Mansions: Multiple Religious Belonging and Christian Identity* (Maryknoll, NY: Orbis, 2003).

states gives voice to this space. Its logic can be elaborated through the epistemology of complementarity thinking. Born in the realm of quantum physics, complementary reasoning allows the simultaneous existence of two apparently contradictory ideas: light as wave and light as particle, for instance. Rather than excluding one another, "'wave' and 'particle' become co-referential and take on new significance."[47] Like John Hick in an earlier discussion of religious pluralism,[48] Sydnor applies this reasoning to differing accounts of reality offered by Buddhists and Christians. The accounts of Buddhism and Christianity may both be true; likewise, neither may be absolutely true. The subject matter of theology necessitates that our knowledge of ultimate reality is always partial and incomplete.

Paradox is not the enemy. We need not explain away the fascination that seemingly incompatible points of view hold for us. To be sure, strategies to reconcile differing theologies do exist. To help me contemplate the saving power of Krishna alongside that of Christ, Christian theologies of religious pluralism offer theories that all saviors are faces of the cosmic Christ, that both Krishna and Christ manifest a transcendent Real, that they offer genuinely different paths to divinity, or that they represent distinct religious ends. Hindu theologies of religious pluralism convey similar positions. We may adopt such doctrines in advance of interreligious encounters, or we may find them useful after the fact. In the end, however, there is no accounting for taste. This old adage carries a nugget of wisdom: we can train our aesthetic lenses to understand form and style, but we are often at a loss to explain what moves us. And, indeed, once we can explain *why* something is beautiful, it can lose some of its charm. The absorbed Christian spectator relishes the interfaith encounter, and this wonderment remains with her as she continues to live out her commitment to Christ.

Ethical Tensions

Every aesthetic emotion has the potential to transport the attuned spectator to an experience of the divine. Taken up in the religious realm,

47. Jon Paul Sydnor, "Complementarity Reasoning and Interreligious Dialogue: A Case Study in Interdisciplinary Reflection," *Studies in Interreligious Dialogue* 15/2 (2005) 169.

48. Cf. John Hick, *An Interpretation of Religion: Human Responses to the Transcendent* (New Haven: Yale University Press, 1989), 245.

*rasa*s offer unique tastes of divinity: love of God, compassion for others, disgust and rage at injustice, courage in the face of despair, and wonder at divine and human mystery. Each *rasa* also carries potential pitfalls or distractions: love and peace have their interior and world-denying aspects, and disgust and anger tempt us to forget the humanity of others. Although wonder opens us up to otherness and embodied particularity, it also partakes of the ethical ambivalence that attends aesthetic emotion.

The predominant critique of aesthetics in religion is that truth gets swallowed up in awe, that thinking gets overwhelmed by feeling. In light of these temptations, Christian theologian Hans Urs von Balthasar labors to develop a theological aesthetics that, in his words, does not "deteriorate into an 'aesthetic theology' by betraying and selling out theological substance to the current viewpoints of an inner-worldly theory of beauty."[49] Contemporary Hindu theologian Rita Sherma similar argues for this possibility: "*rasa* requires vulnerability, openness, sensitivity, passion, and emotion. For, *rasa* is not hedonism; it is . . . not always evocative of delight. A moving and tragic story is capable of bringing about *rasa*; here it would be the *rasa* of deep compassion."[50] Because *rasa* theory is not a theory of the beautiful but attends to every human emotion and experience, it helps participants in interreligious dialogue resist the temptations of a shallow or superficial aesthetics.

Wonder's special temptation is that, even as it opens us to that which is beyond ourselves, it threatens to close off critical inquiry. Aristotle's cautions on this point reverberate throughout Western philosophy, and the strategic employment of music and film by the Third Reich illustrate it painfully well. Recognizing, as Joseph Goebbels did, that "the moment that propaganda becomes conscious, it is ineffective," Nazi officials exercised tight control over the production, funding, marketing, and censorship of the arts. Art sanctioned by the regime comforted and inspired audiences while numbing them to the insidious realities around them.[51]

49. Hans Urs von Balthasar, *The Glory of the Lord: A Theological Aesthetics, Volume I: Seeing the Form*, Erasmo Leiva-Merikakis, trans., Joseph Fessio, SJ and John Riches eds., 7 vols. (San Francisco: Ignatius, 1982), 38.

50. Rita Dasgupta Sherma, "Eros, Ethics, and Enlightenment: Towards a Reconstructive Approach to Ultimate and Penultimate Goals in Hindu Theology," http://www.infinityfoundation.com/mandala/s_es/s_es_sherm_eros_frameset.htm.

51. Goebbels cited in Mary-Elizabeth O'Brien, *Nazi Cinema as Enchantment: The*

It is perhaps no accident that Martin Heidegger, the Western philosopher who ardently strove to reopen wonder, initially fell headlong into the ideology of National Socialism. Hannah Arendt finds four risks inherent to wonder encapsulated in Heidegger's error: wonder can tempt us to escape from the messy obligations of reality, it allows us to become star struck by dictators and tyrants, it can alienate us from the world to the extent that we can hardly relate to it in language, and it can obstruct our ability to form beliefs or make decisions.[52] In Mary-Jane Rubenstein's assessment of the history of wonder, however, she observes that proper attention to the object of emotion is what resists the temptations of the aesthetic: "any unquestioning capitulation to ideology, Heidegger's included, is a matter not of too much wonder, but rather of too little."[53] She advises that we delay resolution and certainty to remain within the unsettling "wound" of wonder: "just as a wound ceases to be itself when it heals, wonder is only wonder when it remains open."[54] The bandages of certainty and the sutures of belief offer the comforting but dangerous illusion that we are self-contained and whole.

Wonder in the face of religious difference occasions similar temptations. On the one hand, wonder can give way to emotional evaluations such as admiration, fear, or disgust. Rather than following these feelings uncritically, we must discern ethical responses to the persons whose beliefs and practices strike us as appealing, strange, or revolting. On the other hand, if we first set out to articulate a coherent theology through critical dialogue, we will be lost if we cease to be amazed by difference. The razor's edge lies somewhere between the willingness to be uncritically swept away and the struggle to find language for what fascinates us. The ethics of this *rasa* demands a "wondrous openness to alterity [that] can be sustained only by ... a tireless refusal to ground once and for all the identity of the self, the other, our god, this nation,

---

Politics of Entertainment in the Third Reich (Rochester, NY: Camden House, 2004), 8. The opening scene of the film *Schindler's List* stuns the viewer with the paradox of beauty alongside evil: over the horrors of a pogrom in a Jewish ghetto in Poland waft strands of a Bach piano sonata perfectly executed by an SS trooper who has discovered a piano in someone's living room. Michael H. Kater, *The Twisted Muse: Musicians and Their Music in the Third Reich* (New York: Oxford University Press, 1997), 3–4.

52. Arendt's concerns are discussed succinctly in Mary-Jane Rubenstein, *Strange Wonder: The Closure of Metaphysics and the Opening of Awe* (New York: Columbia University Press, 2008), 21.

53. Rubenstein, *Strange Wonder*, 23.

54. Ibid., 10.

or that people."[55] When we cultivate the wonder of this edge, we remain open to the mystery of the other and of the divine.

The aesthetic framework I have developed here prevents the theologian from reducing religious differences to aspects of one's own religion. The sympathetic observer's appreciation of Krishna *bhakti* does not mean that she must understand it as another form of worship of the Holy Trinity. It is a distinct religious flavor. If she is willing to learn from her religious neighbors, she learns to savor their faith in its particular idioms. The sympathetic spectator takes in these tastes of the divine in such a way that they nurture the faith formed within her primary community—in part, precisely because it opens this faith up to wonder. The stance of wondrous appreciation heightens the apprehension of the depth and riches of the divine.

The tensions in which aesthetic appreciation entangle us are not meant to be unraveled. Not completely. *Rasa* is not an escapist transcendence, but it transports us nonetheless. Its raptures are firmly planted in bodies: those that evoke it and those that resonate with its frequency. It opens us simultaneously to what is common in the human emotional vocabulary and to the marvel of our irreducible differences. We savor the space between self and other in both its unsettling and complementary aspects.

A Holistic Approach to Dialogue

The holistic and experiential emphases of feminist theology have contributed to the expansion of interreligious dialogue beyond doctrine and ethics. As Pamela Dickey Young observes, "Insofar as we experience a religious tradition as addressed to ourselves as whole human beings rather than as fragmented into discrete parts, we have been grasped by its aesthetic dimension."[56] A broad spectrum of interfaith encounters awakens the senses, from the fascination of unfamiliar rituals or beautiful religious art to participation in trans-religious practices such as meditation, yoga, or service. The interpersonal dimension of dialogue itself awakens wonder, for when we connect with a member of another

55. Rubenstein, *Strange Wonder*, 133.

56. Pamela Dickey Young, *Christ in a Post-Christian World: How Can We Believe in Jesus Christ When Those around Us Believe Differently—Or Not at All?* (Minneapolis: Fortress, 1995), 127.

religious tradition, we obtain a taste of *their* larger reality. These paths to interfaith encounter appeal to us holistically, on the level of body, mind, emotion, and spirit. Everyday encounters such as my ongoing exchange with Lalita are illuminated through attention to the aesthetic, but women are also taking the lead in holistic dialogue focused on aesthetics and the arts. For example, in what she describes as a "journey of wonder," Christian theologian and dancer Angela Yarber has undertaken an embodied dialogue with *bharatanatyam*, *kabuki*, Sufi, and Israeli folk dance with an explicit focus on their expressions and paradoxes of femininity.[57]

As such experiences make their way into mainstream dialogue, the analogy of *rasa* lends specificity to the claim that an aesthetic orientation operates holistically. *Rasa* theory offers categories to analyze the physical, mental, and emotional means of evoking, expressing, and modulating emotion. *Rasa* is rooted in the body through the physical stimuli that cause it to arise and through the appropriate physical responses. *Rasa* theory is culturally inflected, as when particular dance movements carry layers of meaning for cultured Indian viewers that are lost on others, but it also points to shared dimensions of emotion and transcendence through aesthetic experience.

Significantly for women's interfaith relations, *rasa* theory resists the common axiom that the purpose of theological aesthetics is to ascertain the beautiful. Susan Ross muses that an explicit feminist theological aesthetics has been slow to emerge because for feminists the exigencies of justice outweigh beauty.[58] Because *rasa* cannot be reduced to the beautiful, it offers a way to engage in aesthetics that does not prettify life's vicissitudes. Fright, disgust, pathos, fury, humor, and indifference join courage and love as tastes of the divine. Moving beyond the traditional nine *rasas* of Indian theory, emotions identified in other cultural settings, such as the tangle of tragic emotions known as *han* in Korean, or the strong, spontaneous feeling called *qing* in Chinese culture, can also

---

57. Angela M. Yarber, *Embodying the Feminine in the Dances of the World's Religions* (New York: Lang, 2011), 137. In this vein of embodied interreligious appreciation, we may look forward to the translation of Chung Hyun Kyung's two-volume *In the End, Beauty Will Save Us All: A Feminist Spiritual Pilgrimage* (2002, in Korean).

58. Susan A. Ross, "Women, Beauty, and Justice: Moving Beyond von Balthasar," *Journal of the Society of Christian Ethics* 25 (2005) 84. Young takes up this challenge with her feminist view of beauty as "fullness of existence." Young, *Christ in a Post-Christian World*, 106.

find a place.[59] In a world where women are associated with beauty in ways that objectify and demean them and subject them to control, this holistic expansion of the aesthetic is a liberating word.

Finally, a holistic feminist approach complexifies unitary notions of religious identity. As understanding deepens, the sympathetic spectator who cultivates existential openness in the presence of the other temporarily forgets herself. Absorbed in another vision of reality, she tastes complementary emotional states (*vyabhicāribhāvas*) that augment the stable emotional tenor (*sthāyibhāva*) of her primary religious identity. Despite *rasa* theory's assurances that the absorption is temporary and that identity remains relatively stable, however, the aesthetic approach can stir fears of the unknown: Does the *sahṛdaya* come back? Will she get lost in interreligious dialogue? Can her existential openness once again be closed? If comparative theology is ideally done by persons rooted in a distinct religious identity, doesn't an aesthetic orientation uproot this identity in favor of an egoless point of view?

Such questions call attention to the shifting and hybrid nature of identity. Religious identity is not a static thing. Our sense of ourselves undergoes subtle changes over time due to changed circumstances, broader perspectives, and maturing wisdom. The *sahṛdaya*'s primary characteristic in relation to this process is attentiveness: she *notices* the impact interfaith encounters have on her. She notices the distinct emotions these encounters arouse, including the fear of losing her identity. The *sahṛdaya* is a *discerning* as well as sympathetic spectator: she remains aware of the play (and of the religious identities of others) and does not identify its circumstances with her own. From this discerning perspective, whatever epistemic breakthrough occurs from walking imaginatively in the other's shoes can remain with her when she returns to familiar ground. In interreligious encounter as in our openness to the world more generally, identity formation continues as long as the beautiful, confounding, distressing, and wondrous play goes on.

---

59. Jae Hoon Lee, *The Exploration of the Inner Wounds* (Oxford: Oxford University Press, 1994); Pauline C. Lee, *Li Zhi, Confucianism, and the Virtue of Desire* (Albany: SUNY Press, 2012).

11

The Knowing Body

Currents of Connection and Women in Religious Dialogue[1]

Anne Carolyn Klein (Rigzin Drolma)

When we inquire into gender and our lived experience as men and women, we generally use terms like "women" and "feminine" in juxtaposition to "men" and "masculine." These categories are part of a living dialogue, of conversations emerging through shifting sets of culturally determined dichotomies and polarities.

To the extent that this is so, the poles of female and male get lined up with other polarities fundamental to cultural constructions of personhood—mind and body, self and other, intellect and emotion, abstract

1. Excerpt from a manuscript in progress with the working title *The Knowing Body in Love: Currents of Our Lives and the Myth of Isolation* © Anne C. Klein/Rigzin Drolma 2012.

and particular, strong and weak. This has long been recognized in feminist discourse, and I have long been interested in how this plays out for a spiritual life oriented toward deep inquiry into the experience of selfhood. My book, *Meeting the Great Bliss Queen*,[2] explored a conversation between feminist essentialists and constructionists on the one hand and Buddhists discovery and development styles of practice on the other. I saw that the discovery model, like the feminist essential model, was based in a sense that there is in fact something to be discovered within that makes a tremendous difference in experience of self and world. The development model, like the feminist constructionism, emphasizes how experience, including experiences of wisdom, compassion, and beyond, can be cultivated.

Both these models engage mind as well as body, thus calling attention to a powerful cultural categorization of these as polarized, using that mind-body polarity to align the female with the "lower" dimensions of matter, physicality, lust, limited intellectual authority and so forth. Buddhist and other Asian traditions make it clear that mind-body polarization is by no means the only way to frame our human experience. When that paradigm changes, the space between thinking and feeling also shifts and, along with it, the very ground of our sense of self in relation to other. With this in mind, I invite you to explore some subtle aspects of embodied experience that belie mind-body polarity and that also provide a variety of fresh lenses for questions of interest for both personhood and the meaning of dialogue. This exploration focuses on the most fundamental constituents of our sense of who we are—not only our mind and body, but the currents that connect and suffuse them. In discussing this, I draw from Tibetan Buddhist writings in which these currents are a vitally important topic at every level of practice and philosophy. I then look into how this trope pertains to matters of dialogue within and dialogue with others.

The Currents of Our Lives

In Indian, Tibetan and other Asian understandings of perception, every consciousness rides a steed of wind, a current of energy. To understand the dynamic relationship in which body and mind interact, we need

2. Anne Carolyn Klein, *Meeting the Great Bliss Queen: Buddhists, Feminists, and the Art of the Self* (Boston: Beacon, 1995; reprinted, Ithaca, NY: Snow Lion, 2009).

to see that they are always engaged with this third category, *rlung* or *prāṇa*, the wind currents that constantly circulate through the body, and outside it as well. These flows are central to Buddhist perspectives on world, bodies, beings, and consciousness. You cannot understand what you are as an embodied being without understanding and feeling how intrinsic these currents are to your structure, your potential, and all your activities. Interreligious dialogue, as well as personal spiritual practice, involves these elements as well.

A standard definition of a current or wind is "that which is light and moving."[3] As the Dalai Lama puts it: "matter in its most subtle form is *prāṇa* a vital energy which is inseparable from consciousness. These are different aspects of a single reality."[4]

These currents are connected with everything from the most exalted to the most practical aspects of our lives. Sensing into them can yield more precise awareness of the inner states important for spiritual or psychological reflection. Such attention avoids framing our existence through a Cartesian universe in which subject and object have no communication. Likewise, it is different from a Freudian universe in which so much of our inner material is forever hidden, and perhaps most especially, from a Newtonian universe emphasizing discrete individuality. It avoids, in short, the "individual-in-a-disenchanted-world" assumptions associated with these perspectives and much of modernity. Today's science is also contesting these boundaries, so we are in good company.

We are dealing here with "the lived body," as distinct from the material body.[5] And we are focusing on a particular subtle aspect of that lived, experientially crucial body, its currents of energy, the currents of

3. *yang zhing g.yo ba*. See Daniel E. Perdue, *Debate in Tibetan Buddhism* (Ithaca, NY: Snow Lion, 1992), 211. See also Tibetan Text in appendix, 5a.3.

4. HH the Dalai Lama, *The Universe in a Single Atom*, Morgan Road Books (New York: Random House, 2005), 110. This is a very graceful rendering of a technical term *ngo bog cig ltog pa that dad*, "a single entity whose different elements are isolatable by thought." But they cannot be isolated, or separated physically, for example, a table and its impermanence are a single entity yet "table" and "impermanence" can be conceptualized by different thoughts and different times.

5. These terms were originally used by Edmund Husserl in 1907 and are discussed by Elizabeth A. Behnke, "Body," in Lester Embree et al., eds., *Encyclopedia of Phenomenology* (Dordrecht: Kluwer Academic,1997), 66–70. Cited and discussed by Fiona Bowie in "An Anthropology of Religious Experience: Spirituality, Gender and Cultural Transmission in the Focolare Movement," *Ethnos: Journal of Anthropology* 68/1 (2003) 49–72; http://dx.doi.org/10.1080/0014184032000060362. (Thanks to Martijn Van Beek for the reference.)

our very being that move through and pertain to all aspects of body, speech, and mind.

The body and its currents, though interpreted variously in different cultures, are universal across human experience. From the perspective of Buddhist physiology, when we speak of blood pulsing, heart beating, movement across brain synapses, or arms waving, we are describing some type of current. Moreover, the body, along with such currents, is always central to our experience, including religious experience. As Marcel Mauss famously observed "at the bottom of our mystical states there are bodily techniques . . ."[6]

I propose that our bodies, especially the more subtle aspects of embodied experience, are a basis for commonality and dialogue across cultural and religious difference. I am here not referring only to formal or semi-public dialogue programs; religious dialogue these days occurs all the time—when we read a newspaper, watch TV, whenever we encounter someone in the workplace or marketplace from another tradition. We are always in dialogue with each other and our traditions, so the more conscious we can make it, the better. This is one reason why exploring the knowing body—and the currents running through it do include knowing—enhances connection and love for self and for others, both others intimate with us as well as humanity, and even the cosmos, writ large. For these currents are at once the most intimate and subtle aspect of our lived experience. They resonate also with the currents running through space and time, through our inner and outer worlds.[7] This, at least, is a central principle of Buddhist physiology and cosmology.

The Spirit in Our Senses

Buddhists famously articulate three phases of human learning: hearing, reflection and meditation. Each functions through the movement of

6. Marcel Mauss, "Body Techniques," in *Sociology and Psychology: Essays by Marcel Mauss*, trans. Ben Brewster (London: Routledge & Kegan Paul 1979), 95–123; cited and discussed by Bowie, "An Anthropology of Religious Experience," 52.

7. This point is central to many renowned Buddhist practices; for example, the Kālacakra tantra. Essential to its view is that the individual and its environment share the same material basis, *energetic nature* and manner of origination and destruction. See for example Francis Garrett, *Religion, Medicine and the Human Embryo in Tibet*, Critical Studies in Buddhism Series (New York: Routledge, 2008), 32.

their supporting currents. The settling that occurs as one moves from thinking to reflecting has to do with the increasingly gentle flow of these currents; the depths reached in meditation are related with a profound stilling or uniformly even flow of currents deep within the body. This brings about experiences of profound ease and pleasure. These currents, in short, have everything to do with how we think, how we feel, how we react to others, and, finally, how deeply we know ourselves.

Three types of currents. An important Tibetan oral tradition divides our bodily currents or winds into three categories, those currents associated with effort, not associated with effort, and beyond both.[8] The first refers to fairly esoteric practices that explicitly engage the wind-currents, (*rtsa rtlung*), the second, to normal, natural breathing and pranic circulation, and the third, to an enlightened state quite beyond our ken. All such currents are regarded as a subtle type of form. They are crucial to the health of the material body and the flourishing of consciousness.[9] They also play significant roles in the body's development and in the functioning of perception.[10] Likewise, we can gradually hope to better understand how these currents function in meditation, particularly the cultivation of attention, compassion, and insight or wisdom. The cultivated ability to recognize and interpret such currents means we can track subtle bodily sensations in real time. Taking the currents of our lives as a formal category of theory-building shifts our understanding of how we move in the world, and expands our ability to inquire into our deeply felt sense of self. Such sensing includes our awareness of subtle embodied sensations and changes to the self-sensing that arises in the process of dialogue.

In the best case, dialogue yields a fruitful synergy, an animating exchange with others that inspires deeper personal inquiry. I can talk

8. Received from Adzom Paylo Rinpche, June 5, 2012, Chengdu. The three categories are: *brtsol ba'i rlung*; *ma brtsol ba'i rlung*; and *de gnyis las 'das pa'i rlung*.

9. We can see this as a further example of what the philosopher of science Evan Thompson and others, starting with Francisco Varela, speak of as a self-activating system. See Evan Thompson's talk, *First International Symposium on Contemplative Studies*, http://events.powerstream.net/008/00189/2012_ISCS/.

10. In his *Treasury of Philosophical Tenets*, the fifteenth-century Longchen Rabjam writes: "The first step in formation of the physical body occurs when the causal factors from father and mother, white and red bright orbs . . . become inseparable from the subtle energy and mind of the being who is thus conceived." In *Treasury of Philosophical Tenets* (*grub mtha' mdzod*), trans. Richard Barron (Junction City, CA: Padma, 2007), 341.

to you more fulsomely if, right as we speak, I am aware of how our discussion is impacting me, now, in this very moment. Hearing your experience may then become deeply bonding, , whatever our theological differences.

Connecting through Currents, Limbic Resonance, and the Joys of Mimicry

Given their potential importance for spiritual practice as well as religious dialogue, let us look further into what we mean by these inner currents, and how modern science is beginning to approximate analogous categories.

According to classic Tibetan medical and tantric literature, there are five main currents moving through the body.[11] Most briefly these are the: (1) life bearing wind, (2) unequal wind, (3) pervasive wind, (4) upward moving wind, and (5) downward voiding wind. Khetsun Rinpoche further observes:[12]

> As to where they reside, the life-bearing wind dwells in the heart; it makes life stable. The fire wind dwells in the belly and creates heat; the pervasive wind abides everywhere, enhancing the entire body (complexion, strength and capacity).[13] The upward moving wind abides in the upper body and facilitates inhalation and exhalation of the breath . . .[14]
>
> In terms of their functions, they [support] stability in our aggregates, constituents and sensory sources, they are also a basis for

11. Discussed, among other places, in Dr. Yeshi Dondon, *Health through Balance: An Introduction to Tibetan Medicine*, trans. Jeffrey Hopkins (Ithaca, NY: Snow Lion, 1986).

12. Khetsun Sangpo Rinpoche, *Strand of Jewels*, (*bLa ma'i zhal gdams kyi snying po thams cad phyogs gcig tu btus pa'i snying gtam nor bu'i do shal*) trans. Anne Klein (Ithaca, NY: Snow Lion, forthcoming) Tibetan Text 9a.4. Khetsun Rinpoche's disilation of crucial teachings of Dzogchen, the supreme subtle path of the most ancient of Tibetan Buddhist orders.

13. Lama Tenzin Samphel, May 2011.

14. Khetsun Rinpoche notes here that the "meditative stabilization of cessation" occurs when one contemplates only emptiness, the abiding state, and not appearances such as color, shape and so forth. Just emptiness and nothing else. Through such contemplation, all mistaken appearances, all error whatsoever, are ceased. Once all of the defilements have been extinguished, they also provide the basis for the maintenance of the five pure, timeless awarenesses, the five pure wisdoms. Manifestation of "magical displays" then become possible.

> production of the five poisons [desire, hatred, ignorance, pride,
> jealousy] at the time of impurity and, in the context of the path,
> they support the arising of miraculous activities through relying
> on the meditative stabilization that involves extinguishment;
> they also then give rise to the five primordial pure wisdoms.

These currents are considered central to life's functioning, to both the ignominious and the noble—our afflictions and our wisdom. They are the most subtle responders in our repertoire. They intimately express and respond to what is inside us and outside as well.

Practitioners of all contemplative traditions recognize that stilling the body brings stillness to the mind. And stilling the mind, focusing deeply on something, whether in formal meditation or simply attending deeply to a text, garden, conversation, writing or painting—brings stillness to the body.

The currents within us are important elements in any in-depth human encounter, including religious dialogue. Awareness of them can foster dialogue that begins to look beyond ideology and touches into lived experience. Women have an affinity with this process, an orientation to connection and embodiment, as well as a need to bring female experience into the conversation of religions practice in ways that historically are often blocked. Traditional religions have not thematized the experiences of women to the same extent as those of men. And if is correct that experience and emotion often reveal themselves through the felt currents of our lives, it behooves us to look into the significance of these subtle currents that undulate through body and mind, and respond in palpable ways to our lived experience.

The presence of these currents means that subject and object, self and other, mind and body, are not simple polarities. The unique properties of our individual experiences are clearly discernable, yet none possess isolated or separate domains. This holistic perspective is significant for many important endeavors: human relationships, ecology, human rights, cross-cultural, inter-religious understanding, and the interweaving of scientific and humanistic discourse, to name a few. It is also a principle which contemporary women with Western-inflected educations often put forward as a core value in service of peace, effective cooperation, reciprocity, and communication, and the way things really are.[15] Desultory claims about connection have been used to frame

15. See for example, the major works of Helene Cixous, Mary Daly, Carol Gilligan,

women as too "dependent" because they lack western male models of individuality, powerful individuality.

In connecting subject and object, self and other, these currents become fundamental to the most basic structure of our lives. They are always impacting and being impacted in so far as moods, facial expressions, postures, and laughter are all contagious. We instinctively mimic each other. And imitation is one of the deepest human responses, from early childhood through to spiritual unfolding in which we respond to, or imitate, what we hold as ultimate.

Research on human mimicry—which doesn't explicitly name energy currents as its medium—recognizes that even a two-three-week-old infant will engage in an interactive process of miniscule mirroring with a parent.[16] Responsiveness is hard wired into us. It is there almost as soon as we emerge from the womb. Incredibly, "infants as young as 42 minutes can imitate the facial expression of an adult model."[17] And facial expressions, Ekman and others have shown, are associated with a particular pattern of "physiological arousal."[18] In the West, psychiatrists are beginning to speak of "limbic resonance." Thomas Lewis and his co-authors define this as: "a symphony of mutual exchange and internal adaptation whereby two mammals become attuned to each other's inner states . . . Eye contact, although it occurs over a gap of yards, is not a metaphor. When we meet the gaze of another, two nervous systems achieve a palpable and intimate apposition."[19] We sense another's feelings, and our feelings shift in response. Communication is taking place. This is not merely a communication of ideas, but of affect. Thus, "affects are in the air as well as the individual psyche" as Teresa Brennan writes in her study of the psychological implications of this process.[20]

Luce Irigaray, Anne Klein.

16. Samples from video recordings of two-three-week-old infants imitating adult in their view ©Meltzoff & Moore, 1977. In Ivri Kumin, *Pre-Object Relatedness: Early Attachment and the Psychoanalytic Situation* (New York: Guilford 1996), 54.

17. Beatrice Beebe, Frank M. Lachmann, *Infant Research and Adult Treatment* (Hillsdale, NJ: Analytic Press, 2002), 36.

18. Ibid., 38.

19. Thomas Lewis, Fari Amini, and Richard Lannon, *A General Theory of Love* (Toronto: Vintage, 2001), 63.

20. Teresa Brennan, *The Transmission of Affect* (Ithaca, NY: Cornell University Press, 2004), 113. As she also points out, on the same page, "These affects are what threaten the distinctness of persons, the things that divert their psyches (or souls) from their distinct paths and ways of being." My point, which accords also with a

Our eye consciousness rides a current to visible forms. Likewise, our cognitive and emotional experience of other living beings ride currents of their own. For Buddhists, affective contact which comes as these currents transmit affect through gesture, speech, and countenance is as necessary for human life as food and water.[21]

Perceiving emotion in someone else creates a resonant emotional state in the perceiver.[22] This makes it hard to deny that in some meaningful sense, there is something passing between us. And from a Buddhist perspective, that is not our imagination, nor is it just our brain. Something is moving through us in subtle and immediate response to our surroundings.[23]

Tibetan traditions, drawing from Indian and other ancient systems, emphasize that the more subtle the wind or energy, the more subtle the mind it carries. This is because of the close relationship between flowing and knowing. Energy flows, mind knows. The flow is the agile blind horse, which the lame yet perceptive mind will ride. Mind, characterized as "clear and knowing" requires the movement of this wind-horse energy to meet the objects of its knowing. Perhaps this is why in ancient Sanskrit terminology, verbs of going are also always verbs of knowing. And why the spiritual endeavor is called a path. Like any action of locomotion, knowing takes you somewhere. And what is known energetically is at the core of living. The Sufi sage Rumi, living on the edges of Indian culture, seems to express a similar idea:

> The morning wind spreads its fresh smell
> We must get up to take that in,
> The wind that let's us live
> Breathe, before it's gone.[24]

general Buddhist perspective, is that these currents of shifting affective orientation *constitute* our distinct paths and ways of being. They are the currents of our lives.

21. Lewis et. al., *A General Theory of Love*, 68–70.

22. Ibid., 37.

23. Ibid. They add, "So familiar and expected is the neural attunement of limbic resonance that people finds its absence disturbing. Scrutinize the eyes of a shark or a sunbathing salamander and . . . The vacuity behind those glances sends a chill down the mammalian spine" (63–64). This, they suggest, is the origin of the myths of mythic creatures who kill with their gaze—Medusa—as if they can project their own immunity to the stirrings of limbic life to stunt into immobility the living world.

24. Rumi, *The Book of Love*, trans. and commentary by Coleman Barks (New York: HarperCollins, 2003), 98.

In the 1600s, European physicians began dissecting cadavers to further their understanding of the body. This enterprise revealed the body as a marvelous machine of interlocking parts. Traditional Asian medicine gained its knowledge principally through careful observation of living bodies. In those living bodies, movement and responsiveness, systems of connection, are always in evidence. Concomitantly, the religious as well as medical systems of Asia propose dynamic flows known as chi in China, *prāṇa* in India, and *lung* (rhymes with rung) in Tibet.

The inner currents or energies are not a well formed category in the modern West, yet all movement divulges their presence. Breath, heart-beat, the tense feeling in our stomach, our "gut" sense that something is going to happen—all this is the flow of currents. While science is able to measure movement in the brain, it does not call such movement "currents" or "energy." It is not an exotic or noetic category, movement in brain and body is something science already knows how to measure. And, to paraphrase what Gregory Bateson famously said in another context, that naming would be a difference that makes a difference.[25]

How this naming could help inflect scientific research is beyond the scope of our discussion. We can however consider the benefit in identifying this category in its own right, when it comes to spiritual exploration, including cross-cultural and inter-religious conversation, and the role of women therein. Even though the human body is variously interpreted across cultures, there are important commonalities that all embodied beings seek: survival, safety, kindness. Further, women take a special interest in the body. We do so because our life stages demand it, because our bodies are a special source of contestation within male culture, and thus within cultural and legal norms generally. We do so also because of a wide-spread tendency to assimilate women's whole identity to the material and bodily, and to see these as something lesser. Acknowledging the intelligence of the subtle currents discovered in the

---

25. Gregory Bateson, *Steps to an Ecology of Mind* (Chicago: University of Chicago Press, 1972), 336.

Bateson famously writes: "What we mean by information—the elementary unit of information—is a difference which makes a difference, and it is able to make a difference because the neural pathways along which it travels and is continually transformed are themselves provided with energy." Thus from our perspective, the currency of energy is profoundly implicated in all information processing, and therefore in communication. As Bateson adds, "The pathways are ready to be triggered. We may even say that the question is already implicit in them."

lived body thus has special significance for women. It also has an important place in religious dialogue.

The kind of spiritual presence that animates and inspires religious seekers requires stillness and receptivity. Even before Buddhism was introduced to the West, the stillness of the contemplative has been confused, in the mind of the public, with mere peace, even passivity. However, such stillness possesses enormous strength by virtue of its sustaining currents. [26] This was famously demonstrated in a now iconic Bill Moyers program, when a strapping twenty-something Western athlete proved unable to push over a frail-looking elderly T'ai Ch'i master.[27] The explanation, from the T'ai Ch'i tradition, is that the master becomes unassailable because he knows how to anchor his energy in the earth, like the deep roots of tree. This exemplifies a kind of power quite different from the "over and against" strength associated with masculinized Western, individuality."

Currents of Being: Personal and Cosmic

The body is suffused with energies, and every mental or emotional state rides on its own specific steed of wind. To acknowledge your knowing body is to connect nuanced conceptual understanding with a refined introspection born of bodily sensing. Sitting quietly and noticing our breath shelters us from fraying distraction. It lends depth to our experience of the present. The mindfulness that arrives is not just "mind," it is an enriched and embodied presence. Without this, we stay on the surface of our lives, isolated from our own depths and from deep connections with others. This flowing sensibility is both knower and object known. As such, it opens to a knowing suffused with connection in a way that a strictly subject-object knowing can never attain.

Our awareness of these currents, and the energy steed it rides, is our energetic sensibility. This sensibility is neither fully mind nor simply body. Encompassing both, it is a perspective of connectivity and

26. In Buddhist texts, the steadfast presence of mindfulness provides a strength that counters the dissolving of the erroneous sense of self Buddhists equate with ignorance, and that feminists have worried is a deconstruction of women's selfhood at the very moment we were gaining the power to proclaim it. See Chapter II of my *Meeting the Great Bliss Queen: Buddhists, Feminists and the Art of the Self* (Boston: Beacon, 1995; reprinted, Itahca, NY: Snow Lion, 2009).

27. *Healing the Mind: The Mystery of Chi*, with Bill Moyers, October 2009.

wholeness. It holds even the most disparate parts, including our own conflicting emotions, in implicit coherence.

Our energetic sensibility is a powerful, be-mused and embodied knowing. Mystics from every tradition describe a flowing awareness that is by nature powerful, ecstatic, and radiant. When we touch into our own capacity for such creative knowing, we read these works in an entirely new way. Once we see the extent to which sacred testimony is revealed and registered in the body, we experience and understand the power of ritual, prayer, chanting, meditation, or sacrament, differently. These become a mirroring to us of something that we ourselves possess and that we can feel. This is an infinitely open basis for dialogue. An openness that neither assimilates one tradition to another, nor throws up insurmountable obstacles to communication and caring.

When we talk across traditions, and when we connect with our own tradition, it is vital to acknowledge how the heartbeat of that tradition does not derive from ordinary conceptual mind. If our perspective is limited to logic, theory, ritual, history, or cultural context, it is not enough. It impacts us, and our dialogue, differently when we acknowledge the moving currents of deep feeling and embodied presence at the heart of these traditions. Their own literature is a portal to this recognition. We ignore such resonances at great peril—the peril of reducing a powerful sensibility to mere words or empty generalizations. This doesn't mean ideas are not helpful, even essential in understanding, maintaining and entering into dialogue with traditions. But relying on ideas alone risks remaining at the surface of our conversation, and our selves.

Ideas will never be identical across traditions. This is a good thing, it keeps creativity and freshness alive and animates deep feelings of pride and belonging. Several years ago the Dalai Lama, speaking at Rice University, was asked by a student "Do you think there will ever be just one religion in the world?" His Holiness' instantaneous reply was an emphatic "I hope not!" said loudly and with great feeling. [28] We do not all need to think alike. What is needed is that these different ideas and the customs associated with them do not obscure our larger commonalities.

At the level of limbic resonance and the deepest currents of our being, a Christian love of God, for example, can feel very akin to a Sufi's

28. Oral memory. I was moderator during this Q&A period of the Dalai Lama's visit to Rice University following his talk for the Rice community, "Tolerance and Responsibility in a Global Village," May 14, 2007.

love of reality, or a Buddhist's universal compassion for all living beings. In every case, love of something so much larger than ourselves—a Creator, a vastness, the suffering creatures throughout our world—inspires goodness, kindness, generosity, inclusiveness, happiness, balance, and well-being. We cannot engage in interreligious discussion with our minds only. Our bodies and the currents that enliven our lives must be there. That is why they also participate in religious and spiritual literature, art, and practice.

The Cosmic Creative

> Although we are by all odds the most social of all social animal more interdependent, more attached to teach other, more inseparable than bees—we do not often feel our conjoined intelligence.[29]

When we look into the loving eyes of another, we feel love and we feel loved. In Tibetan Buddhist practices, when we look into the knowing eyes of the Teacher, or the Reality embodied by the Teacher—we feel known, and we feel our own knowing. This is a core principle of the central practice of Guru Yoga. The "guru" here is at once an actual person, and also, especially in the context of mature understanding, reality itself.

Several major religious narratives open with evocations of mystery accompanied by descriptions of a fecund and uninterrupted vastness. This is not just theology and these are not just ideas. This is a record of deeply felt human experience. If we can read them that way, our conversation across traditions is bound to be different. Feelings are palpably contagious in ways that intellectual orientations—though influential—are not.[30] So, again, there is a natural distortion when dialogue across traditions relies only on comparative ideas, tenets, theological principles, and iconography. When we talk about how our spiritual life makes us feel, how it expresses itself in our daily lives, we find reservoirs of commonality. These do not elide difference. But they keep difference in perspective, and don't allow such differences to breach a deeper—and more important—sense of human connection. This is especially true when we look at the ecstatic, mind-opening currents running through classic expressions at the heart of several great literatures. Moses' epiphany of

29. Lewis, cited in Lewis, et al. *A General Theory of Love*, 98.
30. Ibid.

the ten commandments, the creation of Genesis and of the Rgveda, for example, can be read as the epiphany of one who sees into the timeless past and experiences its vastness, as can the poem of Samantabhadra below. The Rgveda speaks of how,

> The sages who have searched their hearts with wisdom
> Know that which is kin to that which is not . . .
> Whence all creation had its origin . . .[31]

The study of religion, including cross-cultural studies, cannot simply be a matter of comparing ideas, rules, or protocols. These will never match. But we can recognize that our resonance and attraction to traditions that call us may speak to—and through—the currents of our lives in similar ways. The silent sitting of Quakers, and the loud drumming and chanting of Buddhists look different. But at the end of a session, everyone may feel similarly nourished socially and similarly settled in serenity.

To read religion this way is to gain a perspective not available through other methods, though complementary with them. It offers a different lens. Reading to investigate the psychology, history, cosmology, of a tradition, or how a particular religion's expression at certain times and places reflects or contests cultural or historical context, or is expressed through ritual expression or aesthetic values, is central to religious studies. The importance of these is not diminished by noting that every lens has its limitation. None of these methods directly addresses the power of religious inspiration, the usually invisible way religious writing, ritual, and practice—including academic practices of reading religion[32]—impact our embodied sensibilities.

Given the creative potential of the energetic sensibility and the analogous ultimate creativity which many traditions see as source of our universe, it seems likely that human beings throughout history have seen some such vastness dawn in the intimacy of their own experience.

31. Cited, among many other places, in A. L. Basham, *The Wonder that was India* (New York: Grove, 1954), 247. For the original Sanskrit, see online: http://www.google.com/url?sa=t&rct=j&q=&esrc=s&source=web&cd=5&ved=0CDkQFjAE&url=http%3A%2F%2Fsanskritdocuments.org%2Fall_pdf%2Fnaasadiiya.pdf&ei=6QVHUMonyOfIAZuYgYAD&usg=AFQjCNHwK7N5tnkXlUWG7AWzQ9zzrlGBXQ&sig2=LbHjq-c4BkKzI-VF7mhQEg.

32. For a lively, probing argument that academic study of mysticism is for some a form of mystic practice, see Jeff Kripal, *Roads of Excess, Palaces of Wisdom: Eroticism and Reflexivity in the Study of Mysticism* (Chicago: University of Chicago Press, 2001).

And then concluded that the entire world has arisen from it.[33] Sometime around the eighth century a Tibetan poet put it this way:

> Nothing, not even one thing
> Does not arise from me.
> Nothing, not even one thing
> Dwells not within me.
> Everything, just everything
> Emanates from me
> Thus am I only one
> Knowing me is knowing all
> Great bliss.[34]

The "me" here is the All Good, Samantabhadra, mentioned briefly above and known in Tibetan traditions as the majestic creator and cosmic essence of everything, what Buddhists call the Essential Dimension (*dharma-kāya chos sku*). Samantabhadra is both a particular being and sheer being itself; a creativity immanent in creation.

The Tibetan master Padamsambhava, widely known as Guru Rinoche, was an eight year old child when he was discovered sitting alone inside a giant lotus flower by the fabled Indian King Indrabhuti. Quite naturally, the King asks him who and where are his parents? The child responds:

> My father is the wisdom of spontaneous awareness
> My mother is the Ever-Excellent Lady, the space of all things . . .[35]

Here again spaciousness, "the space of all things" and awareness, which is also a type of illumination, are regarded as one's source.[36]

33. Buddhist texts explicitly call their own sense of originary vastness as an ancestor, the All Good, known as Samantabhadra. See Klein and Wangyal, *Unbounded Wholeness: Dzogchen, Bon, and the Logic of the Nonconceptual* (Oxford: Oxford University Press, 2006).

34. *The Secret Scripture Collection* (*mDo lung gsang ba*): (52.5); cited in Klein and Wangyal, *Unbounded Wholeness*, 229.

35. The verse continues: "I belong to the caste of indivisible space and awareness / I have taken the unborn dharma realm as my homeland. / I belong to the caste of indivisible space and awareness / I have taken the unborn dharma realm as my homeland. See Guru Rinopche, *His Life and Times*, trans. Ngawang Zangpo (Ithaca, NY: Snow Lion, 2002).

36. Pur-bu-jok, expressing a classic view of Indian and Tibetan Buddhism, defines mind as "that which is clear and aware." The word for "clarity" (*gsal*) is, as in English, also a term of illumination. See Lati Rinpoche and Elizabeth Napper, *Mind in Tibetan Buddhism* (Ithaca, NY: Snow Lion, 1981).

Indeed, there seems to be no major religious tradition without significant reference to this dimension, even if such references occur predominantly in the esoteric or rarified expressions of those traditions—the Christian Gnostic,[37] Jewish Kabala, the Muslim Sufi, the Buddhist practitioner of Tantra or Dzogchen. The vibrant variety with which they are expressed strengthens our recognition of their universal appeal.

However different these religions and their ultimate realities might be, they are also profoundly and powerfully similar in their enormity, and the awe-inspiring dawning of the universe which flows forth from them. Consider the following descriptions of transcendently human perception, in the *Gospel of Thomas*,

> Jesus said, "If they say to you, 'Where do you come from?' Say, 'We come from the light; the place where the light [first] came into being . . .'
>
> If they say to you, 'Who are you?' Say, 'We are the children [of the light . . . If they ask you, 'What is the sign of your Father in you?' Say to them, 'Movement and rest."[38]

Like Padmasambhava's description of his parents, this indicates a human sense of being born from something vaster than, and yet immanent in, the immediate causes of fleshy parents, a deeper energetic ancestor. In this light, we read verses cited in an early Tibetan Dzogchen Text, the Authenticity of Open Awareness:[39]

> Prior to all Buddhas and sentient beings
> When even their names do not exist
> Is ancestral wholeness, mindnature . . .
> Essential heart of all that is,
> Mindnature, uncontrived and naturally pure,

37. Karen King's *What Is Gnosticism?* (Cambridge, MA: Belnap, 2003) and others have pointed out the contested nature of this term. I use it in a very general sense, a shorthand way to indicate forms of Christianity oriented toward seeing the divine god within, as much as without.

38. Cited by Pagels, *Beyond Belief: The Secret Gospel of Thomas*, 140–41; she in turn is drawing especially from the historical work of Timothy D. Barnes, especially his *Athanasius and Constantius: Theology and Politics in the Constantian Empire* (Cambridge: Cambridge University Press, 1995). For other relevant sources see Pagels, 223–24, n. 81.

39. Cited in Klein & Wangyal *Unbounded Wholeness*. Tibetan text 50.5; an approximately eighth- to tenth-century text from the Bon-Buddhist tradition of Tibet, which takes this quote from a no longer extant work, *Authentic Scripture (Lung tshad ma)*.

Exists from the first, without start or stop
This is sure.

   Its own state, beyond overlay or detraction,
   Untouched by limits:
   Self-risen open awareness, definitive pith
   Dwells as the heart of the sun.[40]

The Rgveda describes a time before existence, Genesis a time before dark separated from light, Padmasambhava a time when vastness and space came together, and John a time when what is now material was simply light. All of these are times of wholeness. In those times, creation is not yet differentiated from its source. The culmination of these traditions—enlightenment, birth in heaven, union of atman and Brahman, for example—are also times of wholeness. In a similar vein, there is a wholeness that precedes the division between enlightened beings and ordinary unenlightened beings.

In every case, the speaker is inspired to express something more than ordinary experience encompasses. And these same words describes what many of us, at least some of the time, resonate with deeply, whether we are religious or not.

The Ultimate Field

Philosophers have said that we love music
because it resembles the sphere-sounds
of union. We've been part of a harmony
before, so these moments of treble and bass
keep our remembering fresh. But how
does this happen within these dense bodies
full of forgetfulness and doubt?

  —Rumi[41]

From time immemorial and in far-flung parts of the world, the human organism responds powerfully to images of vastness, wholeness, and ongoing creativity. These are nearly ubiquitous characteristics in

40. The unknown Tibetan annotator to this text writes, "The sun is usually an example of open awareness, and space *(nam mkha')* as well as of clarity." A typical use of this metaphor in *the Zhang Zhung snyan rgyud* (273.3) is "Like the sun in the expanse of sky" *(nam mkha'i klong nas nyi ma bzhin)*. This verse describes the base *(kun gzhi)*, as well as its analogue, the mindnature *(sems nyid)* and also the experience of it, which is open awareness *(rig pa)*.

41. Rumi, *The Book of Love: Poems of Ecstasy and Longing*, trans. Coleman Barks (New York: HarpersOne, 2005), 27–28.

religions views of origin. How do we account for this? Perhaps this arises because some sensate dimension of our human organism resonates with vastness, light, and effulgence. Not just as ideas, and not simply because skull-bound brain processes are provoked, but because there is communication between an originary greatness and ourselves. Some find that the outer and inner vastnesses mirror each other. Seeing this mirror clearly would depend very much on training in contemplation, prayer, and deep reflection. This is present in all of the traditions we have named, and others. It is present because humans everywhere yearn for it and express that yearning in their own unique ways. The intimate connection between the vast mysterium with the ordinary everyone is the most compelling element of this mirroring. And there is the potential to meet it afresh in dialogue with ourselves and with others.

Spiritual Mirroring and Real Love

Experiences of dissolution are common across mystic traditions. Words that emerge from a person in that state can help lead another into it. This is a variant on the theme of transmission through an energetic sensibility, analogous to limbic resonance. Once we notice it, the mutual interflowing of body and mind currents is absolutely obvious. Do you fall in love with your mind? With just your body? In fact, the energy of love spills over the narrow confines of these terms with a dynamism that is neither strictly mental nor solely physical. Love is a moving vibration, an all-encompassing vastness embracing everyone in its compass. As an eminent T'ai Ch'i master told his student, a friend of mine, "You think the energy is moving in your body. But you are moving in the energy."[42]

Acknowledging this sensibility has the potential to precipitate a radical reorientation of our identity as knowers, speakers, lovers. It may soften or even dissolve boundaries that otherwise separate individuals, cultures, followers of traditions. This is important for the health of humanity. And, not coincidentally, access to these subtle fluctuations unmasks and eventually dissolves whatever obstructs the divine or ultimate from full presence in our daily experience.

42. Oral communication, Professor William Parsons, Rice University, in the course of explaining traditionally taught principles of T'ai Ch'i to our Contemplative Practicuum.

Feeling vastness in our being is part of what allows us to see our-selves reflected in the words of Buddha, or Christ, or mystics such as Rumi, Milarepa, or Thomas Merton. Through the ultimates they de-scribe, we find a mirror wherein we see our own most profound sen-sibilities. In this way, the currents at play in our energetic sensibility provide an avenue for healing resolution, revealing an expansiveness native to our being, but hidden from plain sight.

The currents of our being are at once the most personal and uni-versal matrix in which we perform the meaning of our lives. Hence the relevance of expansive mystic vision for interpersonal connection and community engagement in the everyday material world.

The great thematizer of Hindu tantra, Abhinavagupta, describes what he calls a pulsation—a very subtle wind-horse—that animates our most subtle consciousness. The ultimate practice, he says, is to allow this subtle consciousness to be sealed by, united with, the ultimate. Ex-periencing this seal means that "the whole world of duality" dissolves into "the great interiority of awareness."[43] The translator of this verse, notes that here "the mind and body of the yogin have been 'melted' by dedicated yogic practice."[44] This is the mystic's limbic-like resonance with being, with divinity, and with reality.

Rumi describes a great sheik on his deathbed as "melting into him-self like a candle."[45] He is engaged with the one reliable love of his life, of anyone's life. Rumi calls this love the Friend, Buddhist practitioners lov-ingly call on the Lama, ultimate reality. Similarly (and also differently), the principle of theosis, central to Greek Orthodox Christianity, means that the purified body can transform as it fills with currents, dissolving into spirit.[46] There is a visceral impact, a shift or recognition in the cur-rents of being. In such cases, that ultimate is itself the ultimate mirror of one's being, one's own nature.

The fourteenth-century Tibetan master Longchen Rabjam and, fol-lowing him, Jigme Lingpa in the eighteenth century, emphasize respon-siveness as a crucial aspect of reality, the spacious matrix (*dharma-dhātu,*

43. "On the Seal of Śambhu: A Poem by Abhinavagupta," in David Gordon White, ed., *Tantra in Practice* (Princeton: Princeton University Press, 2000), 586.

44. Ibid., 580.

45. "The Debtor Sheik" in *The Essential Rumi,* trans. Coleman Barks (San Fran-cisco: HarperSanFrancisco, 1994), 158.

46. For the Alexandrian fathers, influenced by Plato, this was the acme of spiritual furthering.

chos dbyings) that is the ultimate field. This responsiveness is like the rays of the sun—it extends everywhere.[47] These are just a few examples of how spiritual practice, like all other human interactions, involves profound communication which occurs in a field communication. All suggest that we respond to a reality which also responds to us.

And responsiveness is potentially effortless. Rumi, describes the "laziest"—we might say the most relaxed, most unbounded—of three sons who, making no effort to elicit or attend to another's reaction in order to understand him, simply senses into the field between them, and then attends to his own response:

> And so when I start speaking a powerful right arm
> of words sweeping down, I know him from what I say
> and how I say it, because there's a window open
> between us, mixing the night air of our beings.[48]

Recognizing the energetic sensibility and, with it, the currents of our being, helps to de-exoticize mystic experience and brings it into our all-the-time world where we now find an invitation to look more closely at our actual experience in real time. After all, these currents express our most intimate being, they are an organ of knowing already within us. Such knowing can be cultivated and become more subtle through the kinds of training that all traditions offer.

Every major religious or spiritual tradition on the planet, from classic Buddhism, Islam, and Christianity to Alcoholics Anonymous offers its followers a larger field of being. Human beings have always sought to know and to feel this expanse. This is not an exotic topic useful only to distinguished contemplatives. "No philosophy of human personality," observed that brilliant twentieth-century scholar of mysticism H. H. Price, "is worth very much unless it takes full account of the data of mystical experience."[49] William James called psychologists' discovery of such an expansive field the most important in his lifetime. Our under-

---

47. Longchen Rabjam, *Treasury of Philosophical Tenets*, trans. Richard Barron, 360ff. Jigme Lingpa's refuge prayer, directly echoing Longchenpa's point, can be found in *Heart Essence of the Vast Expanse: A Story of Transmission.* trans. and introduction by Anne C. Klein/Rigzin Drolma (Ithaca, NY: Snow Lion, 2010).

48. *The Essential Rumi,* trans. by Coleman Barks, new exp. ed. (New York Harper-SanFrancisco, 2004), 32.

49. Edward F. Kelly et al., *Irreducible Mind: Toward a Psychology for the 21st Century* (Lanham, MD; Rowman & Littlefield, 2009), 52–53.

standing of the human energetic sensibility, the currents that move our lives, has an enormous contribution to make here. First, we identify this as a field of knowing. We also see that this radiant intelligence doesn't always get noticed. Indeed, we become very accustomed to overriding it, even though everyone has the possibility of cultivating awareness of it. With such cultivation, we move toward psychological and spiritual wholeness, as well as deeper cross-cultural understanding.

The Dalai Lama finds compassion to be a precondition of all ethical conduct.[50] For Buddhists, and consistent with those who find the commandment to "Do unto others . . ." an axial guideline, this means not harming others, and helping them when possible. Without exception. This is a big imagining. Yet, as the world grows smaller, it becomes more and more important that we realize that our religious traditions do share vital principles, and that these traditions are much more than ideas, doctrines, positions, debates. Christianity, Judaism, Islam, Hinduism, Buddhism and beyond all have ways of describing an expansive vision possible of what human beings are. It remains for participants in dialogue to interpret what this means for the lives of women and men.

Intimacy across the spaces that would divide us is a central principle of dialogue. This principle is embodied through the connecting currents of conversation. These connections do not stop at the frontier of intellectual or ideological exchange, but incorporate deep seated feelings and commitments that also ride the currents of our experience. These currents, like dialogue itself, sustain the life of intimate communication encompassing the divine, the possible, the all-inclusive reality. Such intimate knowing backlit by this vast horizon feeds dialogue, nourishes spirit, and becomes palpable as the currency of a compassionate heart, whose beat everyone can hear.

---

50. HH The Dalai Lama, *Ethics for the New Millenium* (New York: Riverhead, 1999), 124.

12

What Do Women Bring to the Dialogue Table?

Rita M. Gross

My task in this paper to be to bring together Buddhism, interfaith dialogue, and women/feminism. Let me say at the outset that I find it difficult to juggle all three balls at the same time. I could say a great deal about Buddhism and interfaith dialogue. In fact I am currently well into my next book—*Religious Diversity—What's the Problem? Buddhist Advice for Flourishing with Religious Diversity* and talking about those ideas would be my preference. But what I have to say in that book owes little, if anything, to my being a woman and a feminist, so how do I pull that dimension in? I have already said a great deal about Buddhism and feminism, but that's not the assignment for this chapter. I also have some things to say about interfaith dialogue and women/feminism—in outline, primarily two. First, in previous publications[1] I have chastised women and feminists for not being sufficiently involved in all the issues pertaining to religious diversity. Second, even though I do not think that women/feminists bring unique stances to interfaith issues, I contend passionately that women and feminists *should* nevertheless devote

1. Rita M. Gross, "Feminist Theology: Religiously Diverse Neighborhood or Christian Ghetto?" *Journal of Feminist Studies in Religion* 16/2 (2000) 73–78; Gross, "Feminist Theology as Theology of Religions," in *A Garland of Feminist Reflections: Forty Years of Religious Reflection* (Berkeley: University of California Press, 2009), 211–28.

themselves deeply and consistently to interfaith work. But those views, though not incompatible with Buddhism at all, are not the result of my being a Buddhist.

This chapter will be an expansion of what I wrote for an online forum called "The Interfaith Observer" when asked to contribute a three-hundred-word comment on the question "What do women bring to the interfaith table?" Despite the fact that Buddhist thought could bring unique and valuable ideas to the interfaith table, the focus on women/feminism makes it difficult to focus on those Buddhist insights. Therefore, there is nothing about Buddhism in this short statement. I believe that anyone, male or female, Buddhist or any other religion, could easily write the same thing that I wrote about what women bring to the interfaith table.

In that comment I stressed that the most important thing women bring to the interfaith table is our sheer presence rather than anything essentially due to our being women. Regarding most interfaith issues, I do not think that women offer different insights than men could. But because religions have been such a boys-only club, the *presence* of women at the interfaith table loudly proclaims a critical message that can be proclaimed no other way. Religions are no longer going to be male sanctuaries, closed off to women except for the supportive roles we have traditionally played. Highly publicized meetings of world religious leaders are usually devoid of women. How can such gatherings pretend to represent all humans or have messages relevant for all? I also suggested that if there is anything we women could speak of which men could not, we would speak about the pain of being excluded from something as meaningful as roles of religious leadership. We speak about not having role models who look like us in the religions to which we give our best energies. In other words, we wouldn't bring a specifically *feminine* message, but we do add a *feminist* voice to interfaith discussions. Only then will every chair at the interfaith table be filled.[2]

2. "What Do Women Bring to the Interfaith Table?" Comment in *The Interfaith Observer*; http://theinterfaithobserver.org/journal-articles/2012/3/15/what-do-women-bring-to-the-interfaith-table.html.

The Crucial Nature of Interfaith Work

The point that joins all three concerns is the overriding importance of interfaith work in today's world. I would claim that everyone—male, female, Buddhist, non-Buddhist—should be involved in interfaith activities. Therefore, it follows that women and feminists, Buddhist or non-Buddhist, need to involve themselves in inter-religious dialogue and other activities that would help defuse the tension about religious diversity so prevalent in both the world at large and the North American world today.

Before we even start to talk about dialogue, or about women and interfaith dialogue, I would claim that we need to recognize how disconcerting diversity can be to most people. Most people seem to be hard wired to prefer sameness among human beings, which leads to discomfort with the many kinds of differences always found among humans— difference regarding race, gender, sexual orientation, class, culture, and most especially religion. Additionally, education and enculturation in many families, groups, societies, and religions encourage feelings of in-group superiority and disdain for those in different groups. Probably every person could recount many tales of such childhood indoctrination. Clearly, diversity is very difficult to deal with psychologically, and religious diversity seems to be especially difficult, especially for those who belong to religions that claim to be the only religion valid for all humanity, in other words, those that make exclusive truth claims, and also for many individuals who consider themselves to be deeply religious or especially faithful. Often they regard religious diversity itself as a flaw and a failing, a condition to be overcome rather than the norm or a condition to be celebrated. Unfortunately, religions and religious leaders often encourage rather than discourage such opinions about the reality of religious diversity. Clearly, there must be a paradigm shift in evaluations about religious diversity itself before it is meaningful even to approach the topic of dialogue.

Religious people should be disconcerted about how much suffering has resulted from inappropriate enthusiasm for one's own religion and accompanying attempts to eliminate religious diversity, whether by well-organized and well-funded attempts at large scale conversions or by more militant methods, including political, economic, and social repression of those belonging to minority religions, or even simple harassment and ridicule. Therefore, I regard learning to cope well and to flourish with religious diversity to be one of the most urgent, over-riding issues of our times. This judgment has nothing to do with sex, gender, political orientation, or religion. It applies equally to everyone, whatever peculiar combination of differences they may happen to exhibit.

For these reasons, I have argued that every citizen, and certainly every religious practitioner has an ethical responsibility to learn a great deal about at least one religion besides their own. For defusing discomfort with religious diversity, I suggest that in the beginning, simply learning accurate information about other religions in a neutral context that fosters empathetic understanding of those who are different may well be more effective and less threatening than face-to-face encounters. I also argue that effective dialogue on as loaded a topic as religion requires in-depth, not amateur, knowledge of one's own tradition, highly developed listening skills, a genuine desire to understand the other rather than to argue and debate, and a willingness to be changed in one's dialogical encounter.[3]

Being a student learning about unfamiliar religions in a neutral setting is a more passive, and therefore easier approach. But the accurate, thorough knowledge about other religions gained by this method usually defuses hostility towards and misunderstandings of them. It also helps outsiders to a religion understand it much more as insiders do, giving those outsiders some empathy, some ability to see the world as others see it. Such knowledge is a good start towards becoming comfortable and able to flourish with religious diversity. The great advantage of this approach is that such knowledge is not at all difficult to obtain these days. There are myriad reliable books, DVDs, and university courses available. Other educational venues also offer such courses. Last winter I taught a five week course on Buddhism at the Eau Claire, WI Senior Center. If churches and other religious institutions would begin to get serious concerning such education about the world's diverse religions, discomfort over religious diversity could be dramatically diminished.

As a basis for meaningful discussions of inter-religious dialogue, I would also claim that we need to be clear about what we are searching

3. Those familiar with classic literature on interfaith dialogue will recognize the influence of John Cobb, especially his book *Beyond Dialogue: Toward a Mutual Transformation of Buddhism and Christianity* (1982; reprinted, Eugene, OR: Wipf & Stock, 1998) in these comments.

for in dialogue and other inter-religious projects. Genuine religious diversity is often so disconcerting to people that even inter-religious dialogue becomes an attempt to overcome diversity by finding some underlying, abstract sameness about religions. It often leads to an attempt to demonstrate that at the core, "all religions are the same," that there is some "lowest common denominator" shared by all religions. While the ethical motivations behind such a quest are laudable, I do not think the quest actually comes to terms with the sheer fact of religious diversity. Religions do share many common features, but they are also intractably different, especially when it comes to theology. In my view, attempts to find a lowest common denominator, as evident in John Hick's work, may be relatively successful with theistic religions. But as soon as a non-theistic religion, such as Buddhism, is encountered, the project is less successful.

My more serious objection, however, is that what we need to do, as people and as religious people, is to find methods for living together in peace and harmony, whether or not we agree with one another on fundamentals. In other words, it is far more important to overcome our discomfort with religious diversity than to find some way to pretend or to claim that the diversity doesn't really exist or that it is only superficial. That task is far more difficult. Thus, theologians of each tradition need to find their tradition's internal resources for accepting religious diversity as inevitable, here to stay, not a mistake or failing on the part of human beings, and quite possibly of great benefit for human well-being. Religious diversity is not the problem. The problem is only our discomfort with diversity, especially religious diversity and our tendency to think that in an ideal world, there would be no religious diversity because everyone would join our religion. By exploring how each of our own traditions might solve these problems and then talking with one another across religious lines, we may be able to help each other learn to cope with religious diversity.

Women, Feminists, and Inter-Religious Issues

It is no secret, however, that women and feminists have, thus far, played a limited role in inter-faith gatherings and not contributed much to the literature on religious diversity. Is this because women have been kept out of these venues, because they have kept themselves out, or some combination thereof? Superficially, it might look as if women have been kept out of this arena, as historically they have been kept out of so many others, by the male dominance of religions and by the near monopoly men have on most leadership roles in religious institutions. In the last forty-five years, however, women have broken through many gender barriers in religion, have gained ordination in many denominations, have become bishops and other religious leaders, and have become seminary and university professors of religion and religious studies. Why, then, such a limited advance into the arena of inter-religious dialogue? This is a complex issue and no single or simple answer can be given to this question.

I will suggest that women and feminists have kept themselves out of the inter-religious arena almost as much as they have been kept out. I will also look at the ways in which women have been kept away from the inter-religious dialogue table. I will explore what differences women would make at the dialogue table, strongly suggesting that those changes have much more to do with what the presence of women at the table means than with substantive changes in the discourse that occurs at the table. I will also try to explain why I hold that view.

Although I have been seriously engaged in inter-religious dialogue for thirty years, only two of my nearly two hundred published articles and essays concern women or feminism and interfaith dialogue or any other interfaith issue.[4] Why so little writing revealing a direct connection between feminist theology and inter-religious dialogue? In my case, the answer is quite simple. For most of my career, my colleagues in feminist theology were simply not interested in dialogue or in so-called "non-Western" religions and, for me, trying to bridge my intensive concerns with inter-religious dialogue and with feminism among the same group of colleagues has proved very frustrating, and ultimately unsuccessful. I would have to contend that, although their concerns regarding gender and Western religions were radical and innovative, regarding religious diversity, the outlook and values of my colleagues in feminist theology were quite Eurocentric, in fact quite Christian-centered.

My first direct experience of this lack of interest occurred at the 1975 American Academy of Religion annual meeting. I was the newly appointed section chair of the newly minted section on Women and Religion, a heady and scary responsibility for a 32-year-old who had

4. See note 1 above.

been at the All-But-Dissertation stage when I took on this responsibility.[5] I wanted our first set of sessions as a section to be exemplary, and, in my view, that included a session that went beyond Christian and Eurocentric materials, so I solicited the papers for such a session to occur. I was shocked and disappointed when none of my close colleagues in the fledging feminist theology movement came to that session. When I asked why, they said that materials on women or female imagery in "non-Western" religious traditions were not relevant or interesting to them. On other similar occasions, I would be told that, as feminists, they didn't want to concern themselves with patriarchal religious traditions (even though the Christianity with which they were so concerned is at least as patriarchal), or that reading and listening to papers on "non-Western" religions involved "too many foreign words and unfamiliar terms."

This stance on the part of my feminist colleagues mystified and frustrated me for several reasons. First, it was clear to me, and had been for a long time, that the familiar religions of the West did not have any monopoly on religious concepts and practices that were cogent and meaningful or that might be helpful to women. Many other such concepts and practices were found around the world. Additionally, even if one did not wish to study such materials because of a personal interest in them, I had found Max Müller's motto "to know one religion is to know none" more than accurate. If one thinks about this motto, one sees that even if one's only aim is understanding one's own religion better, it is helpful, perhaps even necessary, to study other religions seriously, in an empathetic and non-judgmental manner. This insight reinforces, from another direction, my claim, made in the previous section of this paper, that everyone has an ethical obligation to learn a great deal about at least one other religion. In the face of these realities, it was and is hard for me to understand such singular Eurocentric attachment to the religions of one's culture of origin. Furthermore, Christianity has one of the worst records of coping well with religious diversity, and in contemporary times, at least in the United States, its skill in doing so is decreasing, not increasing. So how could my largely Christian feminist colleagues ignore such pressing concerns so consistently?

5. My first book, *Beyond Androcentrism: New Essays on Women and Religion* (Missoula MT: Scholars, 1977), came out of that meeting.

In a previous article on "Feminist Theology as Theology of Religions," I presented what I still see as the natural affinity between feminist theology as critique and reformulation of one's own tradition and interest in and concern for diverse religions other than one's own. I suggested that a key feminist value has always been including what had previously been excluded by "mainstream" theologies. This moral value stems from our own experience of having been excluded from theological discourse and leadership roles in our own traditions because we are women. Knowing first hand the inappropriateness of excluding others for arbitrary reasons because it had been done to us as women, how could we then exclude others who happened to belong to other religions? As I stated previously, "a major value of feminist theology is to include the voices that have not been heard, to widen the circle, to learn how to welcome diversity. It makes no sense for those values to stop when they hit the boundary of one's own religion and for another set of values to take over at that point."[6]

The moral incentive to including previously excluded voices from other religious traditions could lead to "widening the canon," which had become a slogan in feminist theology. Feminists generally agreed that neglected and forgotten stories and source materials were important because the received canon contained so little material that was truly empowering for women. At the same time, mainstream theologians were beginning to realize that in a world characterized by religious diversity, one could no longer do reputable theology if one only knew one's own tradition. In the felicitous phrase of one commentator, in the process of seriously studying other religions, we "become a phenomenon to ourselves."[7] To which I added: "For theological reflection, feminist or otherwise, nothing is so useful as becoming a phenomenon to oneself because in that process, we see and understand ourselves much more clearly. Part of that seeing includes seeing the strengths and weaknesses of the perspectives we take for granted. As we begin to experience that there really are religious *alternatives*, our own perspective must also become an *alternative*, not merely the only viable theological position or something with which we are stuck."[8]

6. Gross, "Feminist Theology as Theology of Religions," 216–17.

7. William Paden, *Religious Worlds: The Comparative Study of Religion* (Boston: Beacon, 1988), 165.

8. Gross, "Feminist Theology as Theology of Religions," 219.

In the 1990s, when diversity had finally become a hot topic generally, interest in and concern for non-Western Christianity emerged
among my colleagues in feminist theology. Nevertheless, their concern
was *only* with Christian cultural diversity, not with *religious* diversity.
I found it incomprehensible that when concern with diversity finally
began to emerge in feminist theology, there was still no concern with
religious diversity. In fact, these feminist theologians routinely used the
word "religion" when what they meant was "Christianity." At a number
of meetings with them about "diversity," I consistently called them on
such usage. They found that irritating and just couldn't train themselves
to distinguish between "religion" and "Christianity."

Unfortunately, in this bias, the rhetoric of feminist theology mirrors North American and Christian discourse on religious diversity in
general. Every other kind of diversity is highlighted, but religious diversity is not even regarded as a kind of diversity that deserves recognition,
protection, and encouragement. As the United States grows significantly
more diverse religiously, that fact fails to register. Or if it does register,
it does so negatively, not positively. According to many, this is, after all,
a "Christian nation."

Taking on issues of religious diversity in any theologically serious
way requires each religion, including Christianity, to give up its claims
to unique universal and exclusive relevance. For reasons that I do not
understand, many Christians find that difficult to do. Perhaps, despite
their willingness to be radical on so many other issues, my Christian
feminist colleagues were unwilling to stand against the theological
mainstream on this issue. It has been suggested that Christian feminists,
feeling vulnerable because of their feminism, needed to prove their
Christian orthodoxy to skeptical colleagues. Religious diversity seemed
like an easy place to take a more conventionally Christian stand.[9] But
significant numbers of Christian men do critical and non-conforming
work on religious diversity without jeopardizing their job security. In
any case, when one thinks about how important inter-religious dialogue
and issues of religious diversity are, it is clear that this is not the place
to cut corners to prove one's Christian orthodoxy. Or perhaps I am trying too hard to understand their disinterest in interreligious dialogue.
Perhaps their unwillingness to take these issues seriously reflects more

9. Carol P. Christ, "Response: Roundtable—Feminist Theology and Religious
Diversity," *Journal of Feminist Theology* 16/2 (2000) 79–84.

their immersion in the North American Christian theological milieu than any deeply reflective, conscious choice. After all, almost all of my feminist colleagues had been trained in (Christian) theology at a time when most (Christian) theologians saw no need to know anything about any religion other than their own. They simply did not yet understand the importance of using the 'comparative mirror' in their theologizing.

I remember with great sadness meetings of the editorial board of the *Journal of Feminist Studies in Religion* in which certain board members would complain about lack of diversity among those present or among those who presented papers on women and religion at the American Academy of Religion annual meetings. At the time (late 1990s) I reflected that when I, as a non-Christian, took the floor,

> I felt as if I had momentarily surfaced from underwater in some giant ocean, only to have the waters submerge me again immediately. I also noted that I had felt this way before. In earlier days, it had not been uncommon for men to treat women's observations about religious studies or theology in the same way. One of the few other non-Christian feminists locked eyes with me and whispered, "They just don't get it, do they?" How many times had we said the same thing about men when trying to explain to them what feminism is and why it matters?[10]

Though the article in which these comments appear was eventually published in the book for which it had been an invited contribution, *The Cambridge Companion to Feminist Theology*, that volume's editor initially rejected it because she thought it was too direct and critical.

As it became clear to me that I needed to look beyond my feminist colleagues for scholarly interchange on issues pertaining to religious diversity, beginning in 1980, I started to immerse myself in venues devoted specifically to interreligious dialogue, especially Buddhist–Christian dialogue. Interestingly, these venues, while not concerned with feminism or with gender issues, were not anti-feminist either. In fact, I found those primarily oriented to interreligious exchange far more receptive to feminist concerns than feminists were to interreligious issues. When feminism was appropriate to the topic at hand, it easily received slots in the program at these gatherings devoted to dialogue and interreligious exchange. In these venues, especially in the world of Buddhist–Christian dialogue, I also enjoyed many years of supportive,

10. Rita M. Gross, "Feminist Theology as Theology of Religions," 211.

friendly, non-competitive collegiality. I cannot explain this difference between the two sets of colleagues and will not attempt to do so, though I continue to regard this blind spot as feminist theology's greatest failing. My dual immersion in these two sets of colleagues and concerns eventually led to a schedule conflict every year at the American Academy of Religion annual meetings between an event in the world of feminist theology and an event in the world of Buddhist–Christian dialogue. I usually chose to attend the Buddhist–Christian Studies meeting.

Ironically, I encountered the colleague in feminist theology with whom I have worked most closely over the last twenty-five years, Rosemary Reuther, in the interreligious exchange world, not the feminist theology world. Rosemary agreed to join the prestigious and formerly all male Cobb–Abe International Buddhist–Christian Theological Encounter after protests from the floor of the larger conference with which it was meeting concurrently, resulted, in 1983, in its gender integration. For many years after that, we met annually for meetings of that group and were often asked to do a Buddhist–Christian–feminist dialogue as a public program. Eventually, we led such a dialogue as a weekend-long program together at the Grailville retreat center. This program resulted in a book we co-authored, *Religious Feminism and the Future of the Planet: A Buddhist–Christian–Feminist Dialogue.*[11] It is a good example of what sustained feminist inter-religious dialogue between various traditions could be. But, to my knowledge this book has had very little, if any impact on the world of feminist theology. Nor has that workshop, which would be an ideal way for seminaries to educate their students about feminism and interreligious dialogue, ever been repeated.

From this narrative, I think it is clear that women and feminists cannot simply blame their lack of involvement in interreligious dialogue on being excluded by male dominant religions. Women have also excluded themselves, which does not mean that there are not real obstacles to women's full participation in interreligious dialogue. A major dis-incentive for feminists is the male monopoly on religious institutions and positions of religious leadership in them. As a result of this monopoly, almost all, if not all, the participants in the flashy meetings of world religious leaders are men. Because religious institutions in all cases are

11. Rita M. Gross and Rosemary Radford Ruether, *Religious Feminism and the Future of the Planet: A Buddhist–Christian–Feminist Dialogue* (New York: Continuum, 2001).

so male dominated, women do not have leadership roles at the highest levels and have virtually no chance to participate in these forums. Casual observers of this situation can be forgiven for concluding that women are out of the picture in the world of interreligious exchange. However, I would urge another conclusion. These flashy meetings may produce good news copy and interesting photographs, as well as a few pious resolutions. But that is not where the serious interreligious work is going on, and so it doesn't matter too much that women are locked out of these venues.

Instead, I suggest that for serious interreligious dialogue we rely less on official religious leaders and more on thoughtful, well-educated scholar-practitioners, many of whom are women and more of whom are now interested in dialogue and religious diversity.[12] Things have changed a great deal from thirty years ago when, in 1983, I was the lone female participant in the Cobb–Abe International Buddhist–Christian Theological Encounter and was there by demand from the floor of the larger concurrently running conference, not because I had been invited by the male leadership. By the time of its last meeting twenty years later, the group was almost half female. The same pertains for meetings of the Society for Buddhist–Christian Studies and the other interreligious forums in which I have participated over the years. As far as I can tell, women come to these discussions because we are interested in and care about religious diversity and interreligious dialogue, not because we are women, though some of us also do feminist and gender-related scholarly studies in other contexts. That also describes me, of course. It is telling that recent movements of women into the world of interreligious dialogue are occurring in venues devoted to dialogue, not to feminism.

We also need to remember, when we despair over the fact that all of the most newsworthy interreligious venues look very male-dominated, not receptive to women at all, that things can change, sometimes very rapidly. In 1971, when feminists packed the business meeting of the American Academy of Religion to elect the first woman president of that organization, it also looked very male-dominated and not receptive to women at all. That tactic would not have been successful and could not have worked if there had not been women already in the

12. For example, see Jeannine Hill Fletcher, *Monopoly on Salvation? A Feminist Approach to Religious Pluralism* (New York: Continuum, 2005); and Catherine Cornille, *The Im-Possibility of Interreligious Dialogue* (New York: Crossroads, 2008).

organization, well-trained, and prepared to step into waiting leadership positions. Probably for some time into the future, organizers of flashy interreligious meetings will think that they should invite the Dalai Lama and the Pope to be chief speakers at such meetings. But those invitations will be turned down in most cases. Women are not going to be the ones next on the list of invitees if we have not already distinguished ourselves in less prestigious interfaith meetings.

Patriarchy and male dominance in the religions are not the only reasons feminists have been discouraged about interfaith issues. I suspect that interreligious dialogue did not seem "gender urgent" enough to many of them. Women were unlikely to penetrate the glass ceiling of prestigious and high-powered dialogue venues soon and very few of the issues generally discussed at such meetings pertain directly to gender issues. It may well have seemed to many such feminists that there was little for them to do, *qua* women or feminists, at such meetings. So why bother putting up with the annoying male dominance of the venue? Especially if, as I contend, it is the case that regarding the most critical and important interfaith issues, women will not offer different insights than men. If women are not going to significantly alter the theological discourse, and if the dialogue table looks inhospitable to women, why should women participate in significant numbers?

But should women or feminists give their energies only to ventures that are explicitly feminist? Although I contend that there is not an explicitly feminist approach to interreligious issues and dialogue, that is not the same thing as saying it is unimportant whether or not women participate in such dialogues. To address these questions further, we need to discuss the relationship between gendered and non-gendered aspects of inter-religious dialogue, which, in my view, is related to issues of the gendered and non-gendered aspects of religions and religious studies in general. I suspect that how one parses out those aspects of religion is closely connected with whether or not one adheres to views of gender essentialism. Both as a feminist and as a Buddhist, I do not hold to gender essentialism.

While culturally constructed gender norms are omnipresent and deeply influential, they do not add up to gender essences. Clearly, when one scores many individuals for certain traits or achievements, average differences between men and women often show up, but those are averages, not gender essences. The averages may discourage or encourage certain individuals, but they do not predetermine what any specific individual could achieve. Instead they give rise to a lot of stereotypes that contribute to the cultural gender norms that limit the individuals who internalize them—but do not limit those who do not buy into them to the same extent. If girls were inherently less capable of achievement in math or science, for example, no woman would ever accomplish anything in those realms, which is not the case, and efforts to alter cultural messages that discourage girls from thinking they could be interested in math or science would be useless.

Though gender essentialist theories were once popular in feminist circles, I always claimed that they were more dangerous than helpful because they are completely dualistic and often simply reverse patriarchal versions of gender essentialism. One of the earlier feminist analyses of Western patriarchy claimed that Western, or at least Christian spirituality, posited a fundamental duality between matter and spirit, lower and higher, and many other dualities as well.[13] It was easy to demonstrate that women were consistently associated with matter and everything on the less favored side of the dichotomy while men were consistently associated with the higher, more preferred side of the dichotomy. But feminist essentialism often turned on a different but similar set of dichotomies in which men were evaluated as more aggressive, women as more innately peaceful.[14] It is hard to see how such gender essentialist dualities could foster human well-being and flourishing. For me, feminism is about "freedom from the prison of gender roles." Nothing is more imprisoning than expectations based on gender, especially when one imposes them on oneself. Rather than finding a better, improved, more equal set of gender roles, why not junk the whole idea of putting so much freight on gender identity?[15] That is the much more liberating alternative.

13. For example, see Rosemary Radford Ruether, "Misogynism and Virginal Feminism in the Fathers of the Church," in Ruether, ed., *Religion and Sexism: Images of Women in the Jewish and Christian Traditions* (New York: Simon & Schuster, 1974), 150–83.

14. This thesis was popular in the 1970s and into the 1980s. No one made it more central to her work than Mary Daly, especially in her book *Gyn/Ecolgy: The Metaethics of Radical Feminism* (Boston: Beacon, 1978). In that book she claimed that men are essentially necrophiliac while women are essentially biophilic. For a brief summary of Daly's thinking on these points, see Rita M. Gross, *Feminism and Religion: An Introduction* (Boston: Beacon, 1996), 223–25.

15. I have written a great deal on this point. Two articles that I especially recommend are "What Went Wrong? Feminism and Freedom from the Prison of Gender

From the Buddhist side, of course, the case for gender essentialism is even weaker. Even if 100 percent of humans actually conformed to a cultural gender stereotype, which happens rarely, if ever, their behavior would still be assessed as a "dependently arisen mere appearance," to use the technical language, not something inherently, truly existing. In Buddhist thought, for something to *truly, essentially* exist, rather than to have only mere apparent existence, it would have to be *independent, uncaused, solitary,* and *permanent.* That is what "essence" means in Buddhist thought. Thus, a gender essence would have to involve behavior or traits that are always found in every woman or man, that do not vary across cultures, and that never change. Such a thing, of course, does not exist. Because gender-based behavior is an appearance rather than a reality, it can change at any time. If this were not the case, there would be no hope for any feminist improvements in the status quo. For example, it would have been impossible for the first woman who ever received a *geshe* degree in Tibetan Buddhism to have done so, but she did in 2011. It would have been impossible for *bhikkhuni* ordinations for nuns to have been restored in Theravada Buddhism, but they have started again, albeit amidst great controversy and hesitation. Furthermore, for Buddhism, positing duality as the final reality is a fundamental mistake. No phenomenon is different from any other in a fundamental, ultimately real way. Instead, they are all equal in lacking inherent existence though their appearances are manifold, diverse, and various.

A reasonable question at this point is why, if Buddhist logic against essentialism is so strong, there is so much patriarchy and sexism, so many negative comments about women, in popular Buddhist literature? Given comments about women in such literature, one could wonder if those who made these sexist comments had ever read and studied Buddhist literature about lack of essence! But this is simply the contrast between what religions proclaim as their ideals and what they deliver "on the ground." All religions face the same problem. Such a strong theoretical foundation at least gives Buddhist feminists a strong basis from which to protest gender essentialist teachings and practices that disfavor women.

Roles," in *Garland of Feminist Reflections*, 250–62; and "How Clinging to Gender Subverts Enlightenment," *Inquiring Mind* 27/1 (2010) 18–19, 32. This article is also available on my website: http://ritamgross.com/.

My skepticism about essences fuels my claim that there is no spe-cifically feminist or women's perspectives on issues of religious diversity and the practice of interreligious dialogue. Or perhaps the only specifi-cally feminist position is that women should be at the dialogue table be-cause otherwise religions are once again demonstrating their historical patriarchy rather than their universal human relevance. In other words, questions about selection and self-selection for who sits at the dialogue table *are* questions about gender and there is a clear feminist perspective on these questions.

Once everyone is seated at the dialogue table, the main issues that need to be discussed there include how to overcome the religions' tradi-tional xenophobia and the collective egotism and self-centeredness that fuel their claims of superiority and exclusive relevance to all humans. Regarding this issue, women do not have special insight based on gen-der. Some women, however, will have special insight due to our training, thoughtfulness, and deep commitment to solving problems brought about by fear and dislike of religious diversity. These problems are huge enough to require the thought and energy of all properly trained, com-mitted individuals. It is unlikely that men will solve these problems by themselves, not because of any limitations on them specifically as men, but because the problems are so massive and the issues so serious.

In making these claims, I am not unaware of how much of reli-gion is gendered and of how much is overlooked if we ignore gender in our studies of religions. Certainly my own work as a historian of religions, especially the co-edited volume *Unspoken Worlds: Women's Religious Lives* clearly demonstrates how much difference it makes to pay attention to gender in religious studies.[16] Nevertheless, it is also important to distinguish gendered from non-gendered dimensions of religions. Anything dealing with religion "on the ground," with human subjects, including how people self-select or are selected to participate in dialogue formats, will be gendered. Some more abstract theological concepts, such as pronouns and imagery used to discuss deities, are also gendered—highly gendered. Thus, much Western theological discourse, which uses only male pronouns of deity, whether habitually or delib-erately, is highly gendered. I suspect the fact that Western theological discourse is so pervasively gendered and many feminists are aware of

16. Nancy Auer Falk and Rita M. Gross, eds., *Unspoken Worlds: Women's Religious Lives,* 3rd ed. (Belmont CA: Wadsworth, 2001).

that fact may be the reason why they assume that all religious issues have a gendered dimension and also why they are reluctant to involve themselves in something that does not overtly pertain to gender.

More abstract theological topics, such as how to foster flourishing with religious diversity, simply are much less gendered, even non-gendered, in my view. But cultural stereotypes about gender can obscure some issues that are not especially gendered with a gender overlay that simply isn't there. Recently I attended a Buddhist seminar on the Buddhist philosopher Chandrakirti, whose work is highly abstract and dependent on Madhyamikan logic, which many initially find extremely challenging. A young woman whom I have befriended and who obviously knows my reputation approached me one day and asked, "Isn't this all just a male logic trip?" I simply replied, "No." Not distinguishing between gendered and non-gendered aspects of the whole situation, and also adhering to gender essentialism, she had combined gender stereotypes and her own discomfort with the subject matter to try to find a reason why she should not have to take Chandrakirti seriously. I am afraid such inappropriate gender overlays are often projected onto complex topics.

If issues of religious diversity and the practice of inter-religious dialogue are more non-gendered than gendered and if women are unlikely to have unique things to say about these topics simply because they are women, is it then unimportant whether or not women and feminists concern ourselves about such issues? By now, it should be obvious that my answer is a resounding "no." Thinking about religious diversity and participating in interreligious dialogue are just too important to human well-being for women to exclude themselves or for religions not to involve women and feminists in interreligious exchanges. The most important thing that women bring to the interfaith table is our sheer presence. By being present, we demonstrate that religions are *human* enterprises, not *male* enterprises. If we have to somehow break into those spaces to make that point, that is okay. To back up their claims to speak to all humans, not just to male humans, religions really need women at the dialogue table for those claims to be credible. This is not a case of women rescuing an inherently male-dominated enterprise, thereby making any specific religions look better in press releases and publicity photos, but of women beginning to participate in a discourse that, though not inherently gendered, has mainly been carried out by men until now. Not every issue in religious thought is gendered and whether or not women would actually make different claims than men should not be the reason why women avoid dialogue situations or why they should be included or not included in dialogue venues. In some senses, we declare ourselves irrelevant if we choose not to participate in concerns not directly related to gender.

Women's sheer presence at the interfaith table makes a significant difference in other ways as well. If women are present at the table, our voices can make a difference when gender-related issues do come up in discussion, as they sometimes will. Without our input, men, who are frequently much less aware of how much difference gender makes than we are, will usually gloss over or ignore such topics. They may well not question the habitual male dominance of religions and not be aware of how much suffering that male dominance produces. They will have little to say about what exclusion feels like, or what it feels like to be consistently evaluated as "inferior" or needing supervision. How could they know what it feels like not to have equal rights or not to be self-determining? They may even be unaware of the differential impact war, poverty, or overpopulation have on women. If women are present at the dialogue table, many nuances can and will change.

In many ways these arguments and issues are similar to arguments about a Buddhist issue about which I care passionately. I have long argued that, because of the supreme importance of the role of dharma teacher in Buddhism, the acid test for whether Buddhism has overcome its patriarchal ways is whether or not women become dharma teachers in significant numbers.[17] But others have argued against me, claiming that authentic dharma does not depend on any accidental traits characterizing the dharma teacher, including his or her gender. "If women were gurus, would their dharma be different from that of male gurus?" I have been asked. When I answer in the negative, I have faced a "Gotcha!" reaction. Some claim that, given dharma's liberative potential, it is overridingly important that dharma be taught by competent teachers and irrelevant whether or not any of those teachers happen to be women. Given that "enlightened mind is beyond gender, neither male

17. This case was made recently in my article "Buddhist Women and Teaching Authority," published several times but most accessible in my *Garland of Feminist Reflections*, 281–90.

nor female,"[18] women and men *do* teach essentially the same dharma. Note that the argument is the same: if the discourse itself is not radically changed by women's presence, it does not matter if they are absent. In this case, however, the argument is made by men (and some women) wanting to justify a status quo which excludes women from the discourse.

In the Buddhist case, my rejoinder is multi-faceted but mainly revolves around two points. First, the presence or absence of female role models is crucially important to Buddhist students, both female and male. Again, our sheer presence or absence speaks as loudly as the words being said, perhaps more loudly. Furthermore, in the case of Buddhism, when gendered subjects of Buddhist institutions who happen to be women speak, they tell us a great deal from their experiences "on the ground" that cannot be expressed by men. Their abstract dharma teachings may not be different from those of men, but how they express their teachings and how those teachings are received may be subtly different. At least we must concede that because each teacher expresses the universal dharma in idiosyncratic ways, the uniquely relevant message of a great teacher may go unheard if women's voices are not part of the conversation. The same is certainly true regarding issues of religious diversity and inter-religious dialogue.

Conclusions

Given that I am currently writing a book about "Buddhist advice for flourishing with religious diversity," I obviously have thought about that topic a great deal and presumably have some cogent things to say about it. In my view, Buddhist thought can contribute some valuable and unique tools to the interfaith discussion—tools that other religions have not contributed and may not be able to contribute. But I simply cannot and will not claim that I am concerned about these issues *because* I am a woman or a feminist, that my conclusions and suggestions derive from my being a woman, or that a male Buddhist could not or would

18. This, Buddhism's most frequently recited cliché about Buddhism and gender, is often used to dismiss feminist critiques of Buddhism as irrelevant and to subtly pressure critics to ignore and overlook extreme male dominance in Buddhist institutions, as if the truth of this slogan at the absolute level renders patriarchy at the relative level non-existent or irrelevant. Exposing this erroneous use of Buddhist ideas of the two truths has been important in my feminist critique of Buddhism.

not have come up with the same conclusions. I can only claim that, to my knowledge, no male Buddhist has made similar claims or proposed similar suggestions, but I do not think that has anything to do with gender. For one thing, only a few male Buddhists have made contributions to modern discussions of religious diversity.[19] But I really have nothing further to say about Buddhist women or being a Buddhist woman and inter-religious exchange.

It is clear from this paper that I would much rather deal with a situation in which women's presence at the dialogue table is not in question—neither from the side of the world's religions nor from the side of women or feminists. While for the foreseeable future, the flashy, high-powered meetings of "world religious leaders" will be dominated by men, I do not regard that as grounds for women and feminists to opt out of the whole enterprise of inter-religious exchange, as they have so often done in the recent past. From the side of women, the importance of participating in inter-religious formats should not be in question. The topic is simply too urgent. Leaving aside the meetings of world religious leaders, to which we may not be invited, there are many, many ways, in our own communities and between communities, that we can help people overcome fear of religious diversity and defuse religious chauvinism. We can help people overcome the belief the world would be a better place if only we all belonged to the same religion—which is always our own! We can help people realize that our sisters and brothers love their religions just as much as we love our own. They find them just as valuable and transformative as we find our own spiritual path. We can help people realize that religious diversity is not a theological mistake. Rather, it is a great gift and resource.

19. For example, see: His Holiness the Dalai Lama, *Toward a True Kinship of Faiths: How the World's Religions Can Come Together* (New York: Random House, 2010); Thich Nhat Hanh, *Living Buddha, Living Christ* (New York: Penguin Group, 2007); and Nhat Hanh, *Going Home: Jesus and Buddha as Brothers* (New York: Riverhead, 1999); Masao Abe and Stephen Heine, *Buddhism and Interfaith Dialogue: Part One of a Two Volume Sequel to Zen and Western Thought* (Honolulu: University of Hawaii Press, 1995); and Abe and Christopher Ives, *Divine Emptiness and Historical Fullness: A Buddhist, Jewish, Christian Conversation with Masao Abe* (Valley Forge, PA: Trinity, 1995).

Contributors

MARA BRECHT is Assistant Professor of Religious Studies at St. Norbert College in De Pere, Wisconsin. She received her doctorate from Fordham University. Her research brings together feminist theology, philosophy of religion, and theology of religious pluralism. She is the author of the forthcoming book *Virtues in Dialogue: Belief, Diversity, and Women's Interreligious Encounter* (2013).

RABBI NANCY FUCHS KREIMER is the Director of the Department of Multifaith Studies and Initiatives at the Reconstructionist Rabbinical College and Associate Professor of Religious Studies. She holds a PhD in Religion from Temple University where her doctoral work was in the field of Jewish–Christian Relations. She serves on the boards of the Interfaith Center of Philadelphia and Clergy Beyond Borders. She is the author of *Parenting as a Spiritual Journey* (1998) and she contributed chapters to *Broken Tablets: Restoring the Ten Commandments* (1999), *Christianity in Jewish Terms* (2000), *The Torah: A Women's Commentary* (2007), and other volumes in the fields of interreligious dialogue, religion and social science, and Jewish thought. She is the co-editor of *Chapters of the Heart: Jewish Women Sharing the Torah of their Lives* (Cascade Books, 2013).

RITA M. GROSS is a Buddhist scholar-practitioner who has specialized in Buddhist critical and constructive thought, especially in the area of Buddhism and gender. She was also a leader in the feminist theology movement and contributed a great deal to the development of that field. Her most important books are *Unspoken Worlds: Women's Religious Lives* (co-edited with Nancy Auer Falk, 2000), *Feminism and Religion: An Introduction* (1996), *Buddhism after Patriarchy: A Feminist History,*

Analysis and Reconstruction of Buddhism (1992), and *A Garland of Feminist Reflections: Forty Years of Religious Exploration* (2009). Her forthcoming book is *Religious Diversity—What's the Problem? Buddhist Advice for Flourishing with Religious Diversity* (Cascade Books). She is Professor Emerita of Comparative Studies in Religion at the University of Wisconsin–Eau Claire.

AYSHA HIDAYATULLAH is Assistant Professor in the Department of Theology and Religious Studies at the Jesuit University of San Francisco, where she teaches courses on Islam, gender, race, and ethics. Her research interests include feminist exegesis of the Qur'an; representations of women in early Islamic history; constructions of femininity and masculinity in various aspects of the Islamic tradition; racial imaginaries of U.S. Islam; popular discourse on Muslim women in the U.S.; and the pedagogy of Islamic studies. Her forthcoming book, *Feminist Edges of the Qur'an* (Oxford University Press, forthcoming 2014), examines the emerging body of Muslim feminist scholarship on the Qur'an in North America.

JEANNINE HILL FLETCHER is Professor of Theology at Fordham University, Bronx NY. As a Catholic systematic theologian, she writes at the intersection of theologies of religious pluralism and feminist theology. Her publications include *Monopoly on Salvation: A Feminist Approach to Religious Pluralism* (2005), and *Motherhood as Metaphor: Engendering Interreligious Dialogue* (2013). Jeannine also serves as the Faculty Director of Fordham's service-learning program, collaborating with the Dorothy Day Center for Service and Justice in helping faculty and students connect their scholarship with work in the community.

ZAYN KASSAM is the John Knox McLean Professor of Religious Studies at Pomona College in Claremont, CA. The winner of two Wig Awards for Distinguished Teaching, she has also won the National American Academy of Religion award for Excellence in Teaching. Dr. Kassam has lectured widely on gender issues in Muslim societies in the UK, the USA, and Canada. She has authored a volume on Islam, and edited *Women and Islam* dealing with the intersection between gender, religion, and activism. Her current research investigates contemporary challenges facing Muslim women. She has published articles on Islamic philosophy, on pedagogy, and on Muslim Women and Globalization. She is a board member for the highly acclaimed *Journal of Feminist Studies in Religion*, as well as the *Journal of Religion, Conflict, and Peace*.

ANNE CAROLYN KLEIN (RIGZIN DROLMA) is Professor of Religious Studies at Rice University as well as a founding director and resident teacher of Dawn Mountain Tibetan Buddhist Temple and Dawn Mountain Community Center & Research Institute in Houston. Her scholarly work draws from Tibetan Buddhist texts and oral traditions. Her books include *Knowledge and Liberation, on Buddhist Ways of Knowing* (1987); *Path to the Middle: Oral Madhyamika Philosophy in Tibet* (1994); *Meeting the Great Bliss Queen: Buddhists, Feminists and the Art of the Self* (1995), and with Geshe Tenzin Wangyal Rinopche, *Unbounded Wholeness* (2006). Her most recent publication is *Heart Essence of the Vast Expanse: A Story of Transmission* (2010).

SUE LEVI ELWELL, PhD, is the Founding Director and Founding Rabbinic Director of Jewish women's centers in Los Angeles and New York. She has served as a congregational rabbi and as a congregational consultant for the Union for Reform Judaism. The editor of *Lesbian Rabbis: The First Generation* (2001) and *The Open Door*, the CCAR Haggadah (2002), she served as poetry editor of the award-winning *The Torah: A Women's Commentary* (2008). With Nancy Fuchs Kreimer, she edited *Chapters of the Heart: Jewish Women Sharing the Torah of Our Lives* (2013). She is a graduate of Indiana University and the Hebrew Union College–Jewish Institute of Religion, and a Senior Rabbinic Fellow of the Shalom Hartman Institute.

ROSEMARY RADFORD RUETHER holds a PhD in Classics and Patristics from the Claremont Graduate University. She was the Georgia Harkness Professor in Theology for twenty-seven years at the Garrett School of Theology and Northwestern University in Evanston, Illinois. She also taught at the Graduate Theological Union at Berkeley, California and is presently teaching at the Claremont Graduate University. She is author or editor of forty-seven books, including the epoch making *Sexism and God-Talk: Toward a Feminist Theology* (1983), *The Wrath of Jonah: The Crisis of Religious Nationalism in the Israeli–Palestinian Conflict* (2002), *Integrating Ecofeminism, Globalization, and World Religions* (2005), and mostly recently *My Quests for Hope and Meaning: An Autobiography* (Cascade Books, 2013).

KATHARINA VON KELLENBACH is Professor of Religious Studies at St. Mary's College of Maryland, the Honors College of the State of Maryland. Her areas of expertise include feminist theology, interreligious dialogue, and Jewish-Christian relations in a post-Holocaust world. Previous publications include *Anti-Judaism in Feminist Religious Writings* (1994), essays on the first ordained female Rabbi Regina Jonas of Berlin (1902–1944), and on the theological, ethical and personal implications of the Holocaust. Her book, *"The Mark of Cain: Guilt and Denial in the Lives of Nazi Perpetrators*, examines the effects of genocidal violence on its agents and explores the prospects for moral and spiritual recovery for perpetrators.

MICHELLE VOSS ROBERTS is Assistant Professor of Theology and Culture at the Wake Forest University School of Divinity, where she teaches in the fields of systematic, comparative, and feminist theologies. She received her PhD from Emory University and is the author of *Dualities: A Theology of Difference* (2010), which received the award for the Best Book in Hindu–Christian Studies (2008–2011). Her current research focuses on the role of the emotions in religious experience through the lens of Indian aesthetic theories. She currently serves as Secretary for the Society for Hindu–Christian Studies and is on the steering committee of the Christian Systematic Theology group of the American Academy of Religion.

WAI CHING ANGELA WONG received her PhD in religious studies from the University of Chicago Divinity School. She is Associate Professor of the Department of Cultural and Religious Studies, and Professor of the Chung Chi College Divinity School at the Chinese University of Hong Kong. She is also the Co-Director of Gender Research Centre of the University. Her publications include *"The Poor Woman": A Critical Analysis of Asian Theology and Contemporary Chinese Fiction by Women* (2002), "Negotiating Gender: Postcolonialism and Hong Kong Christian Women," in *Gender and Society in Hong Kong* (2003), and *Chinese Women and Hong Kong Christianity: An Oral History* (in Chinese, 2010).

65204322R00156

Made in the USA
Middletown, DE
23 February 2018